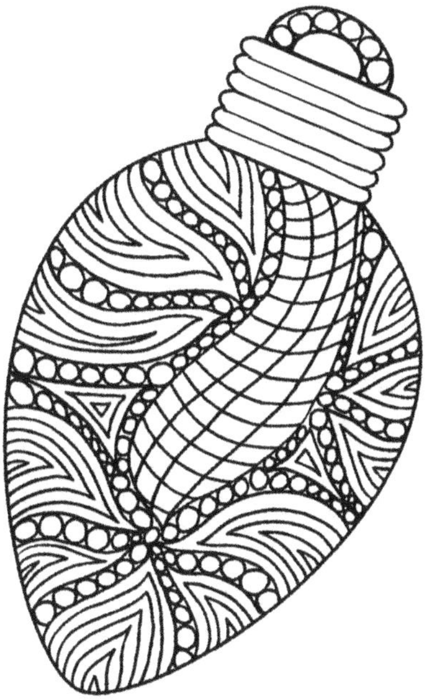

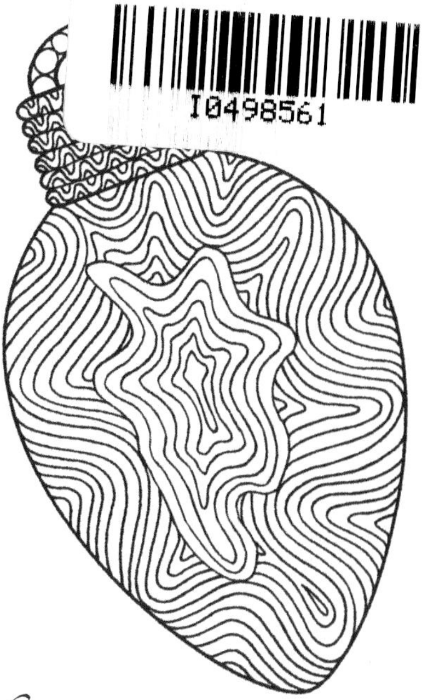

This Book
Belongs to the collection
of

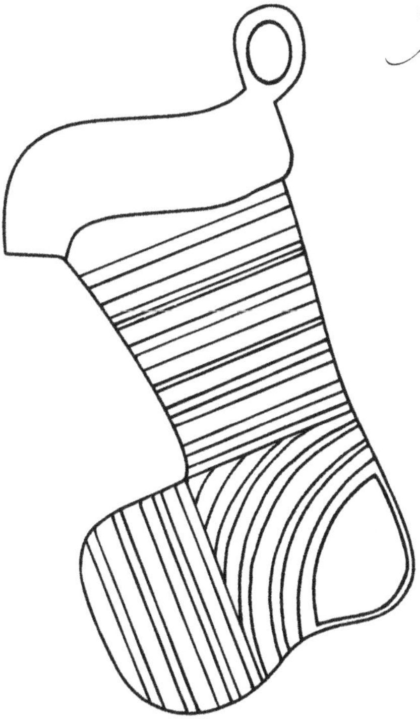

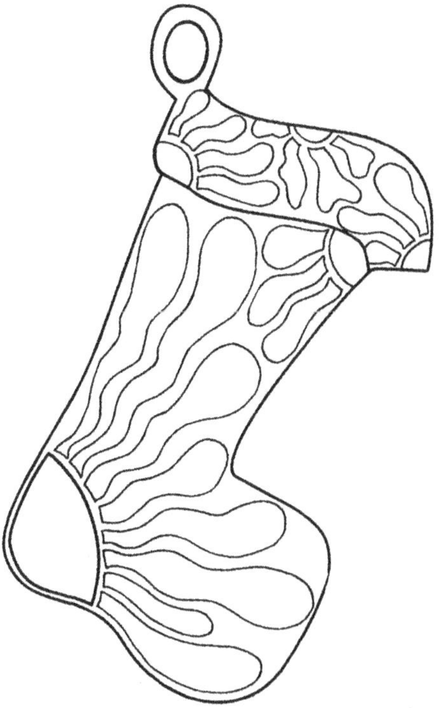

Published by
"GDG©"
Global Doodle Gems

Share your colored versions with us ! We love seeing your results

and hearing from you

we are social !

The Official FB book page, stay on top of what we have in the works !
www.facebook.com/globaldoodlegems
The Community group, share your colored pages, meet the artists, enjoy exclusive freebies, take part in community Charity books and so much more......
www.facebook.com/groups/globaldoodlegems/
Follow us on Twitter.... @GlobalDoodlegem
We are on Instagram too
@globaldoodlegems for instagram
...and if you are not social like that we have a blog
globaldoodlegems.wordpress.com

All of us from the Global Doodle Gems wish you a colortastic time and look forward to seeing your wonderful color results online !

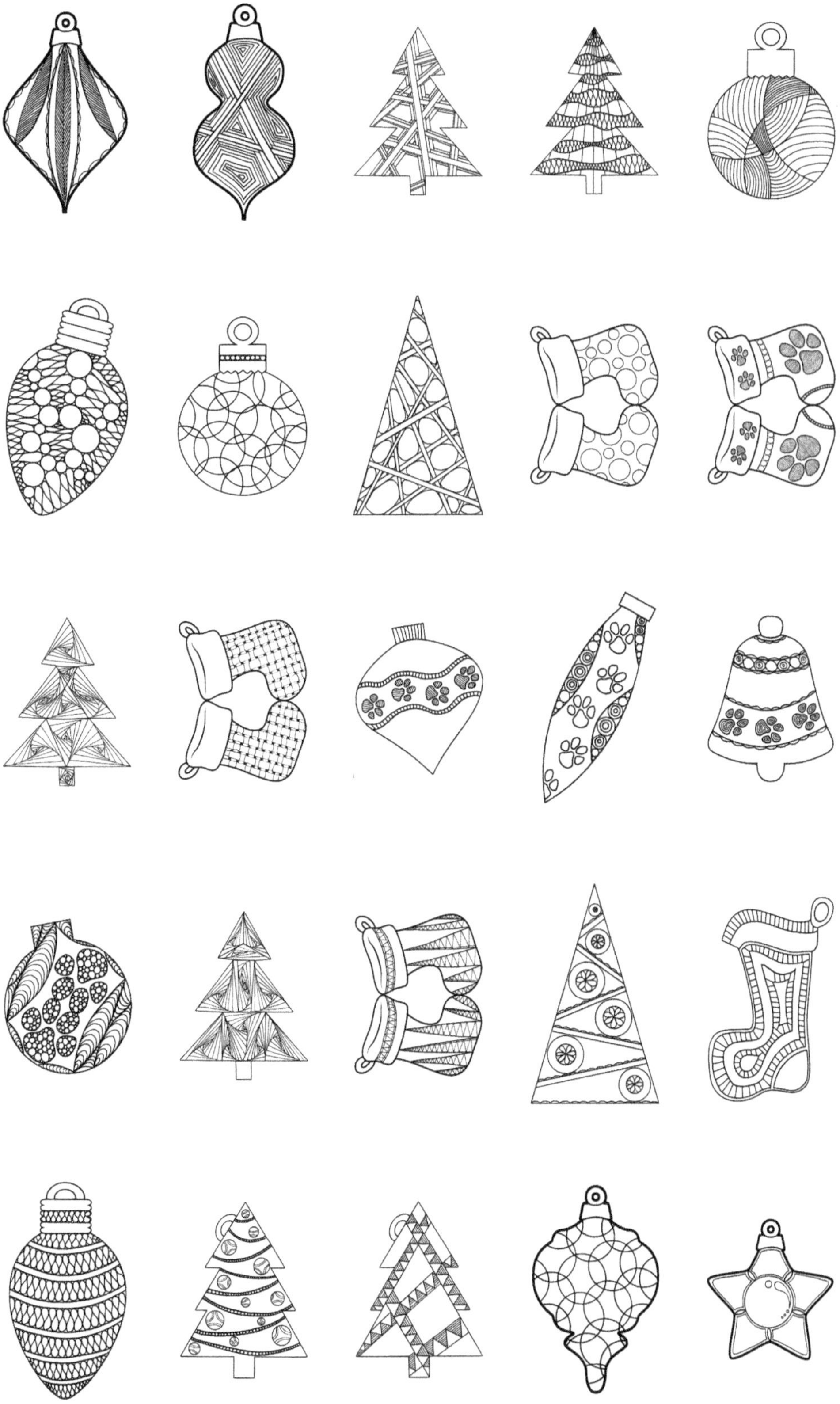

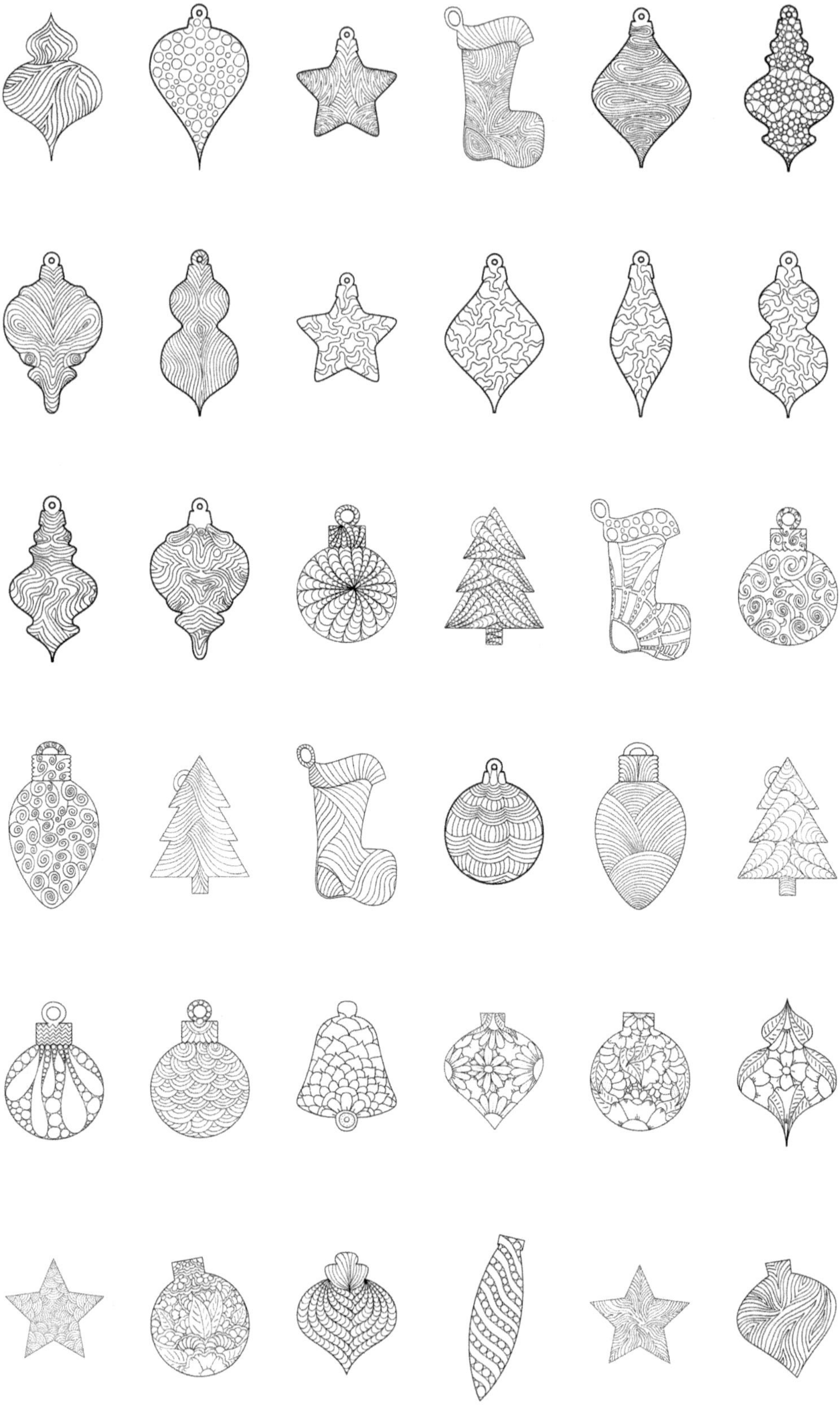

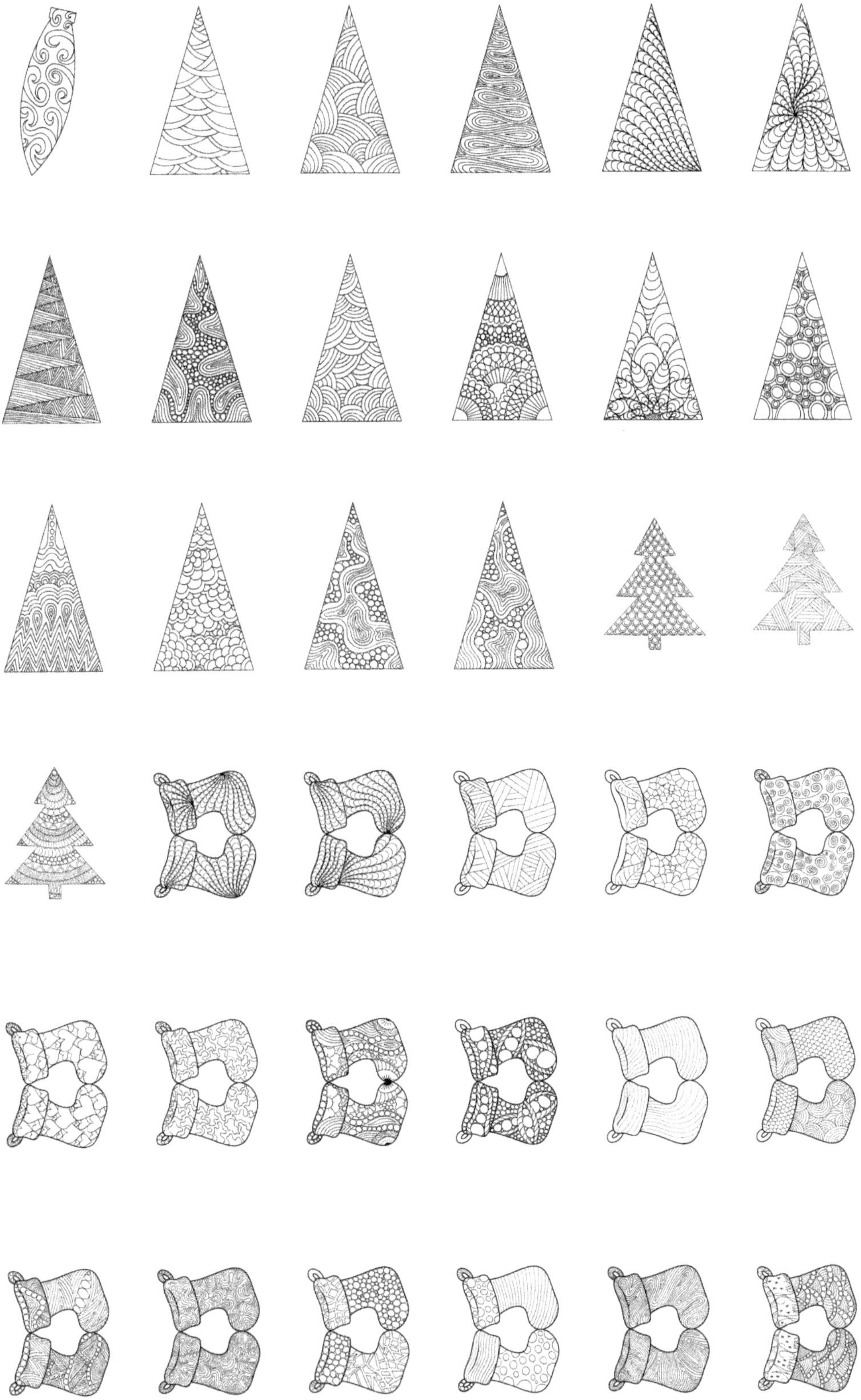

26 Designs from Johanna Ans

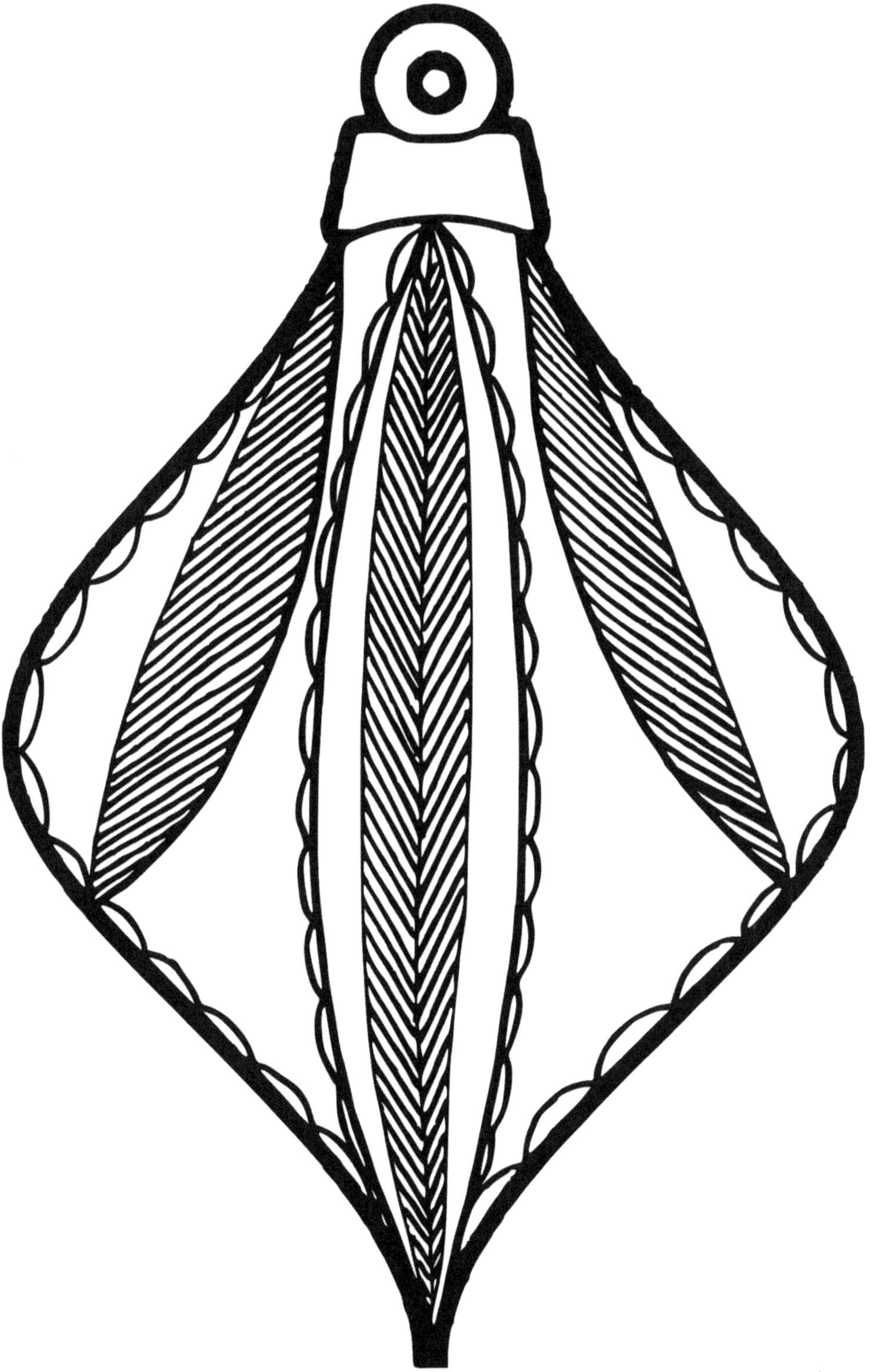

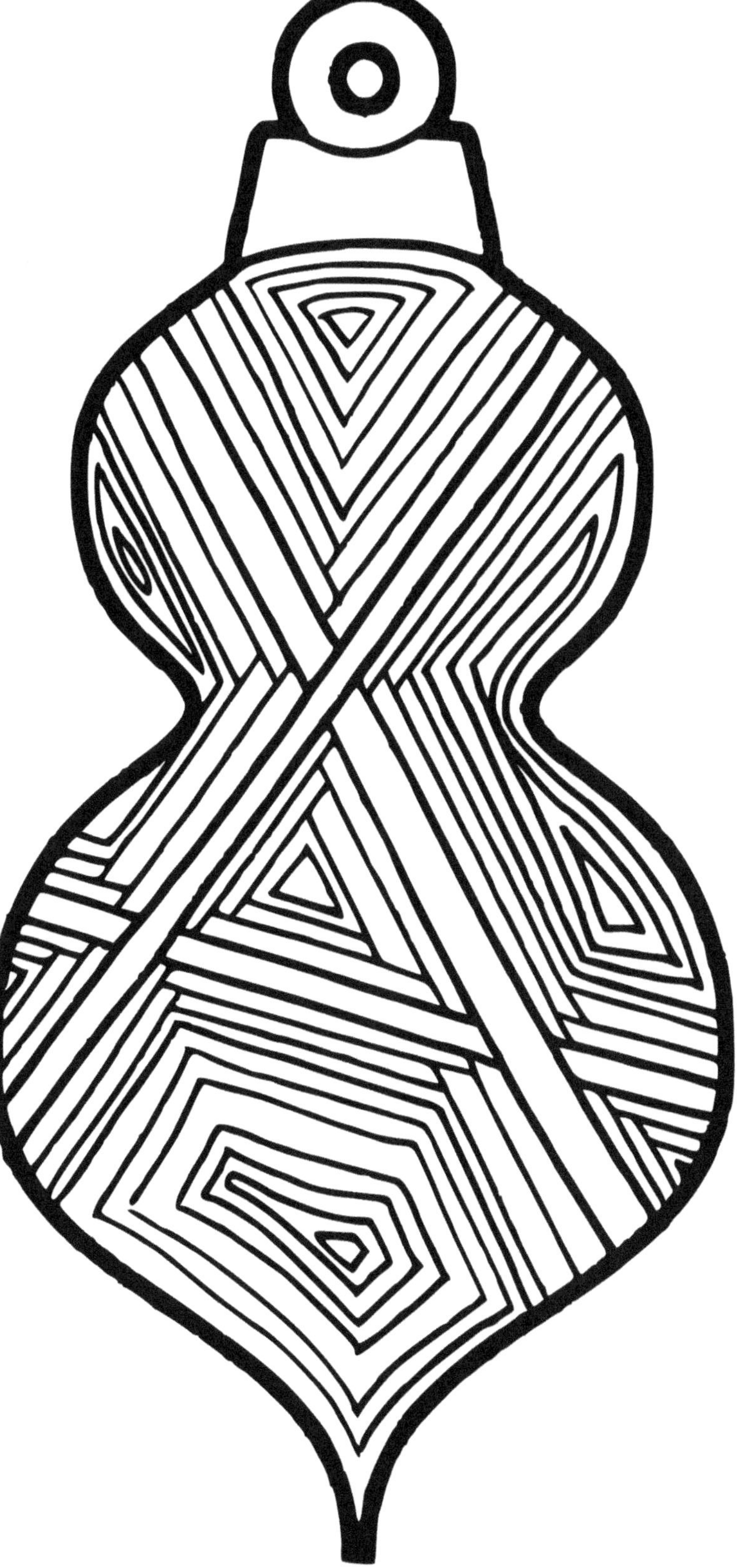

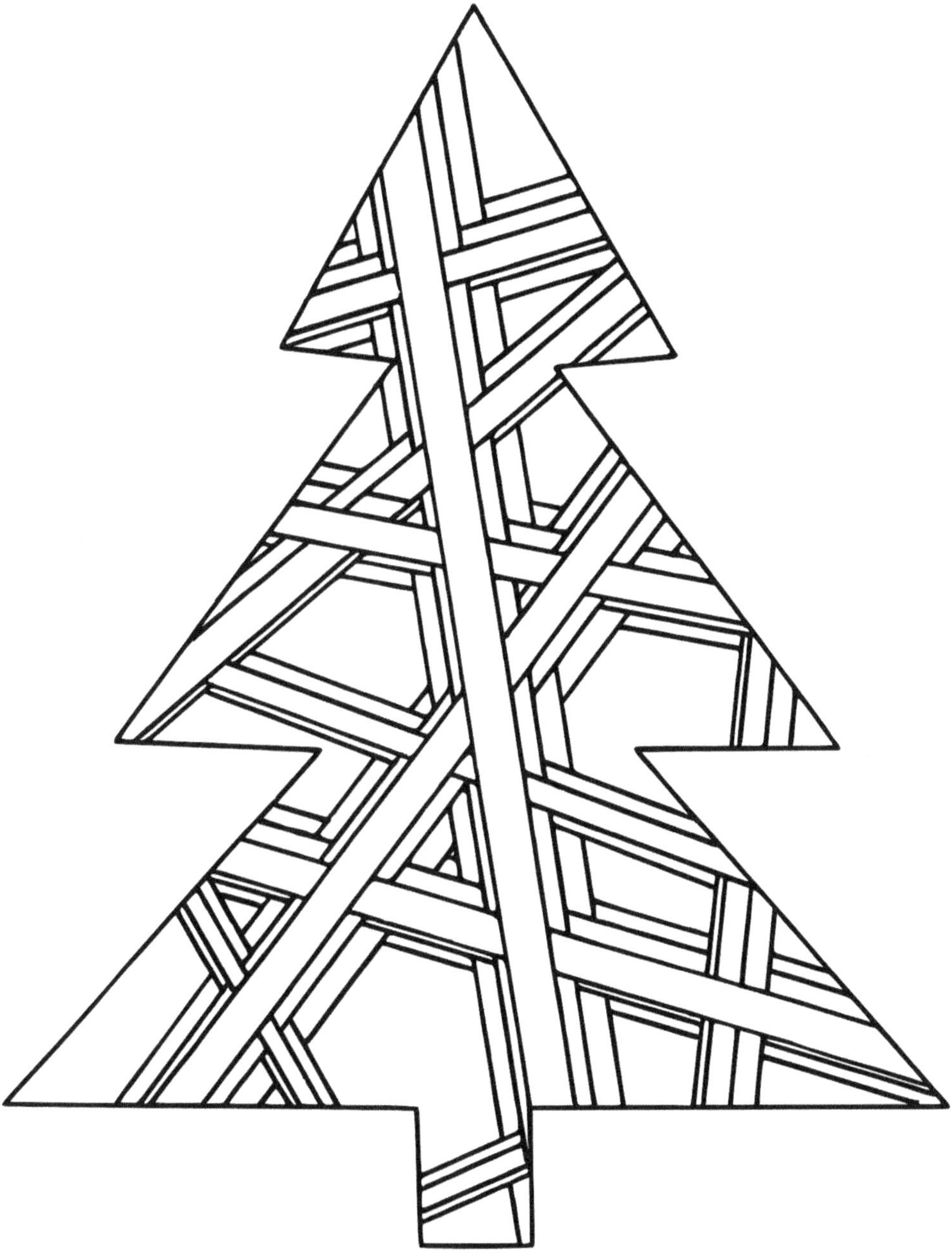

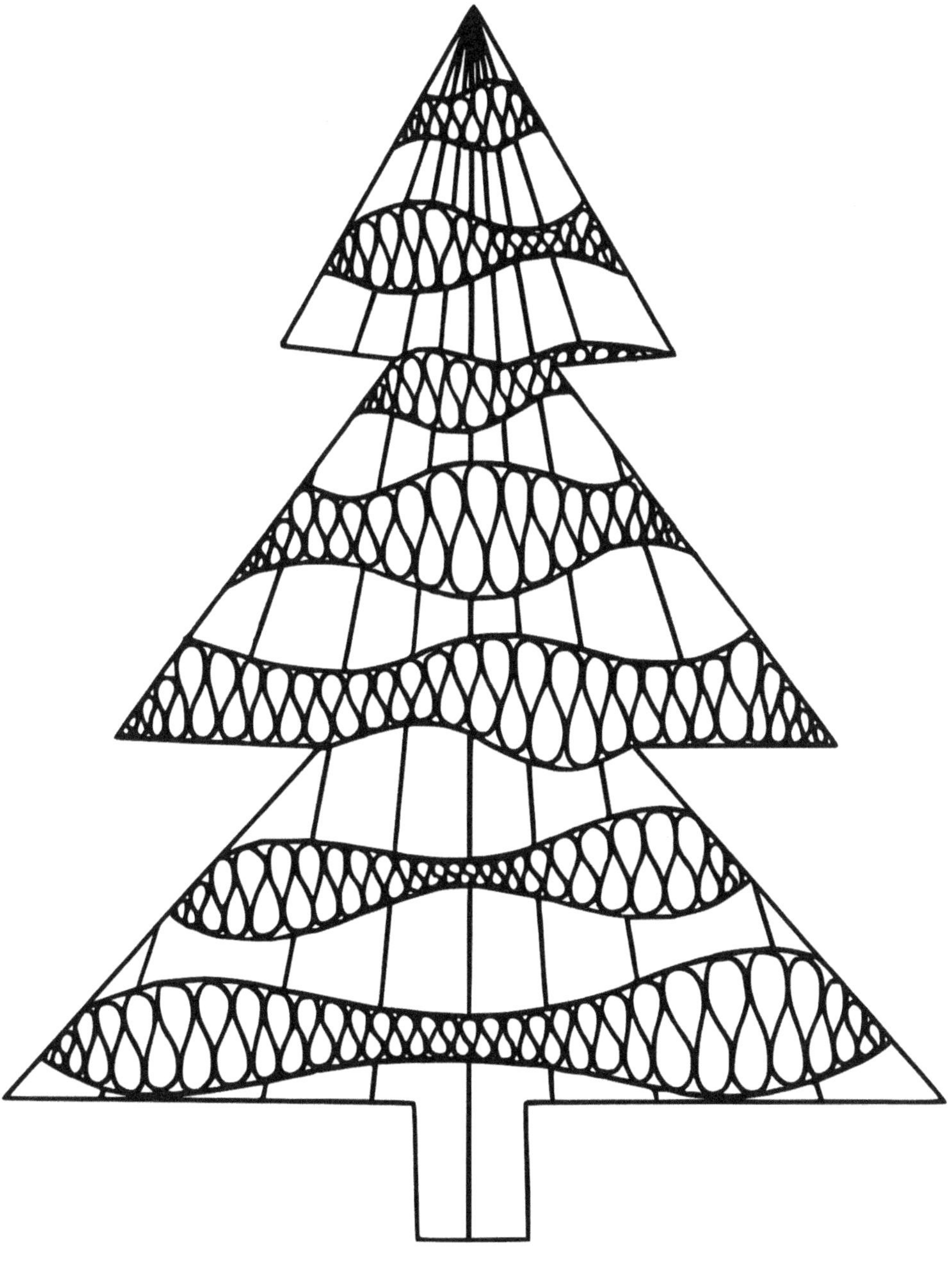

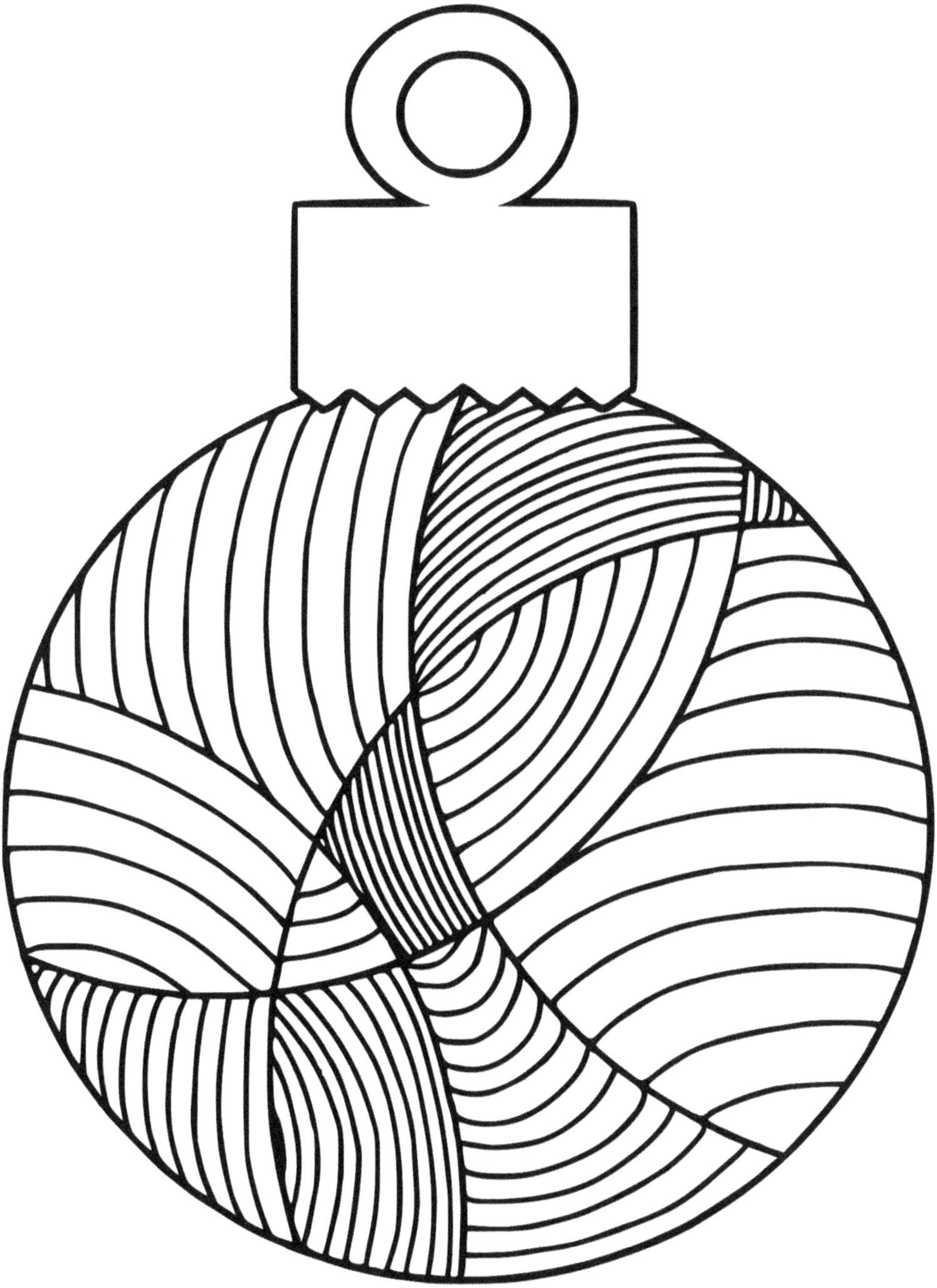

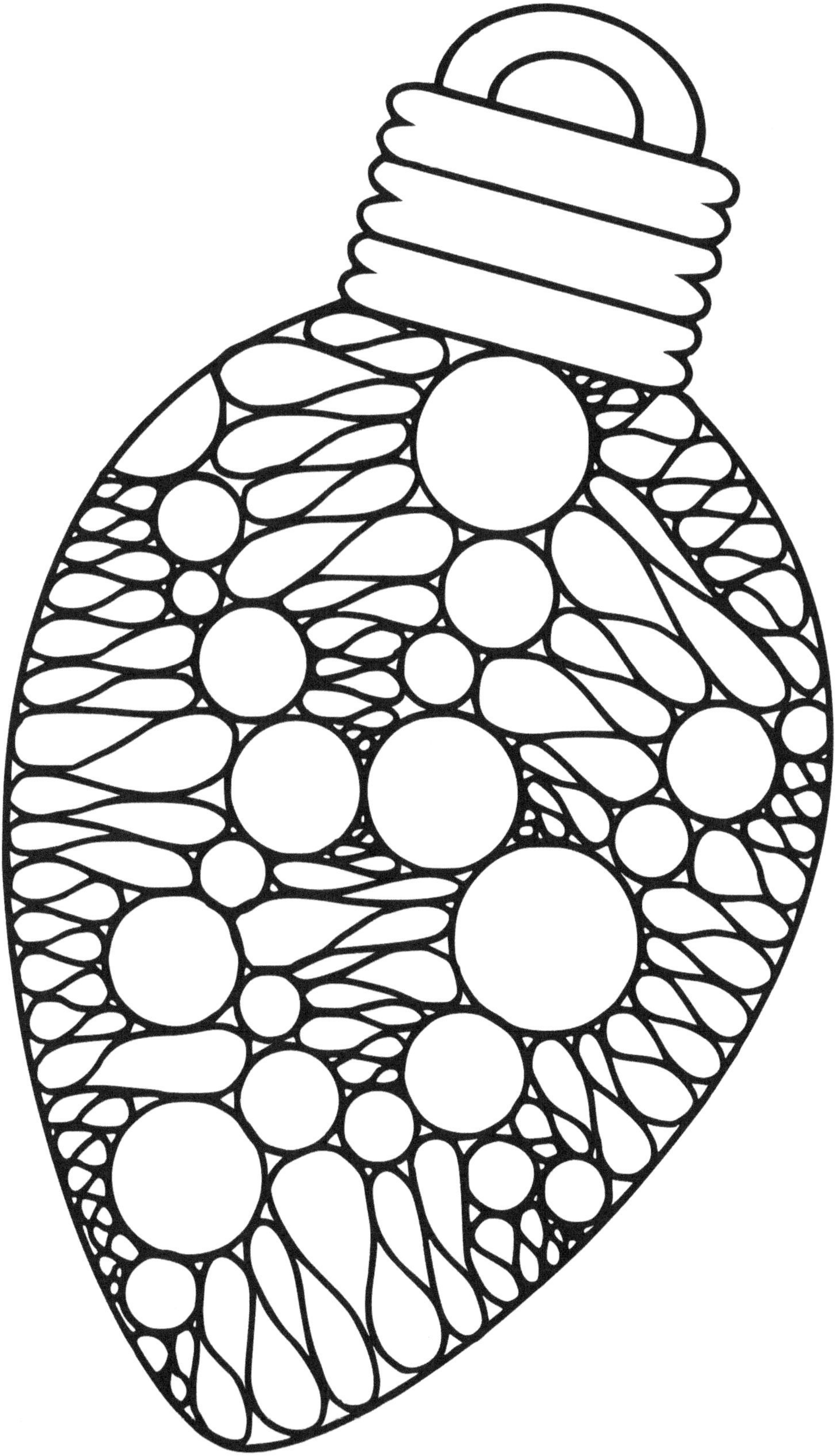

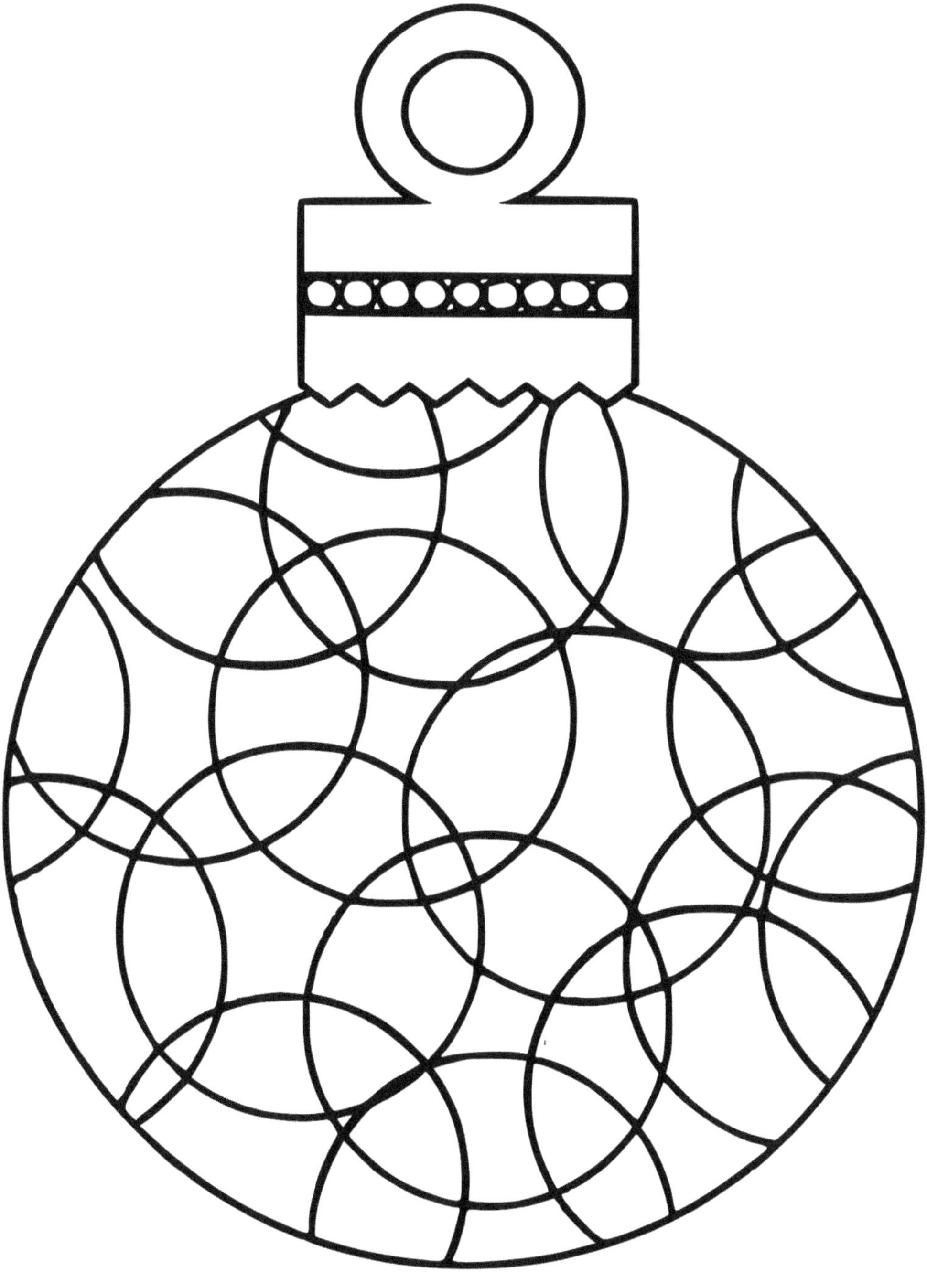

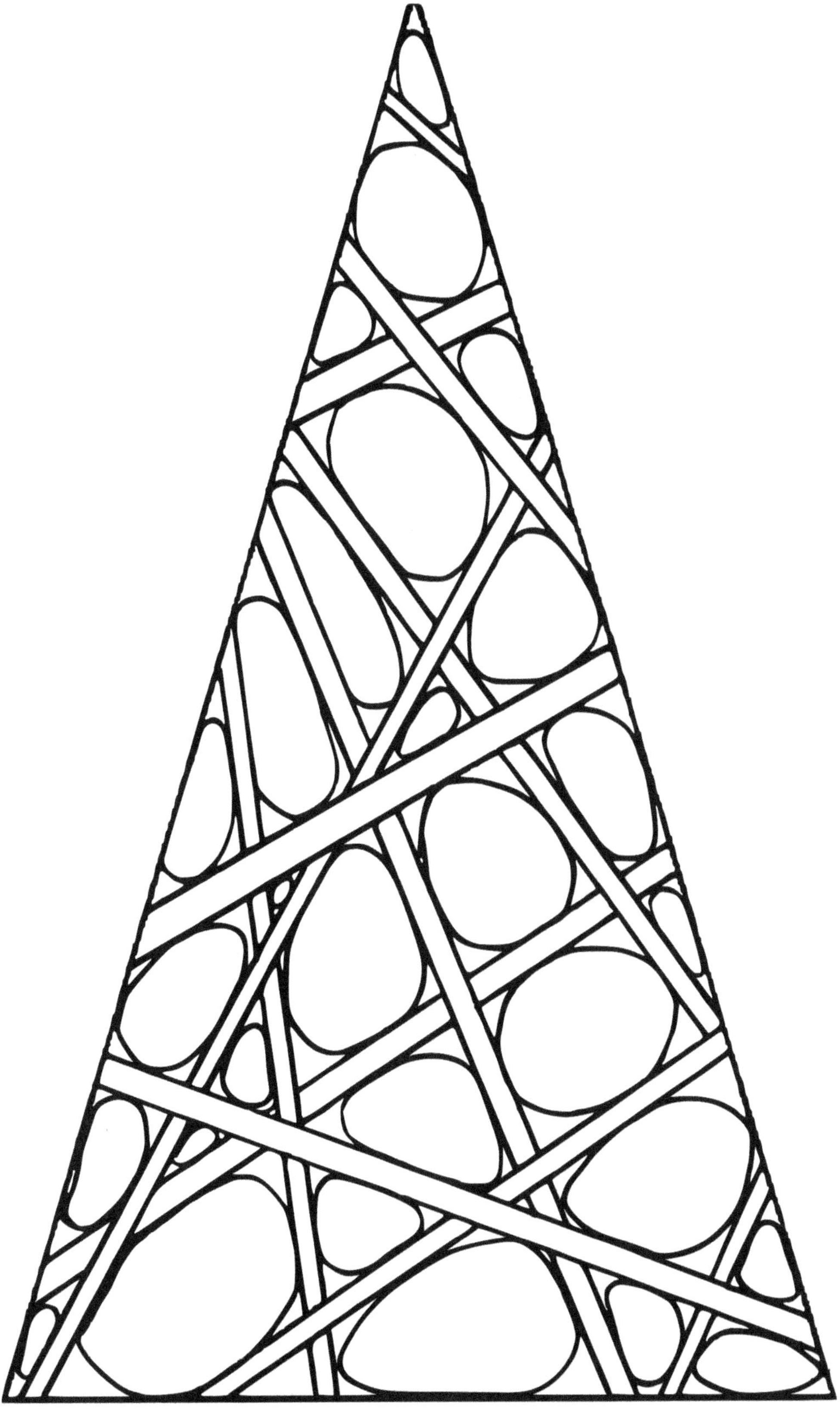

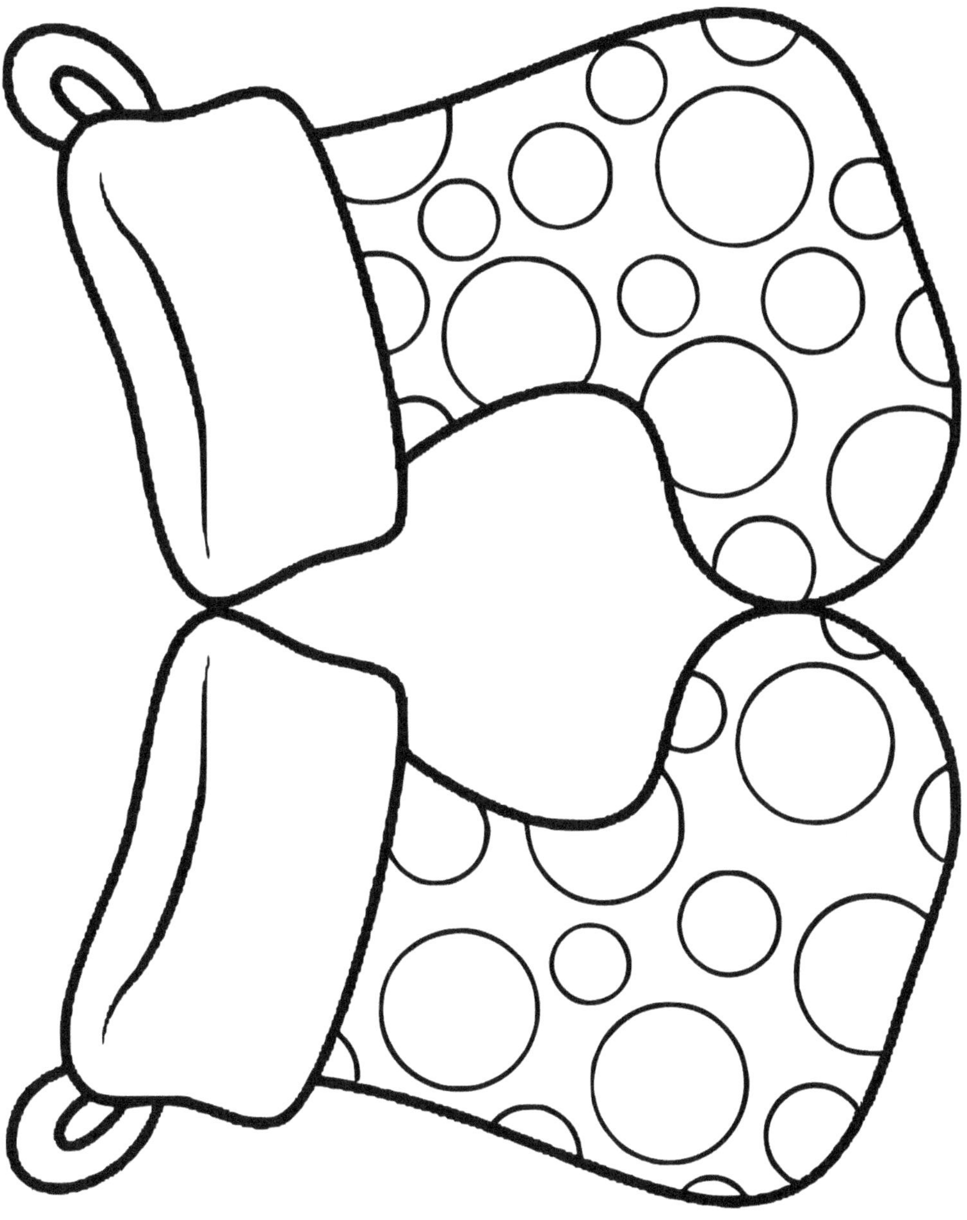

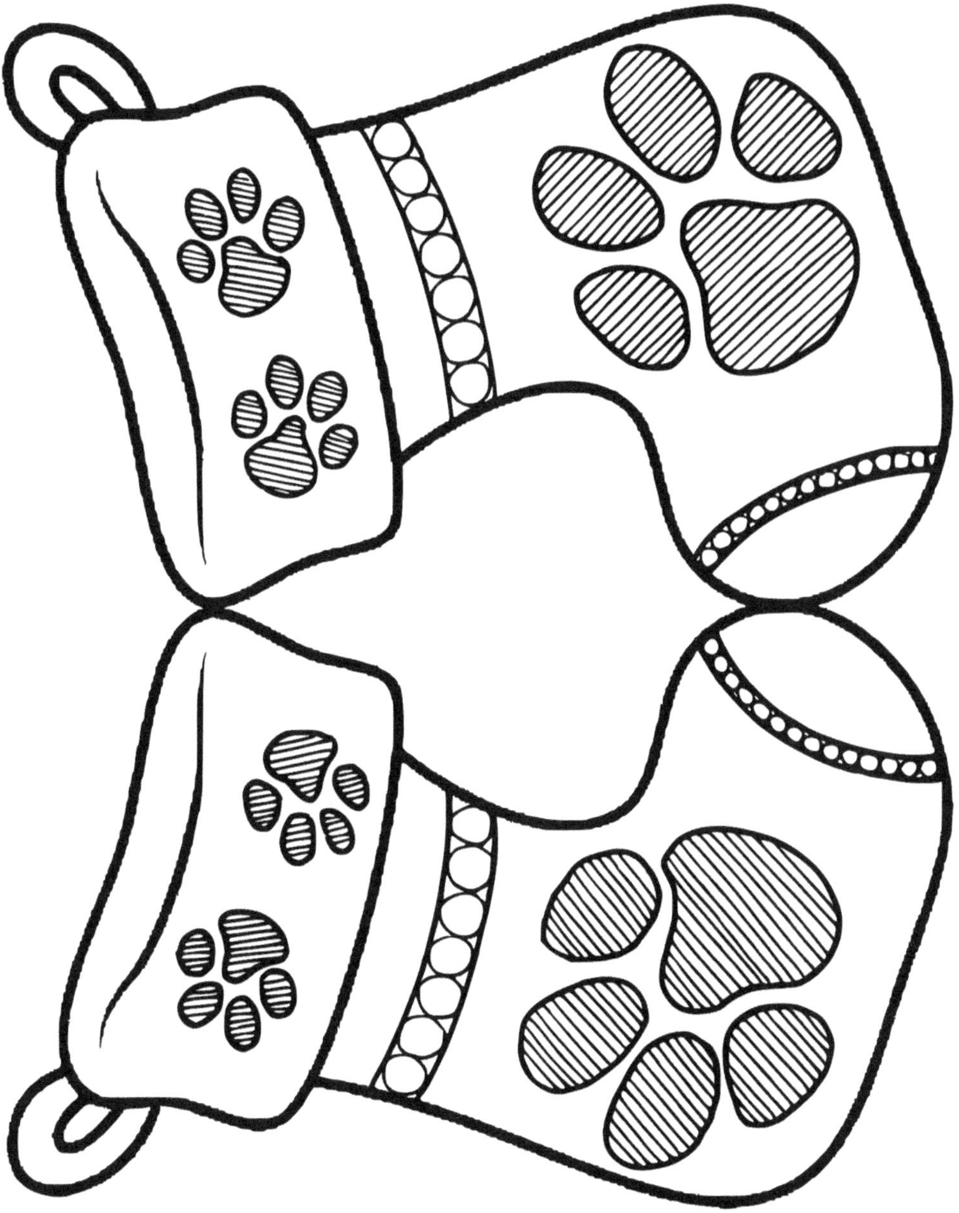

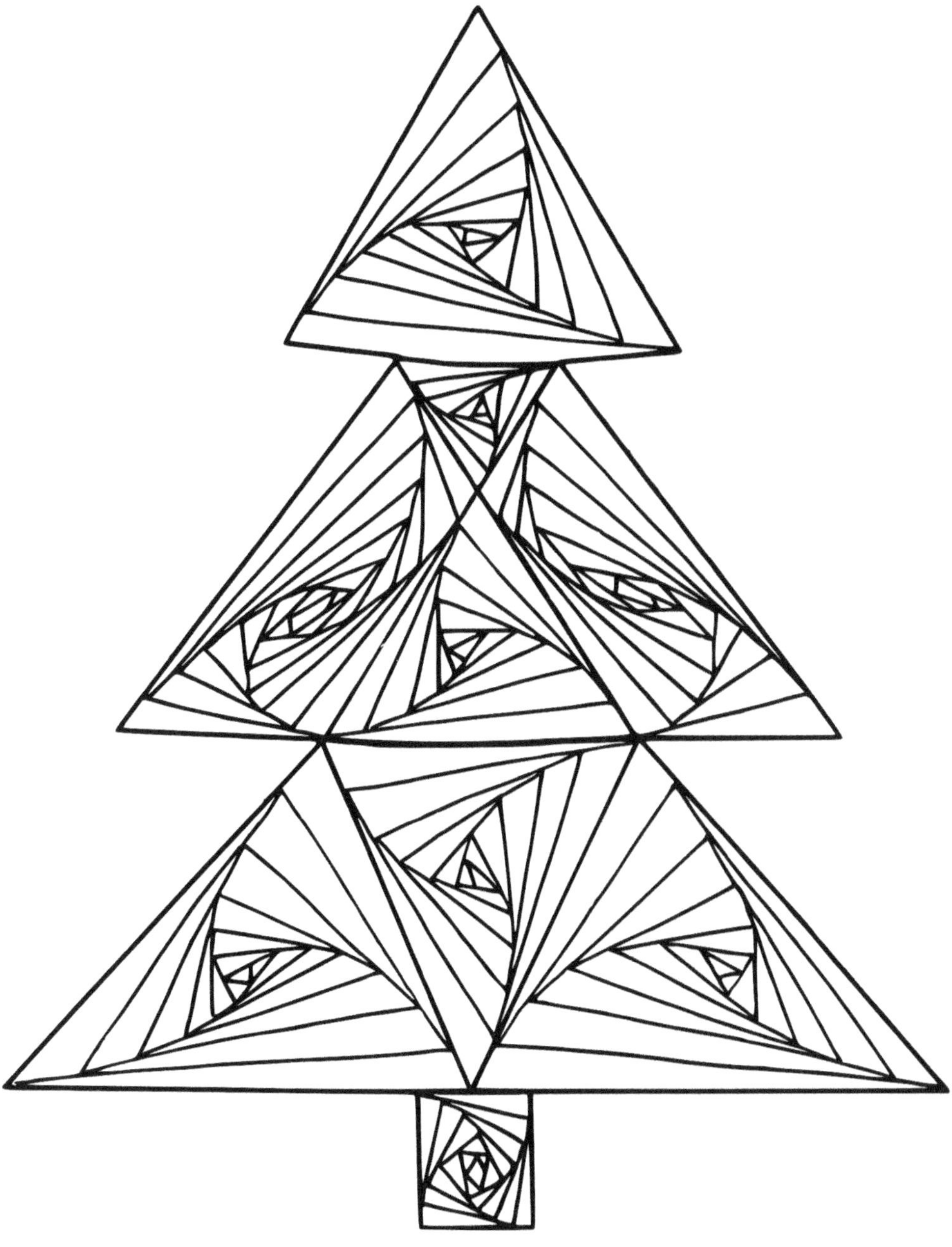

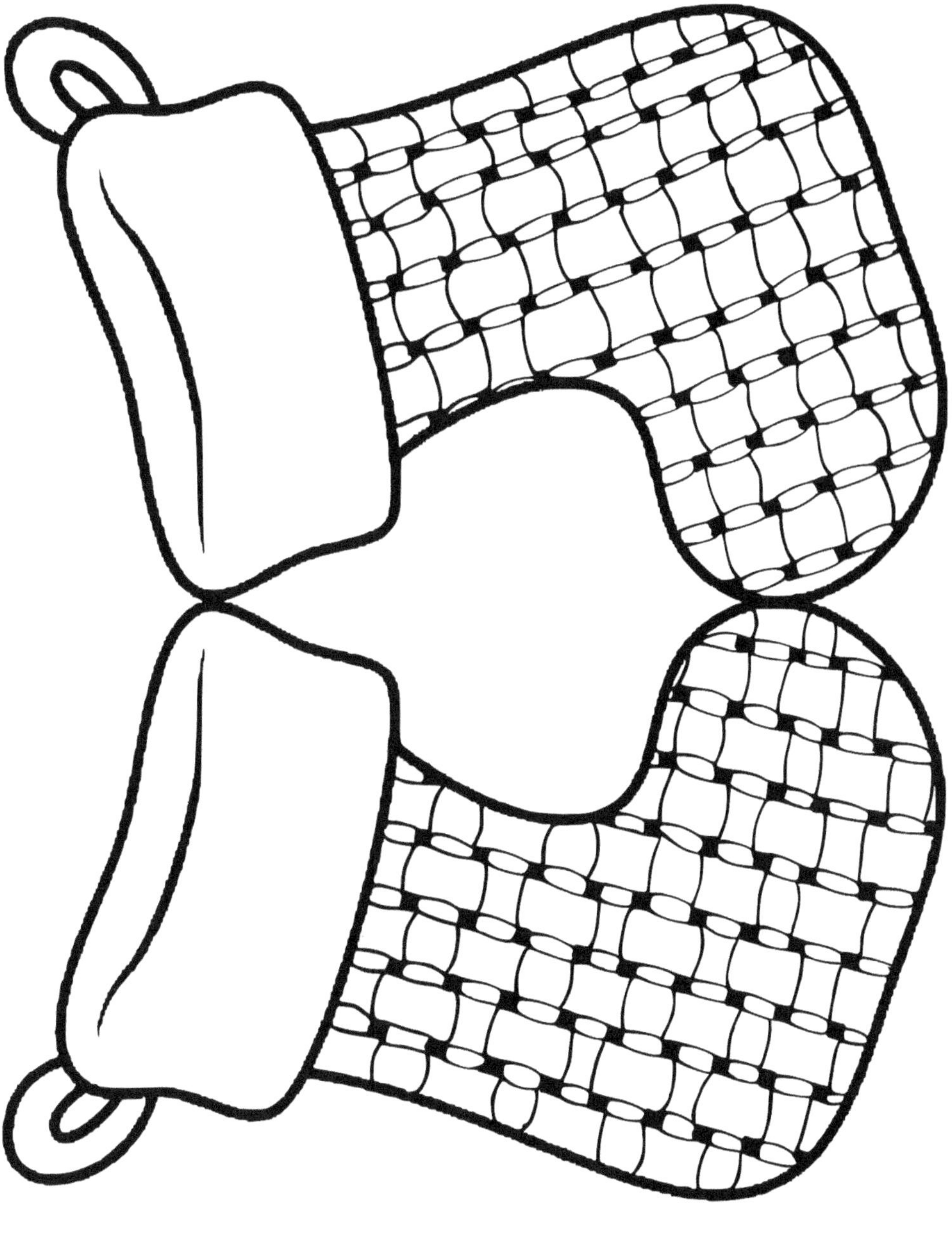

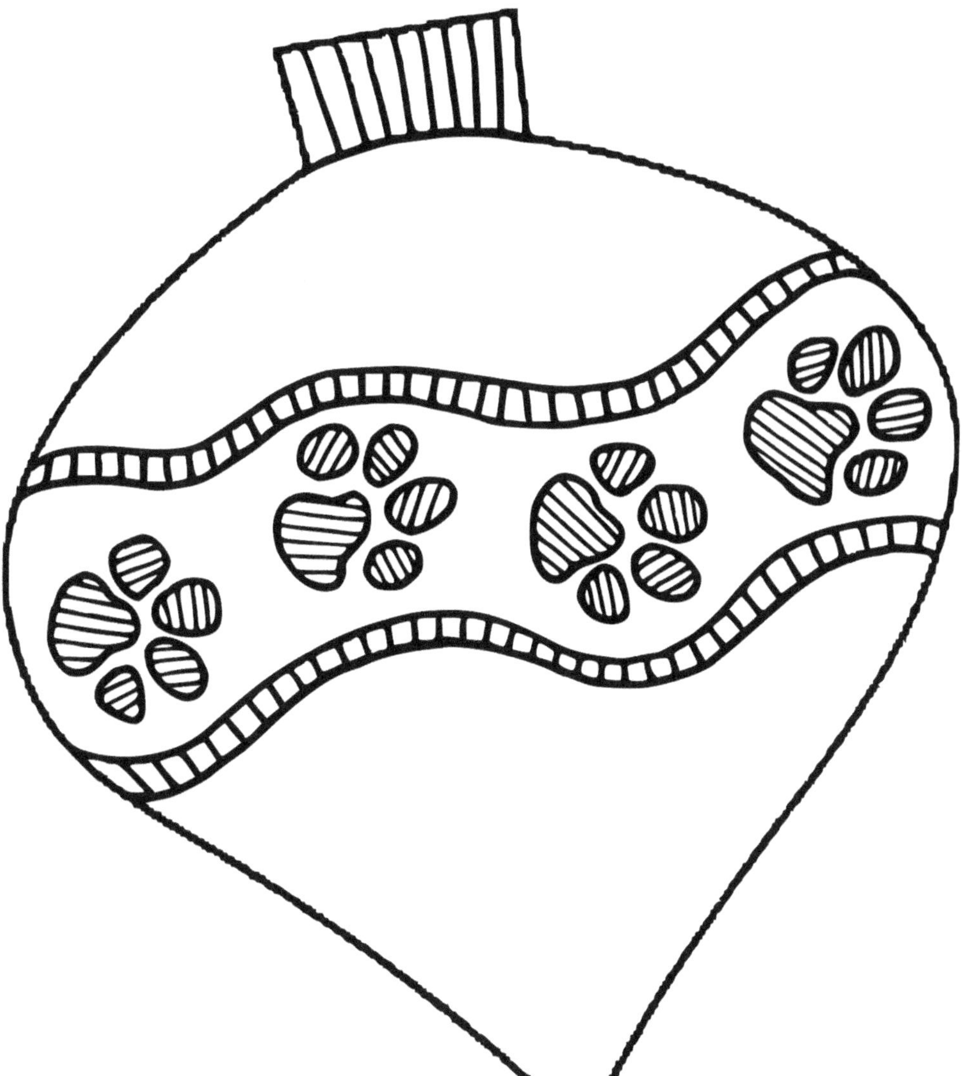

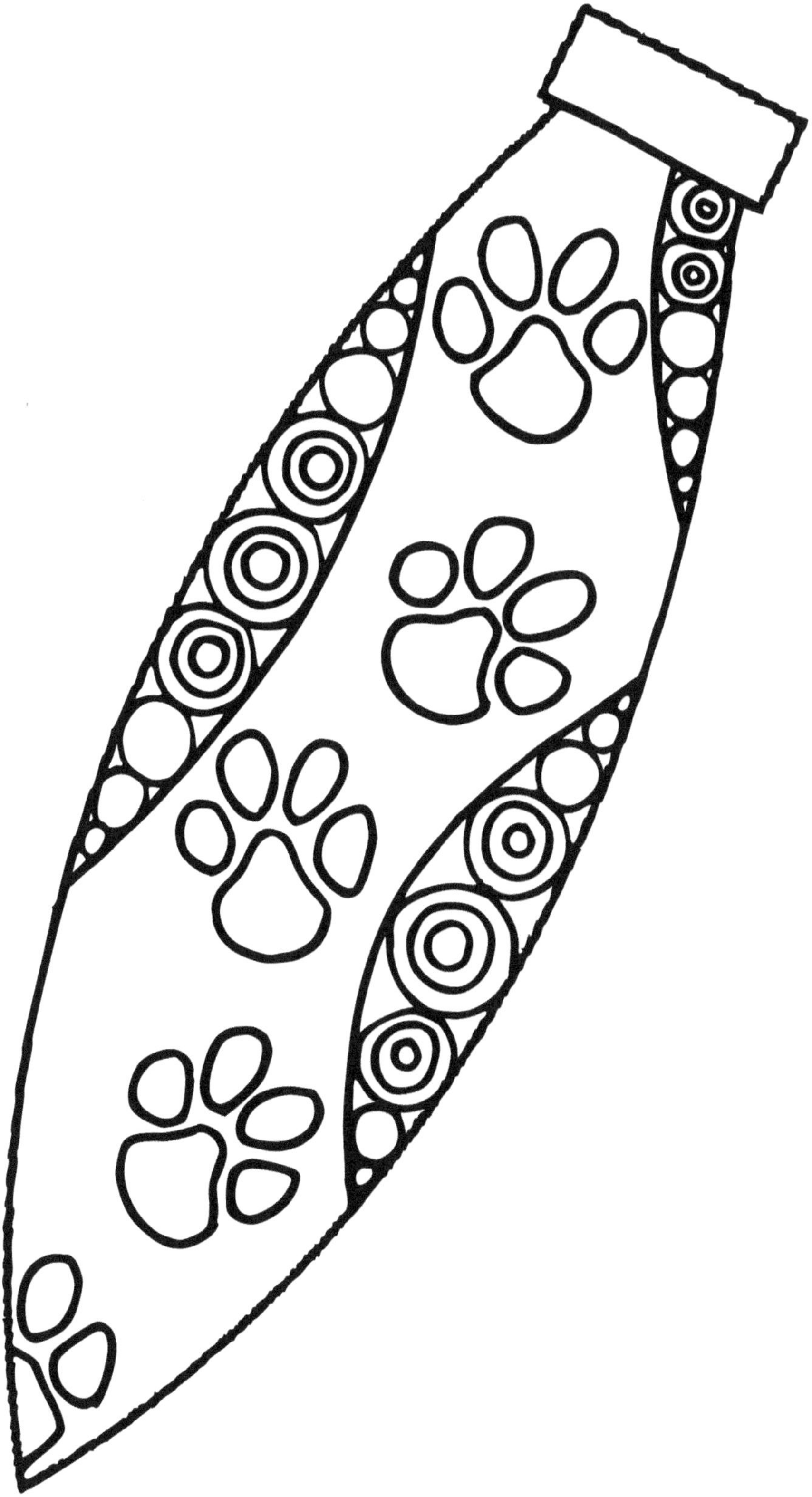

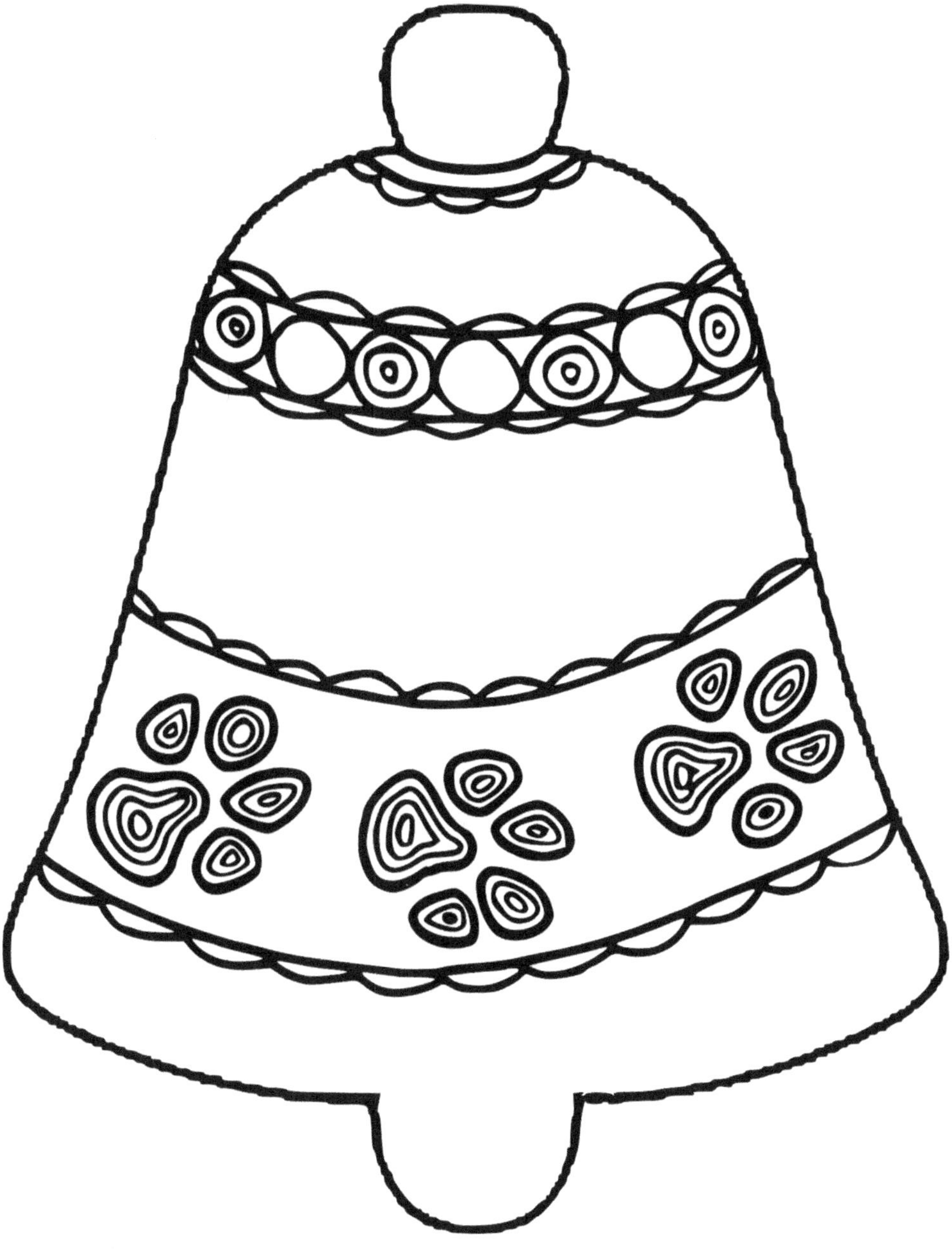

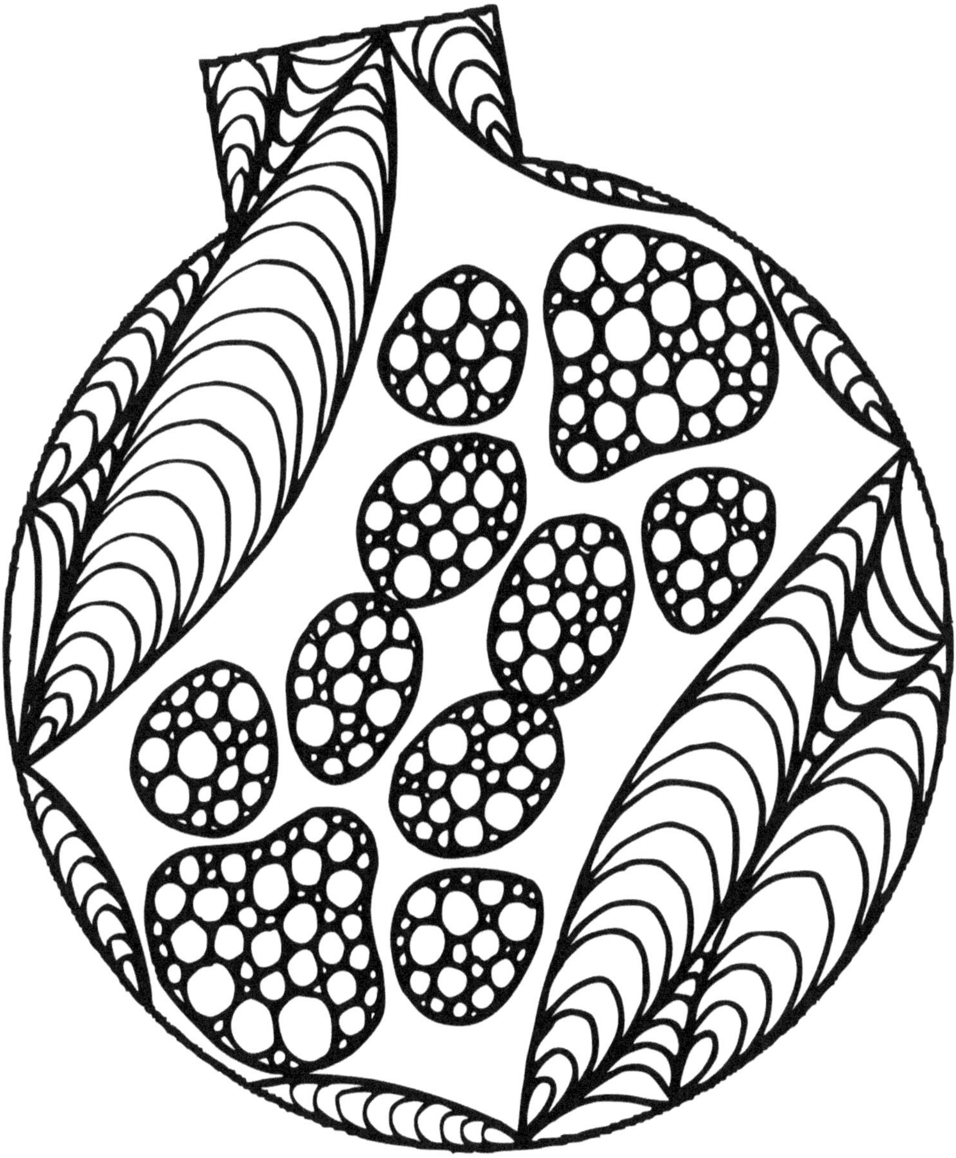

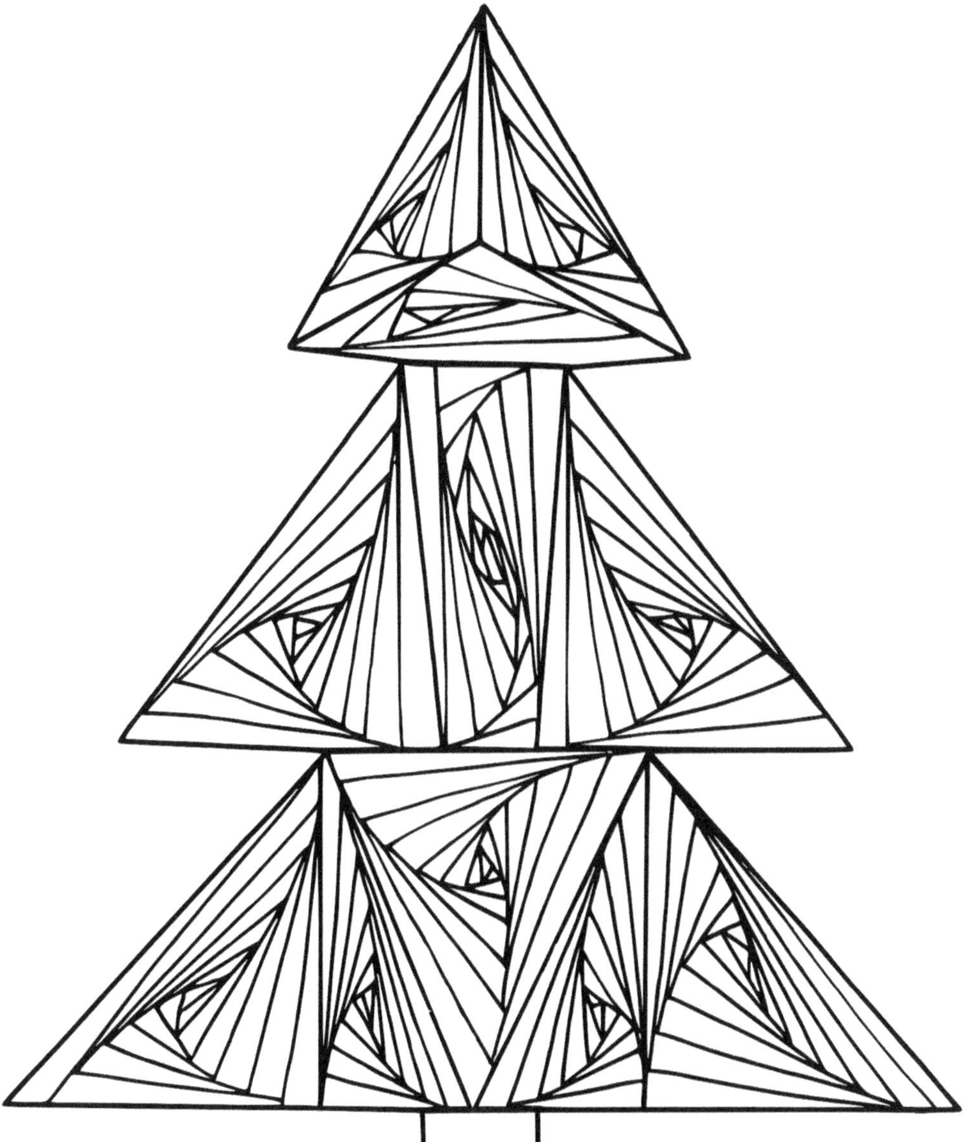

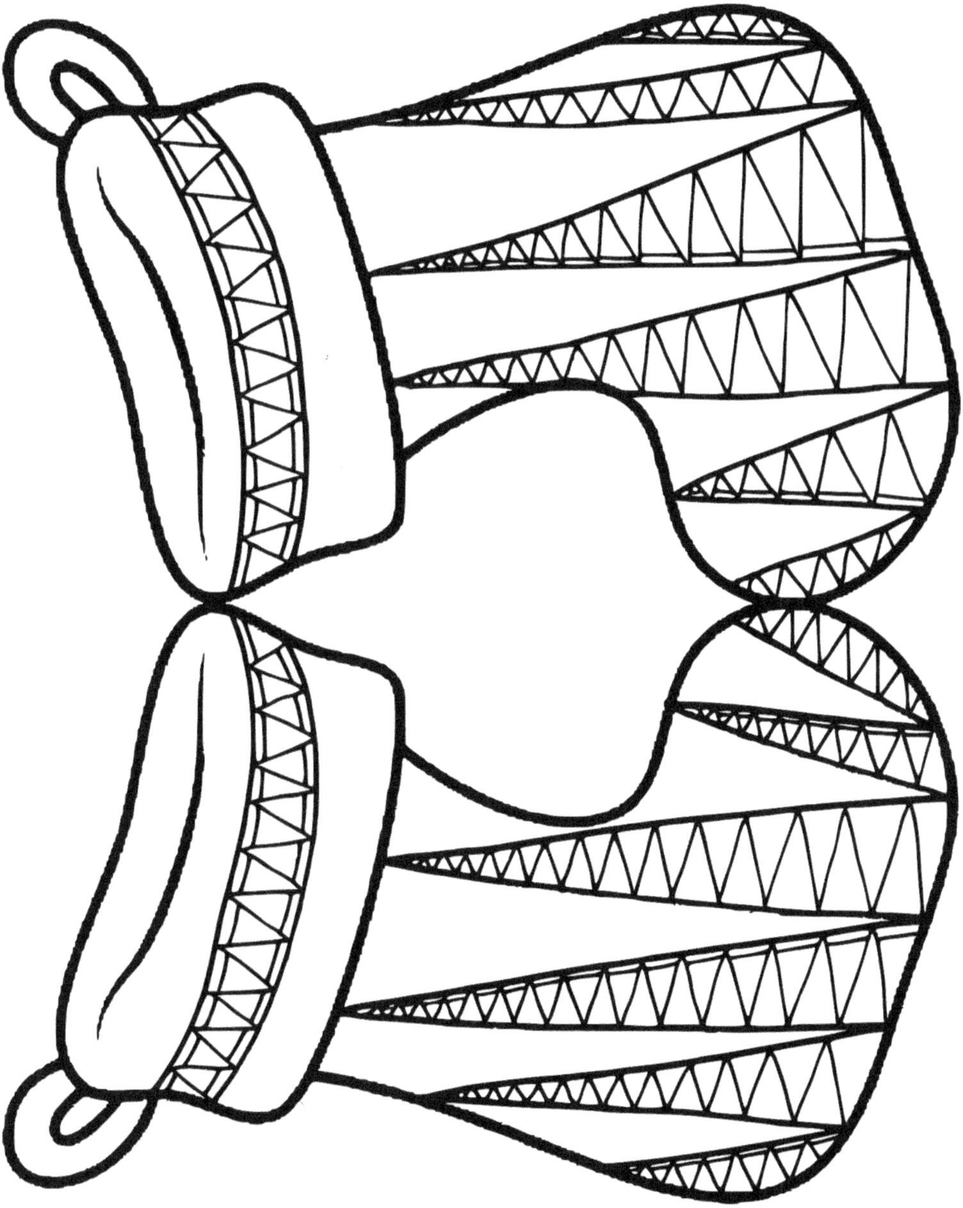

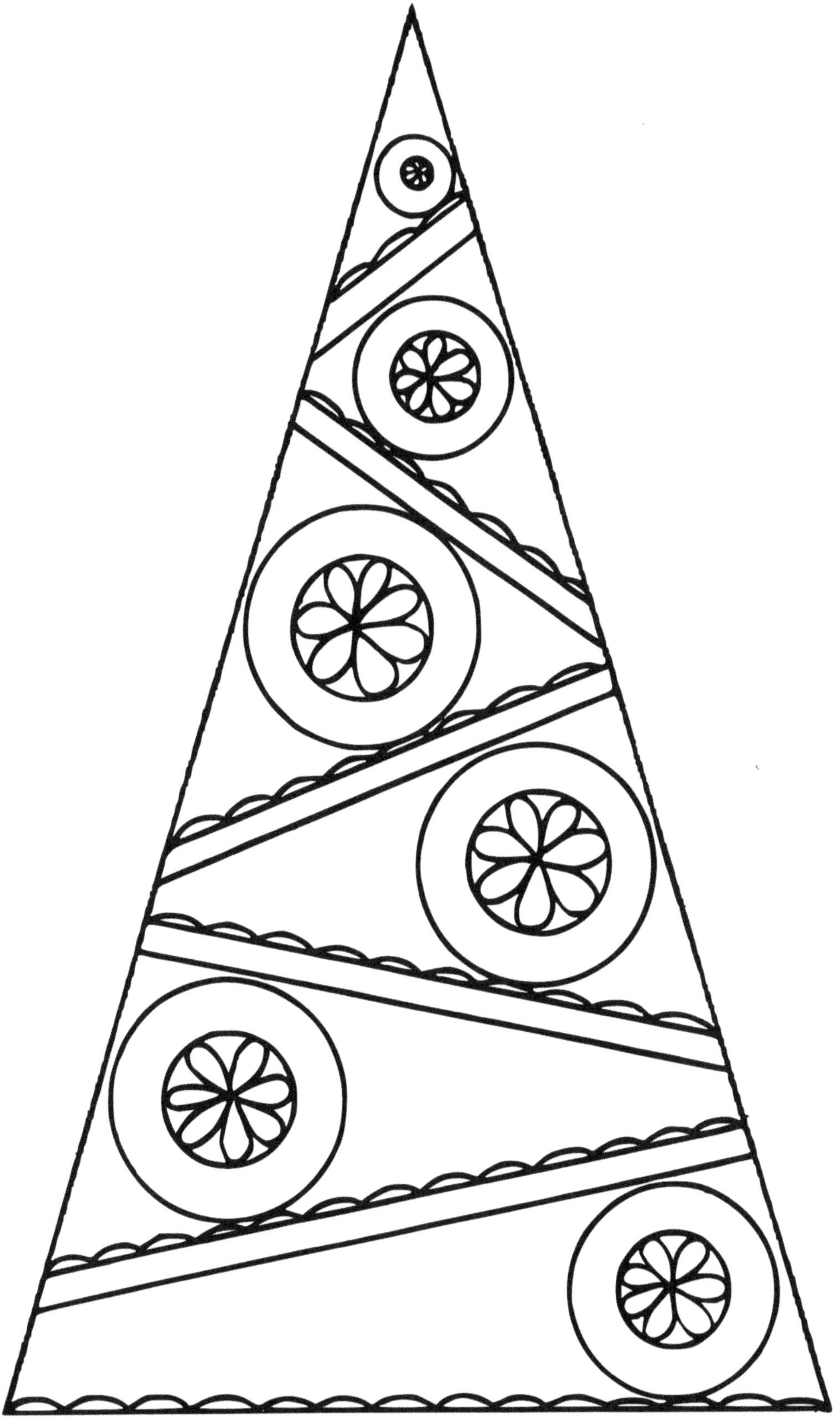

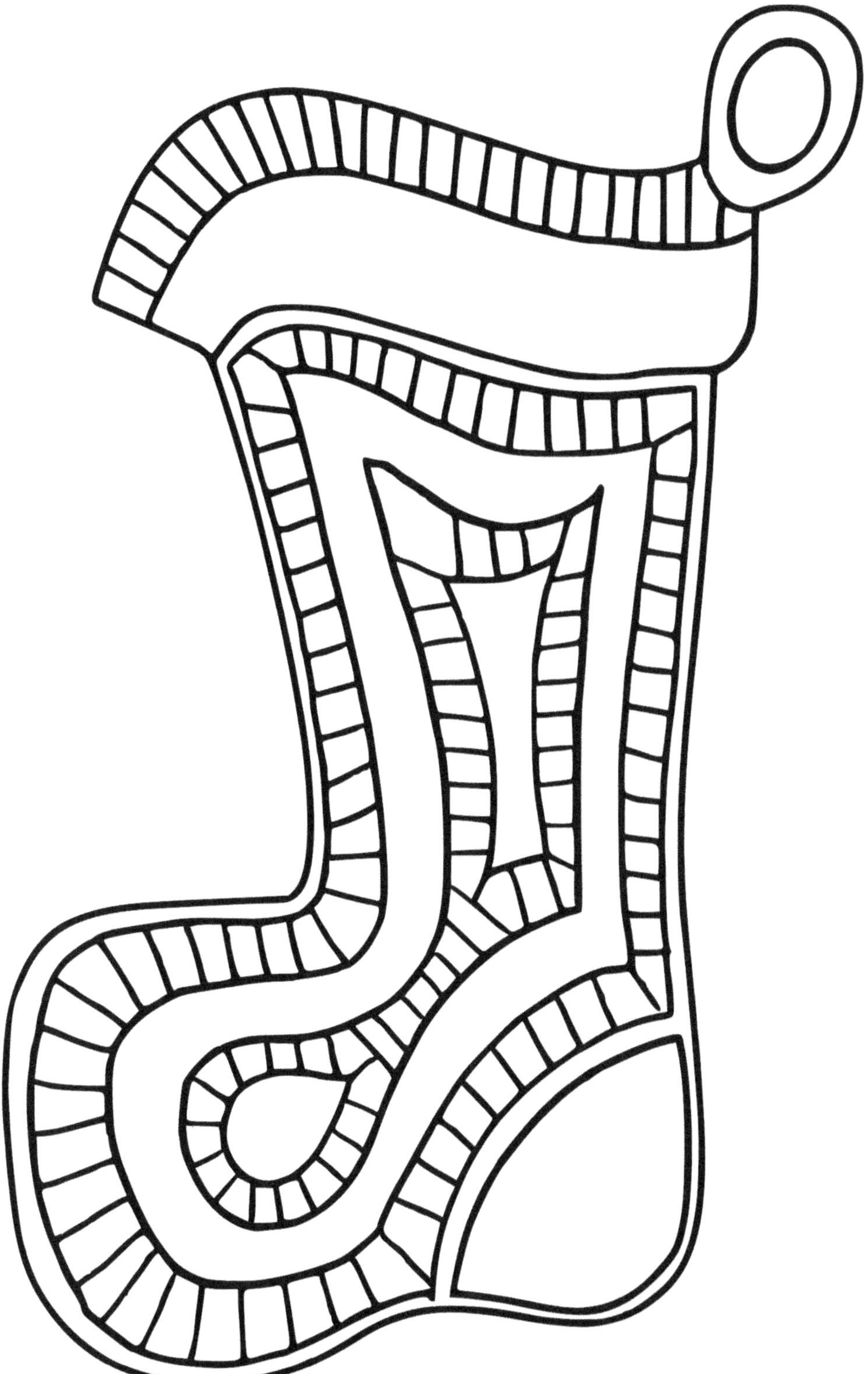

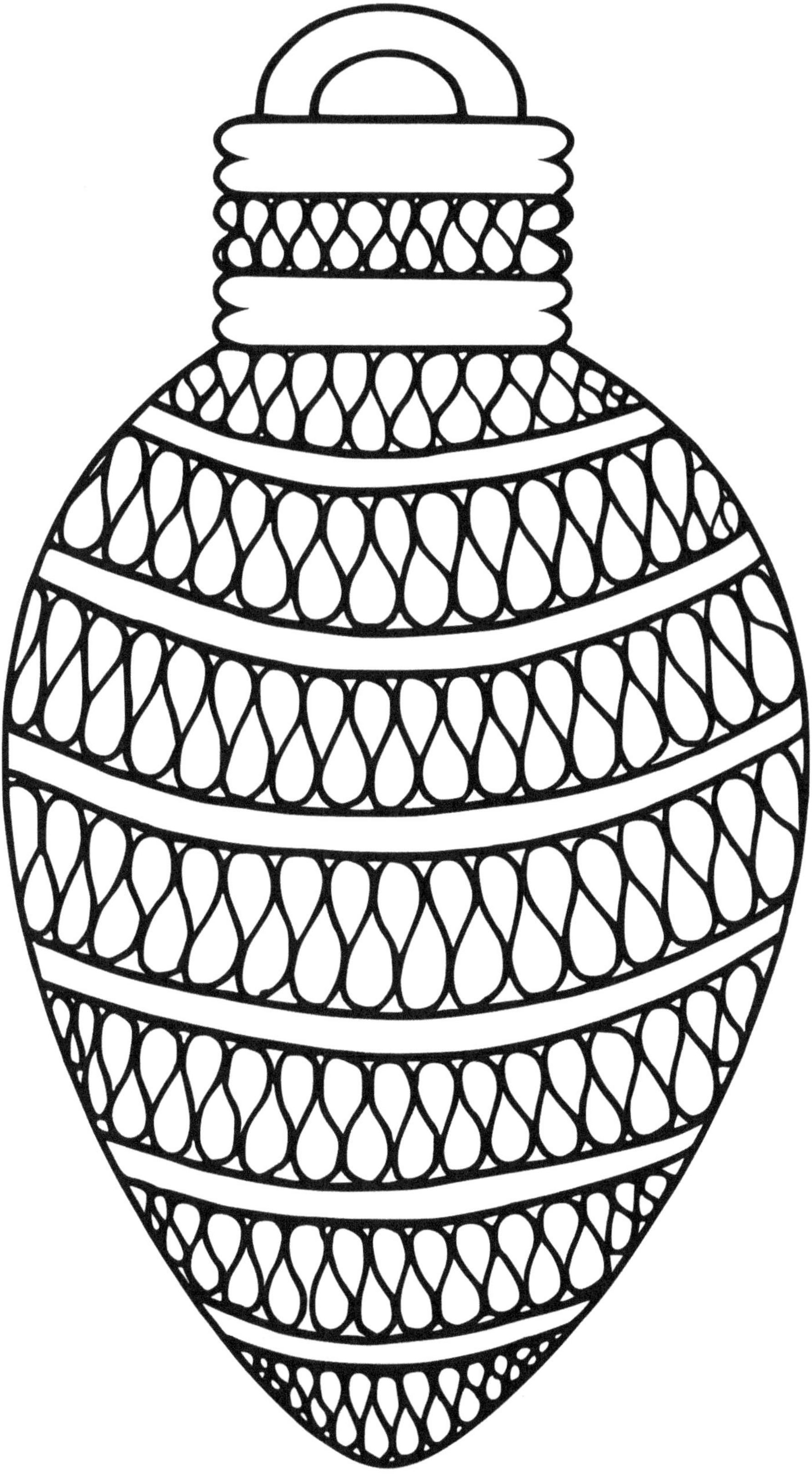

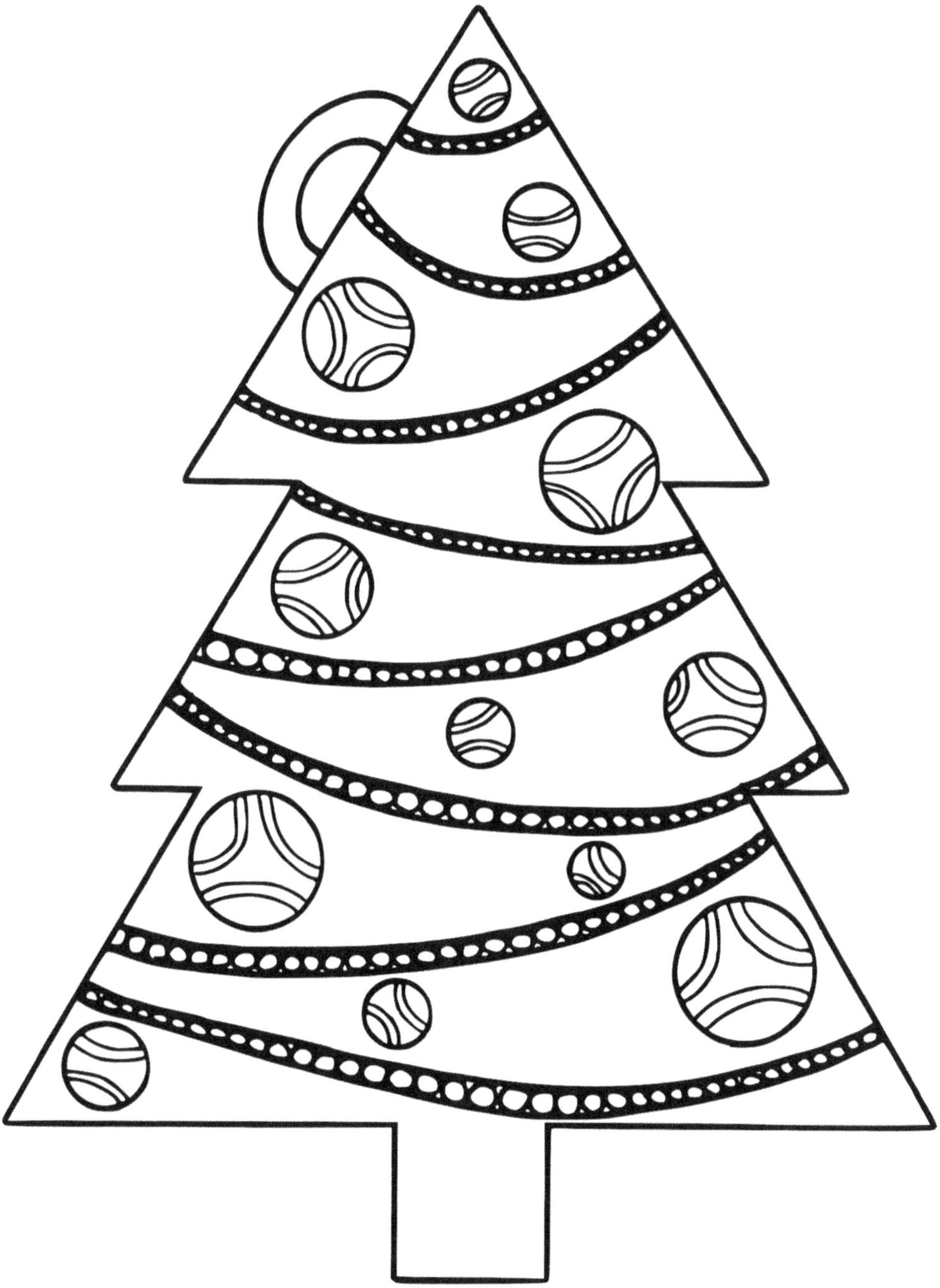

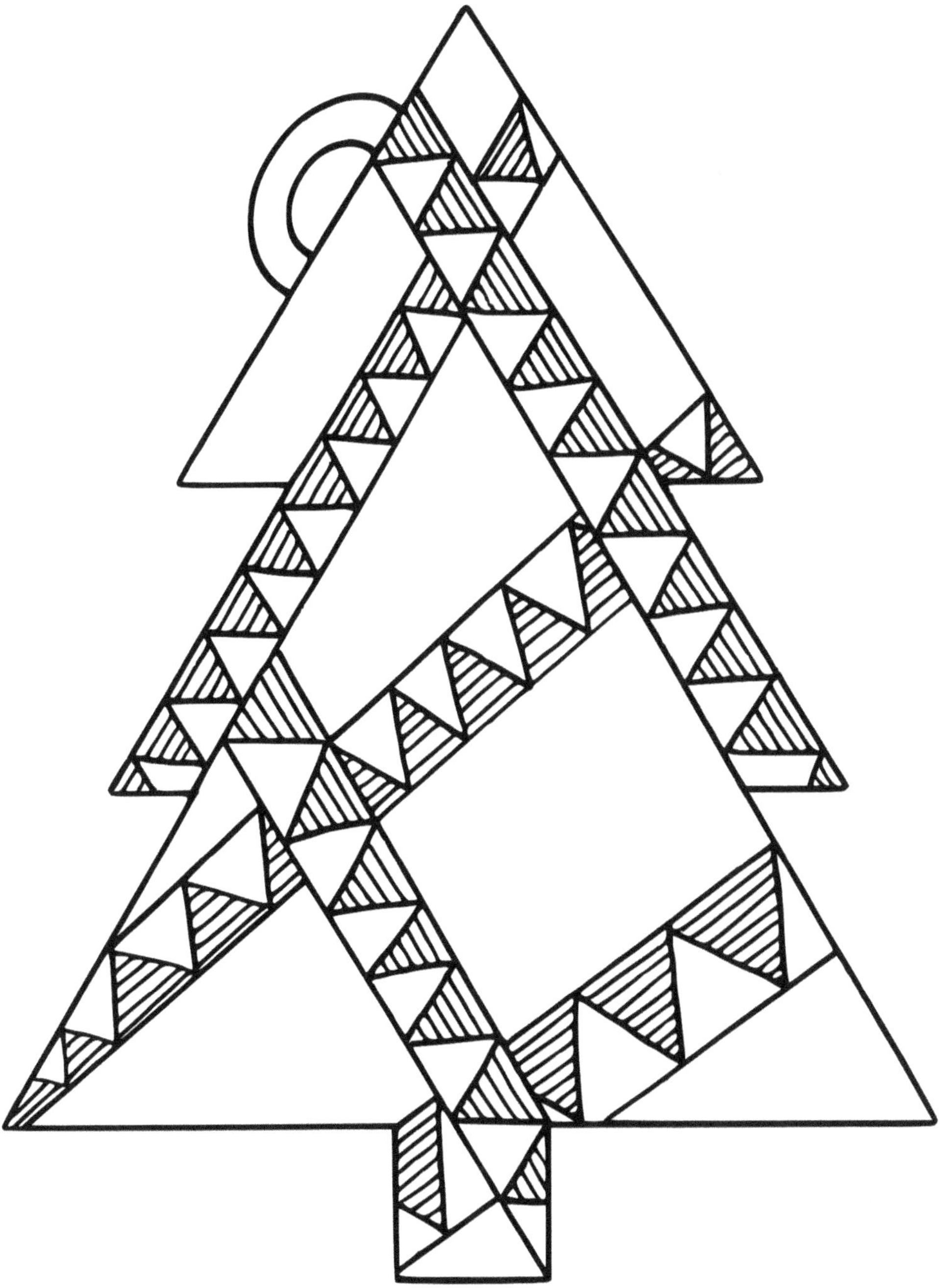

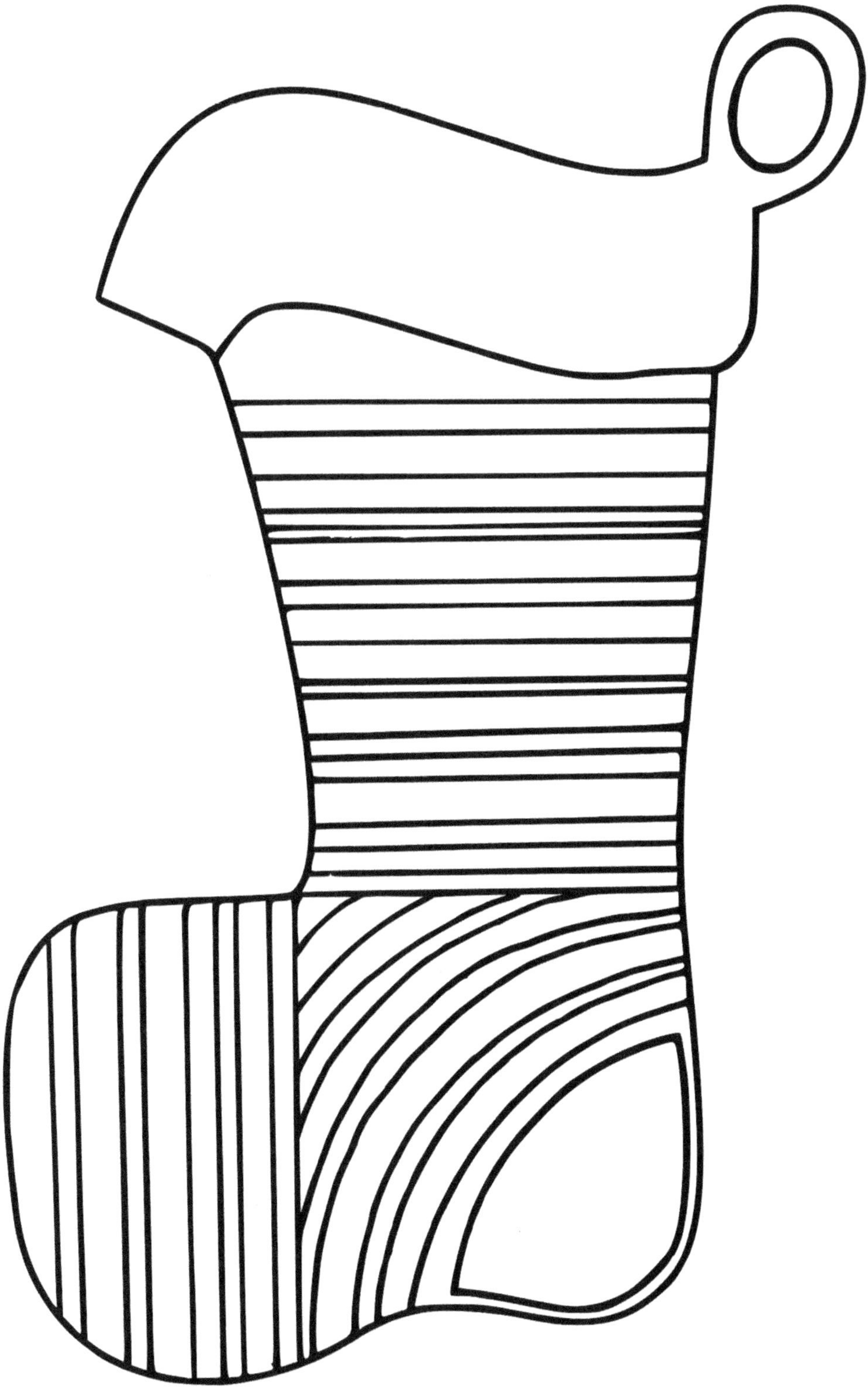

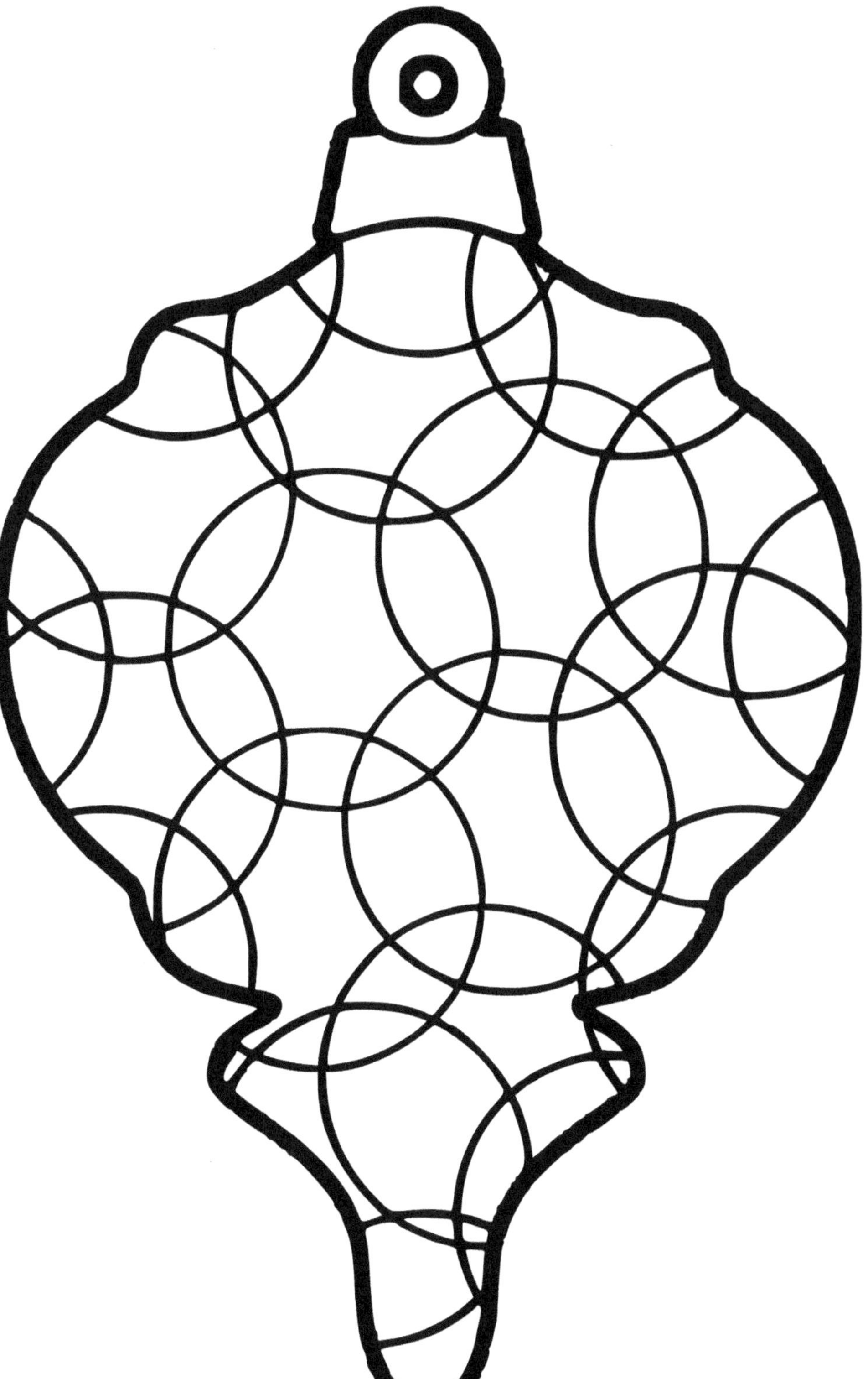

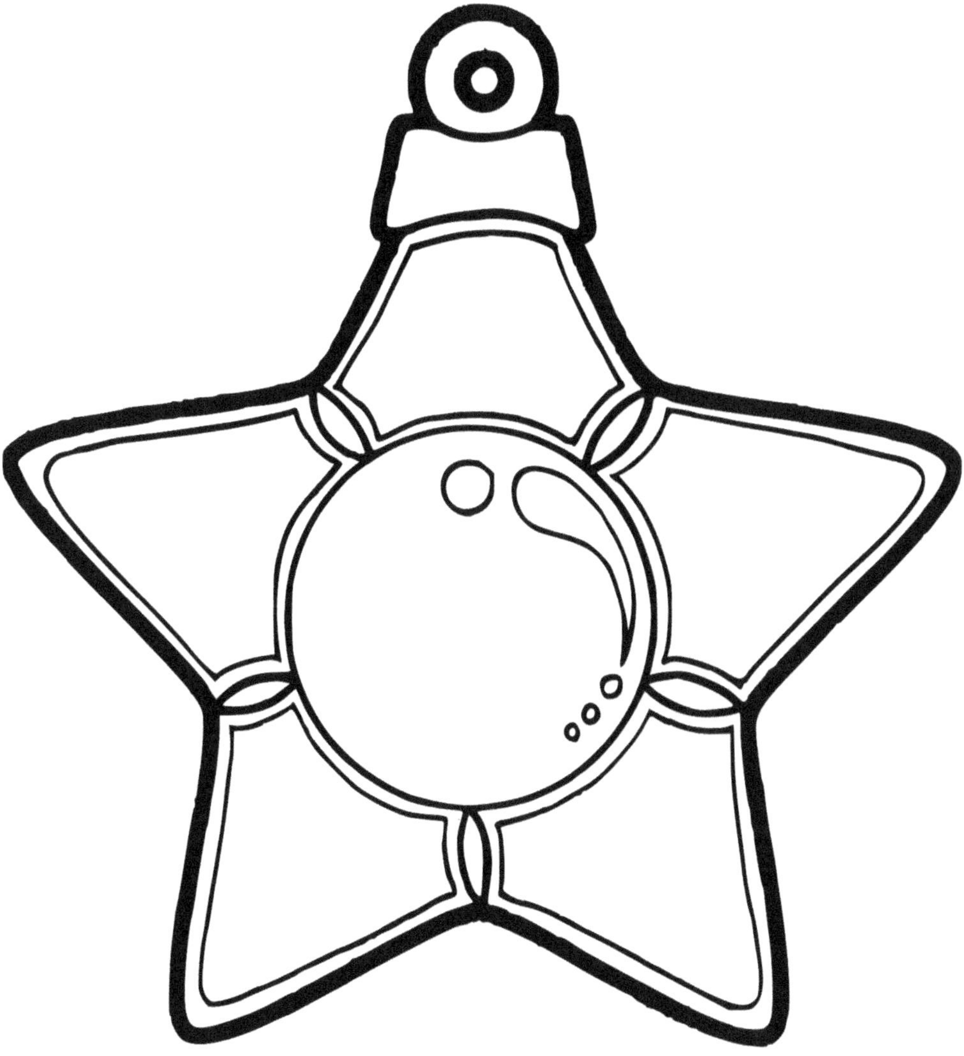

75 Designs from Maria Wedel

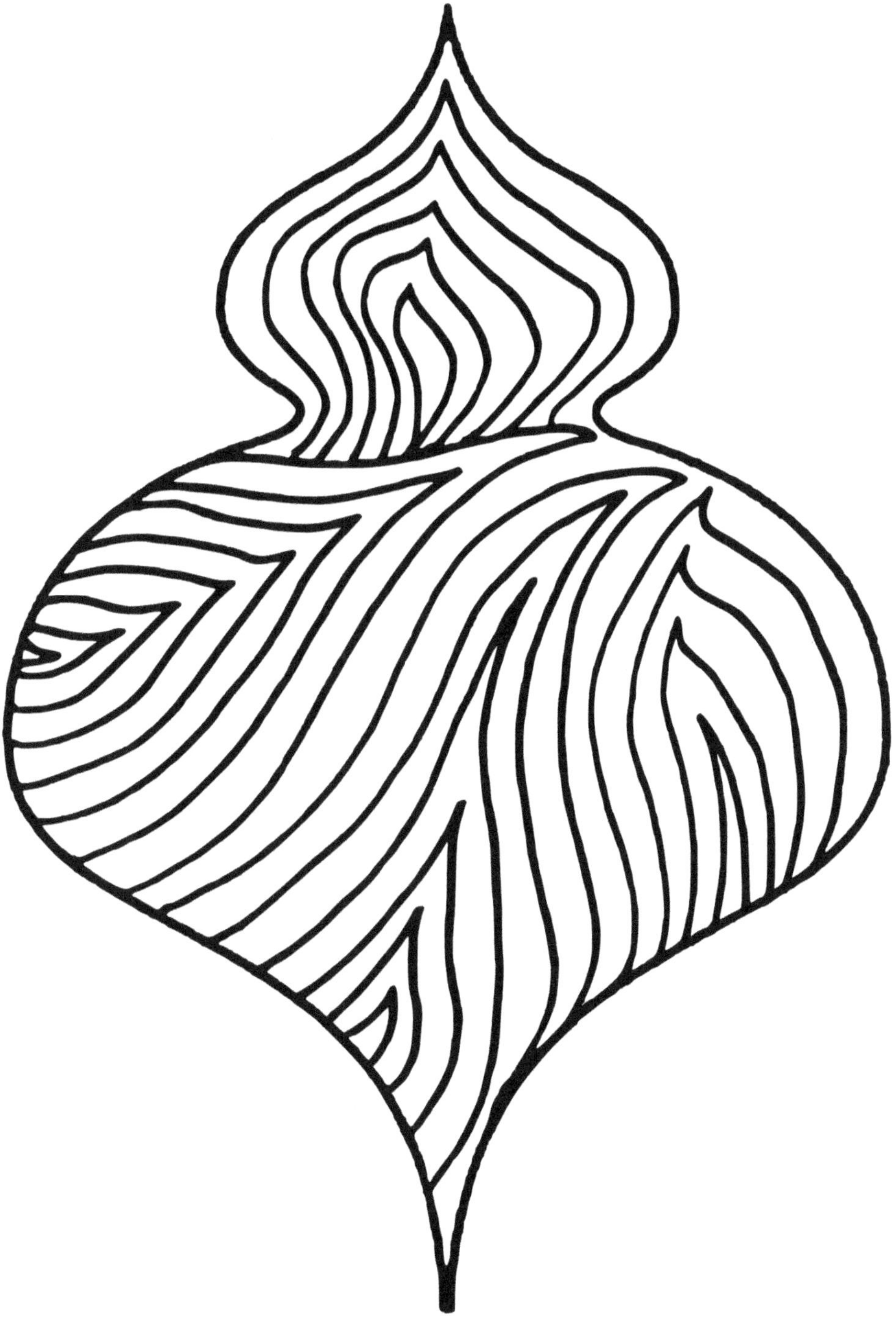

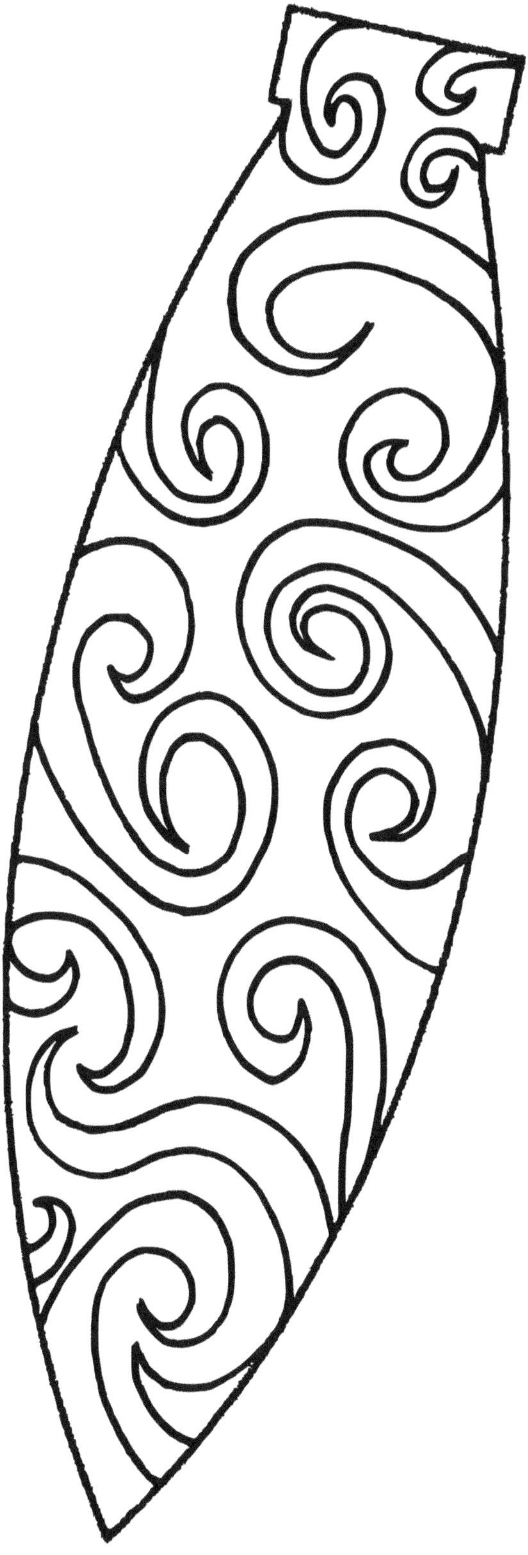

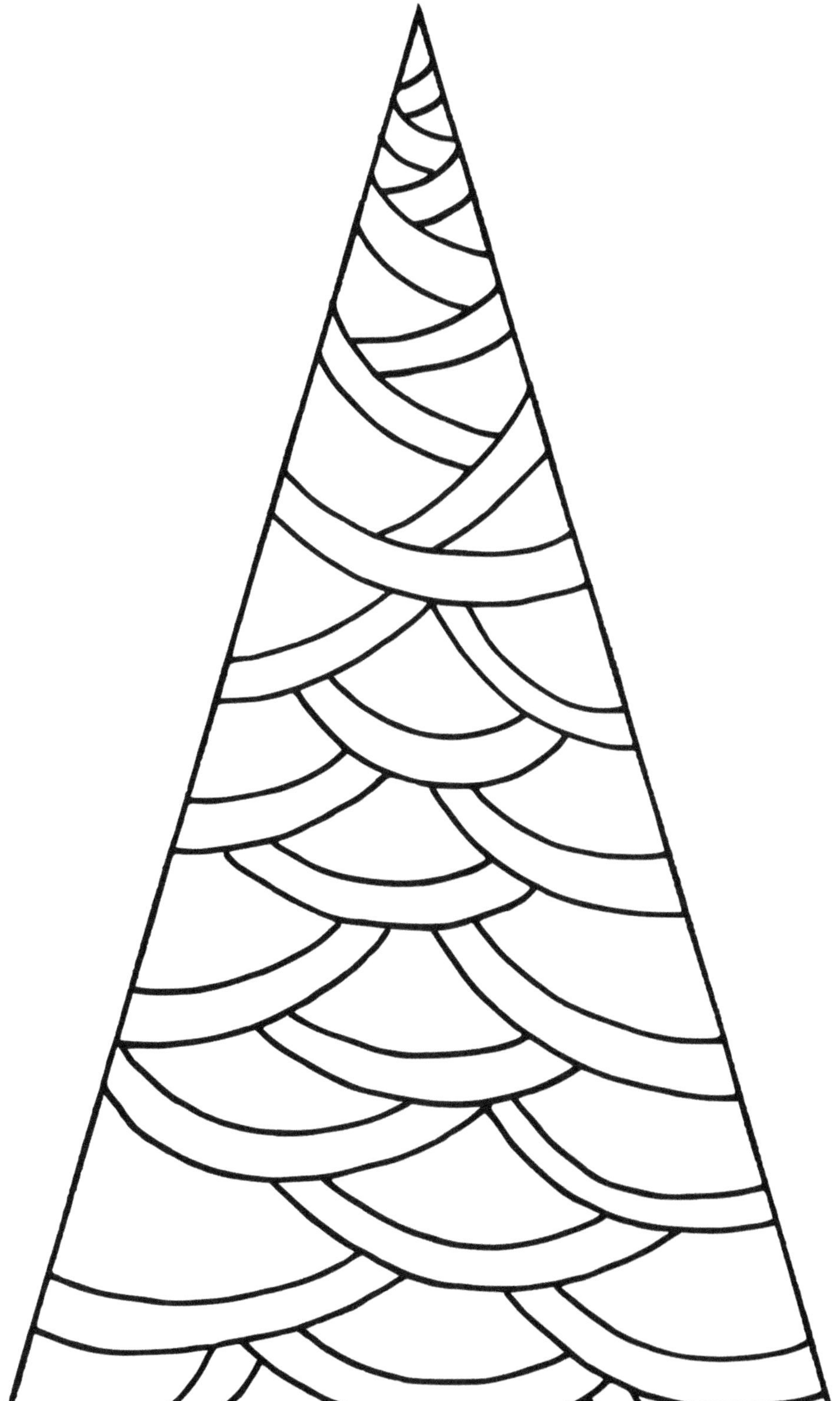

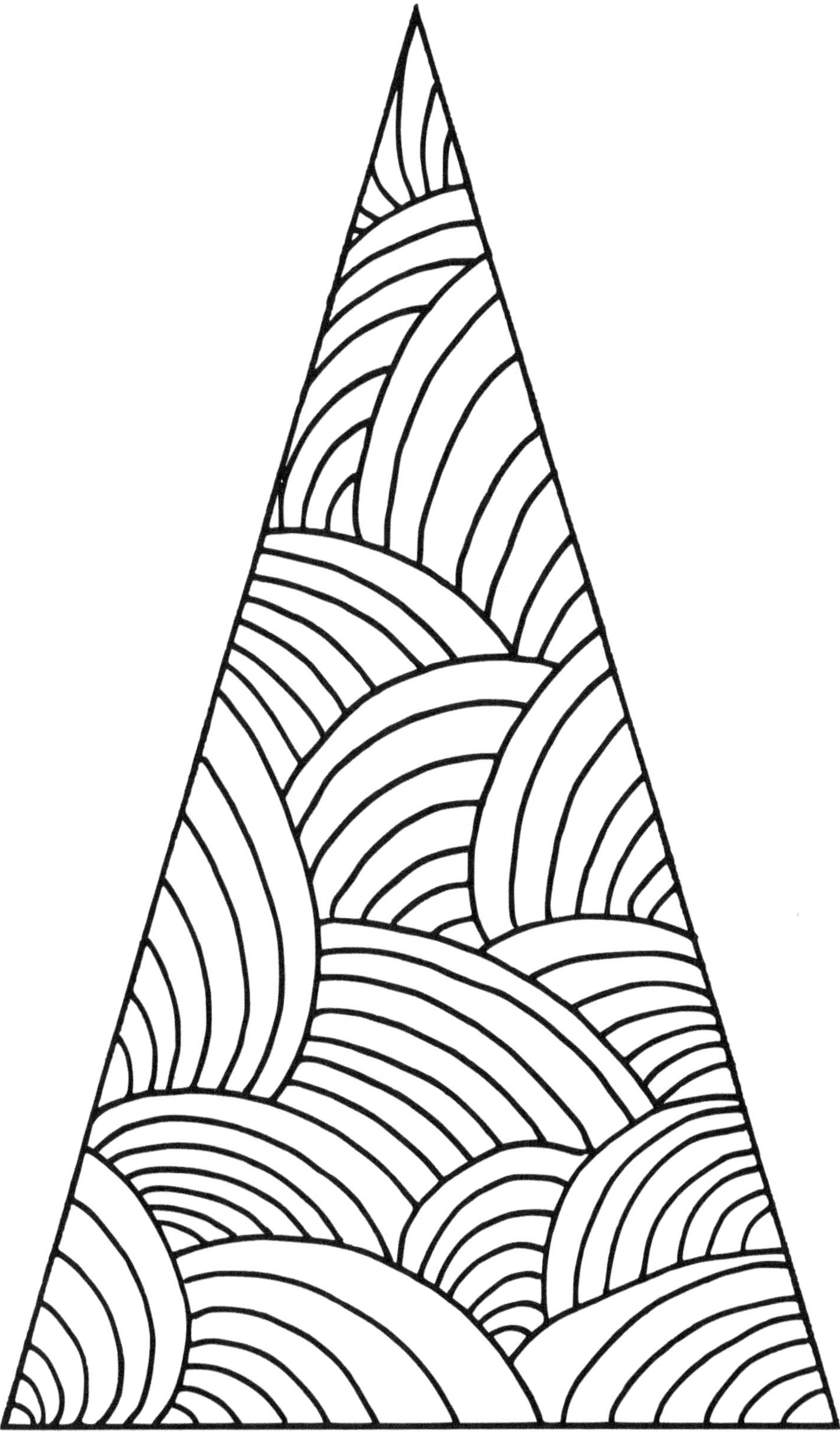

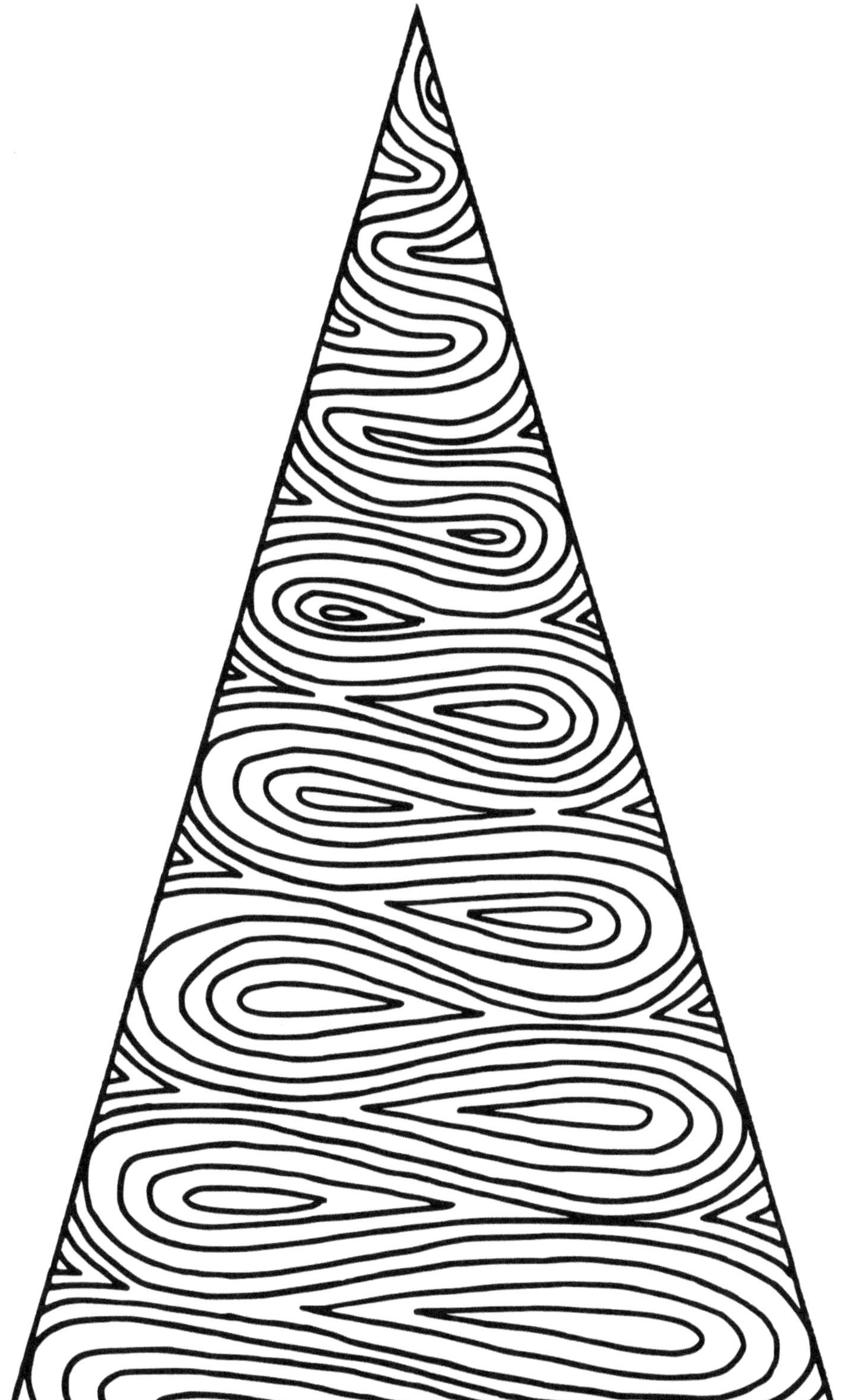

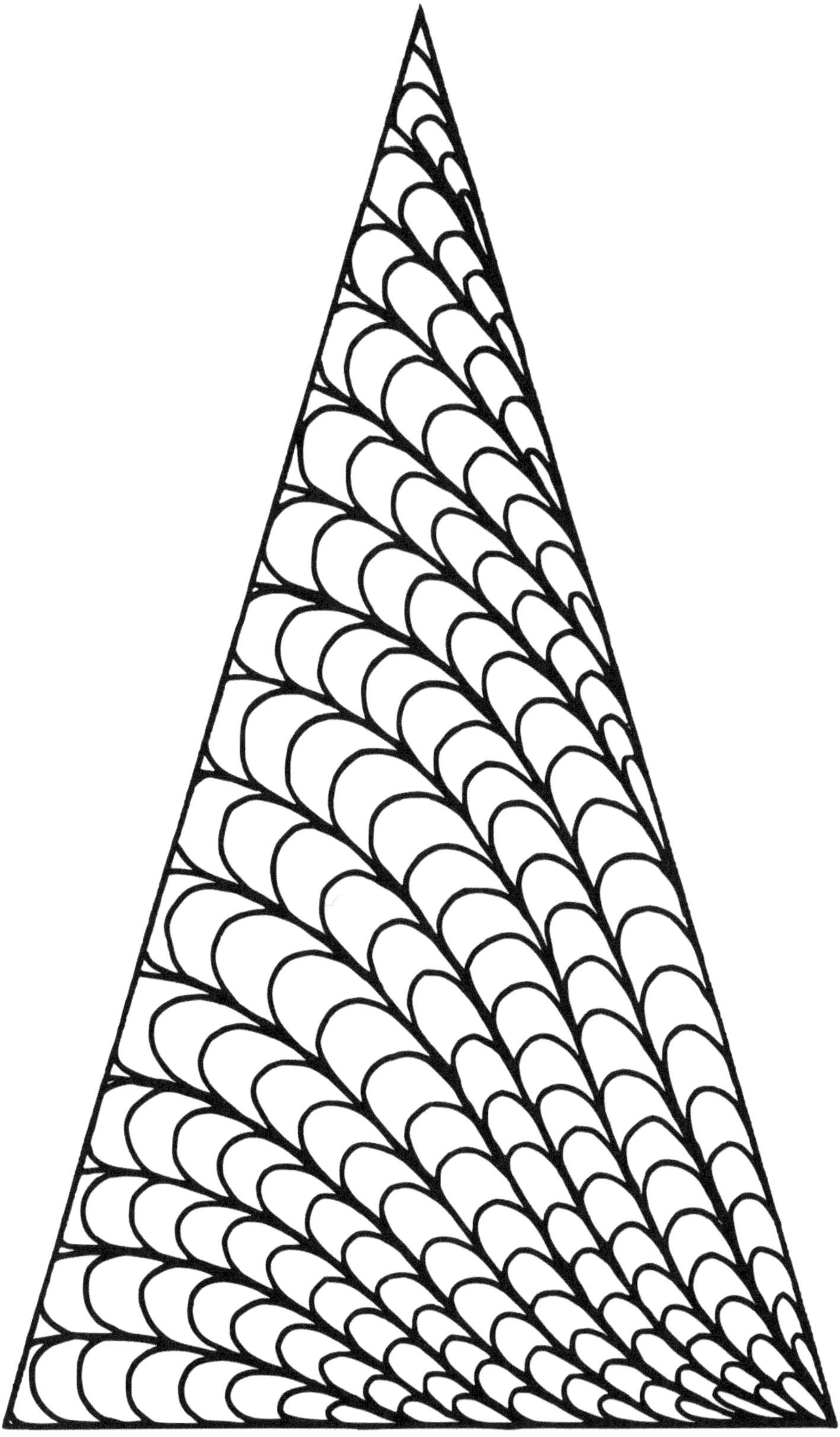

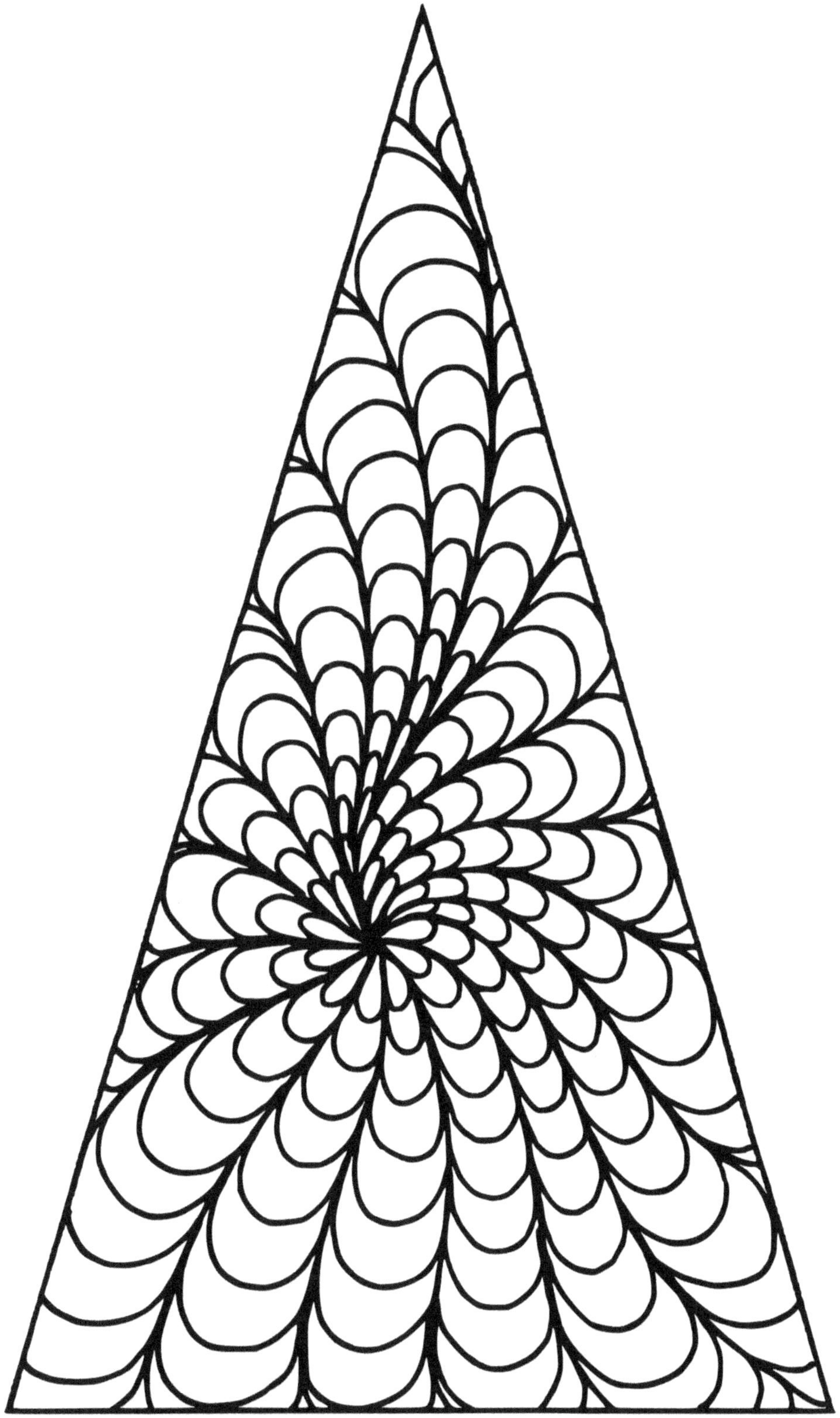

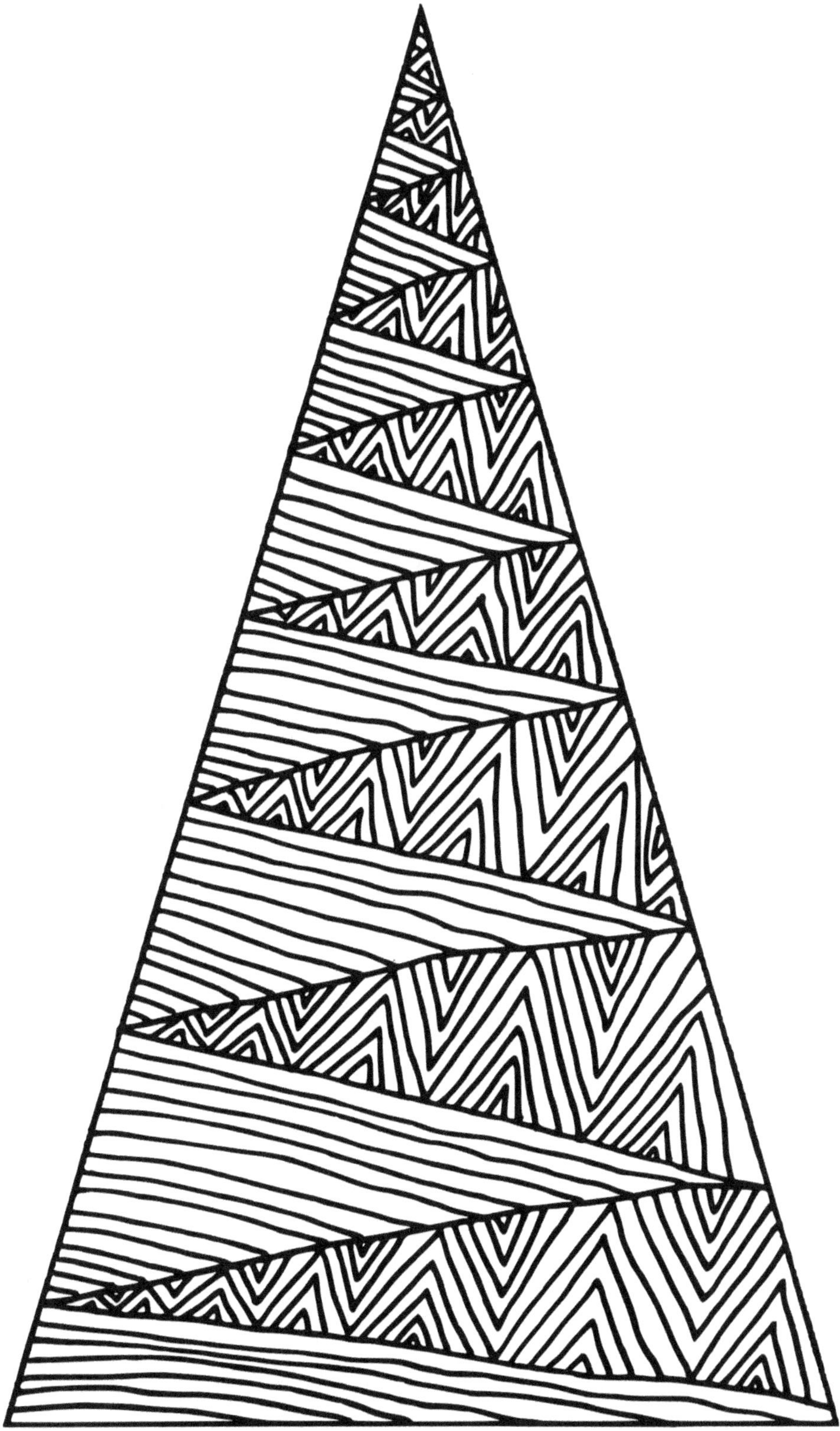

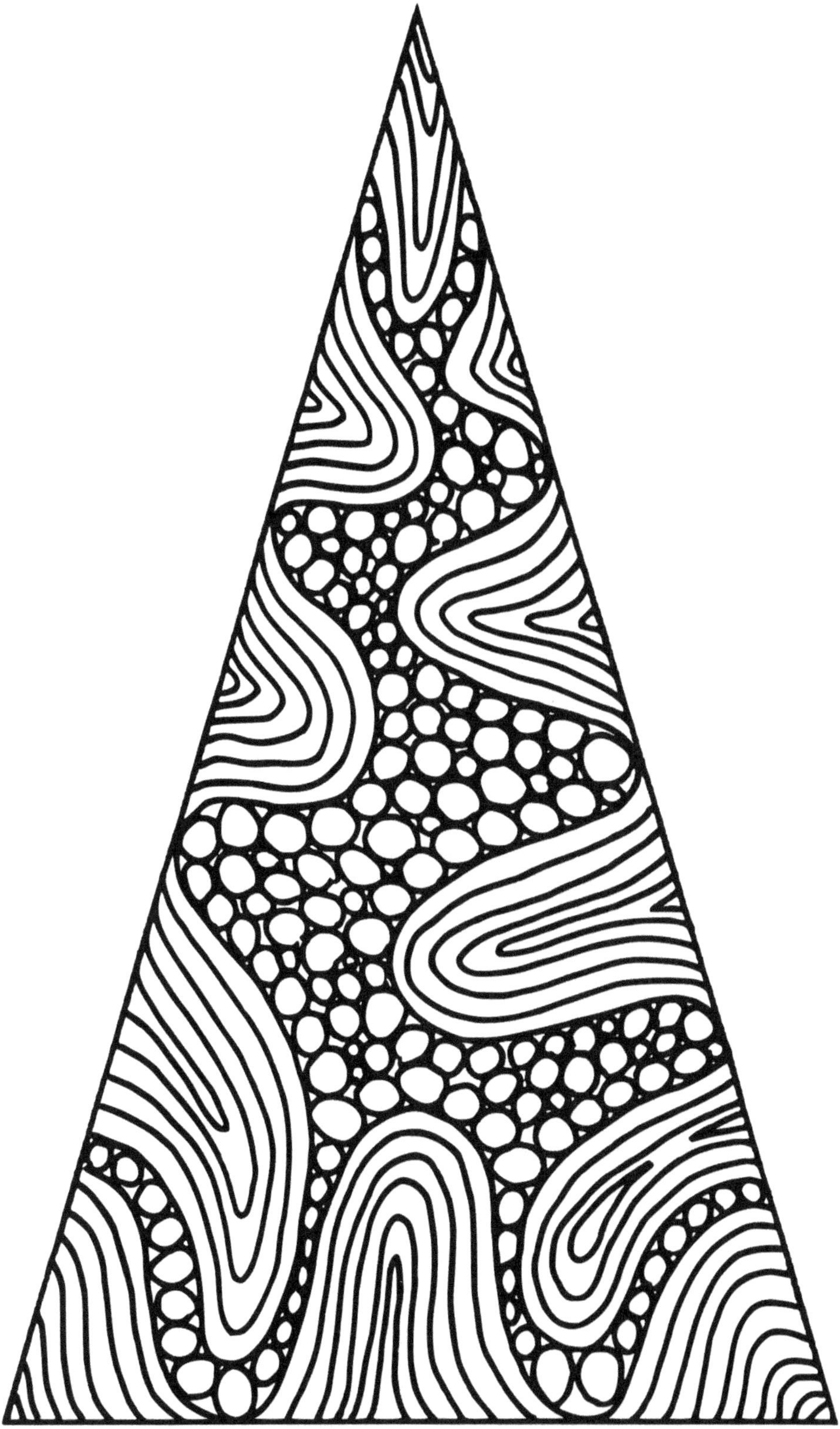

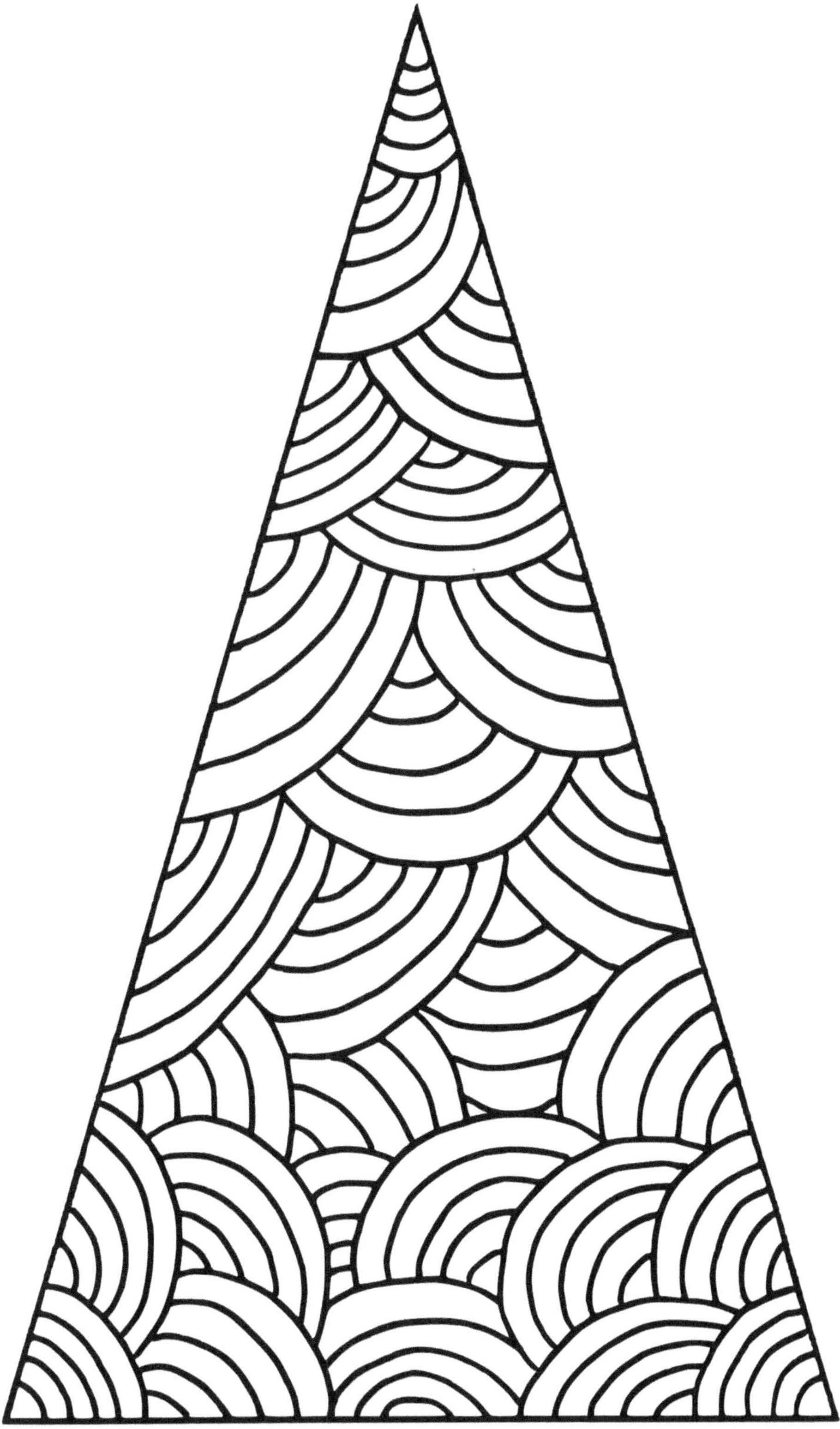

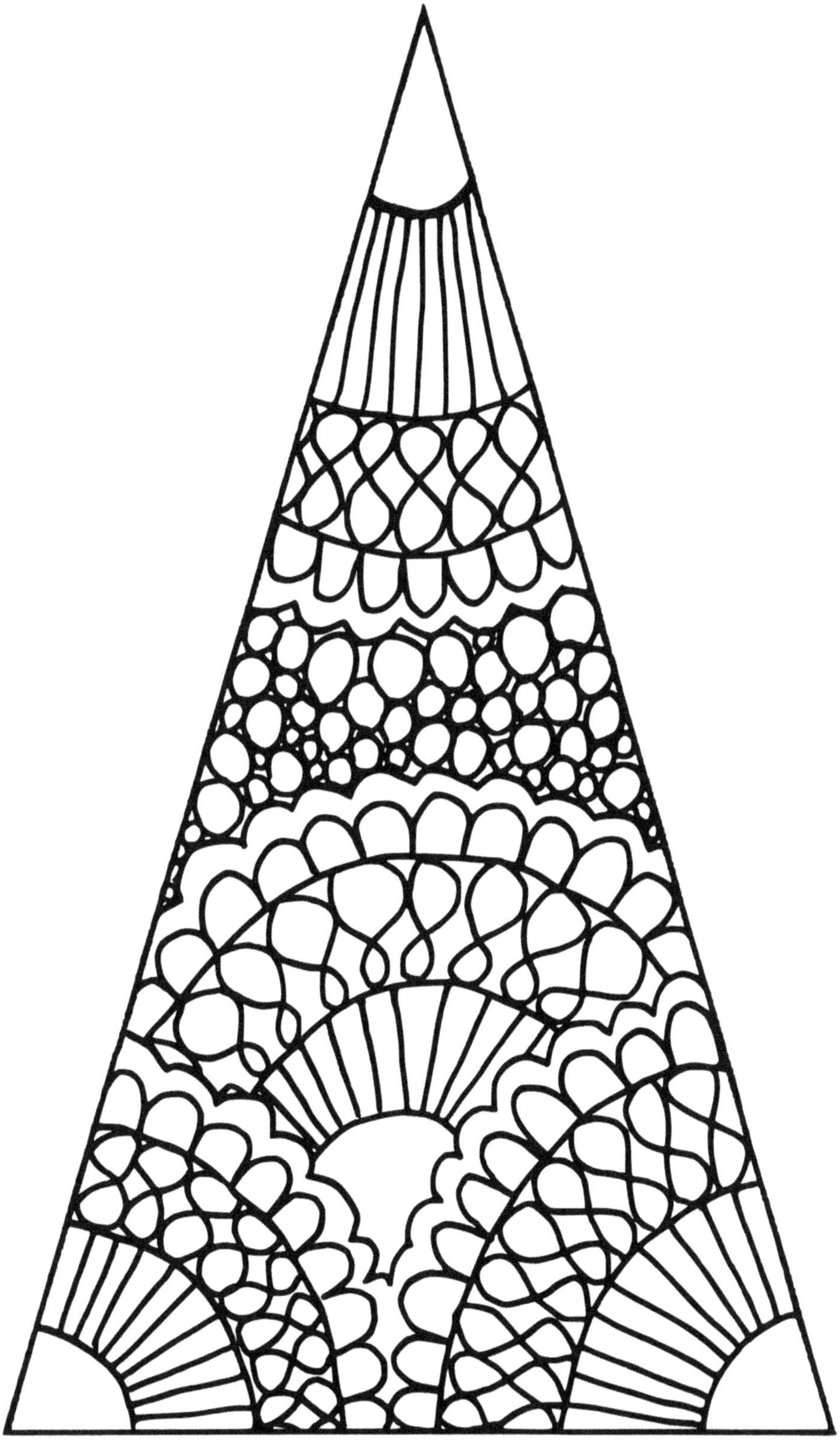

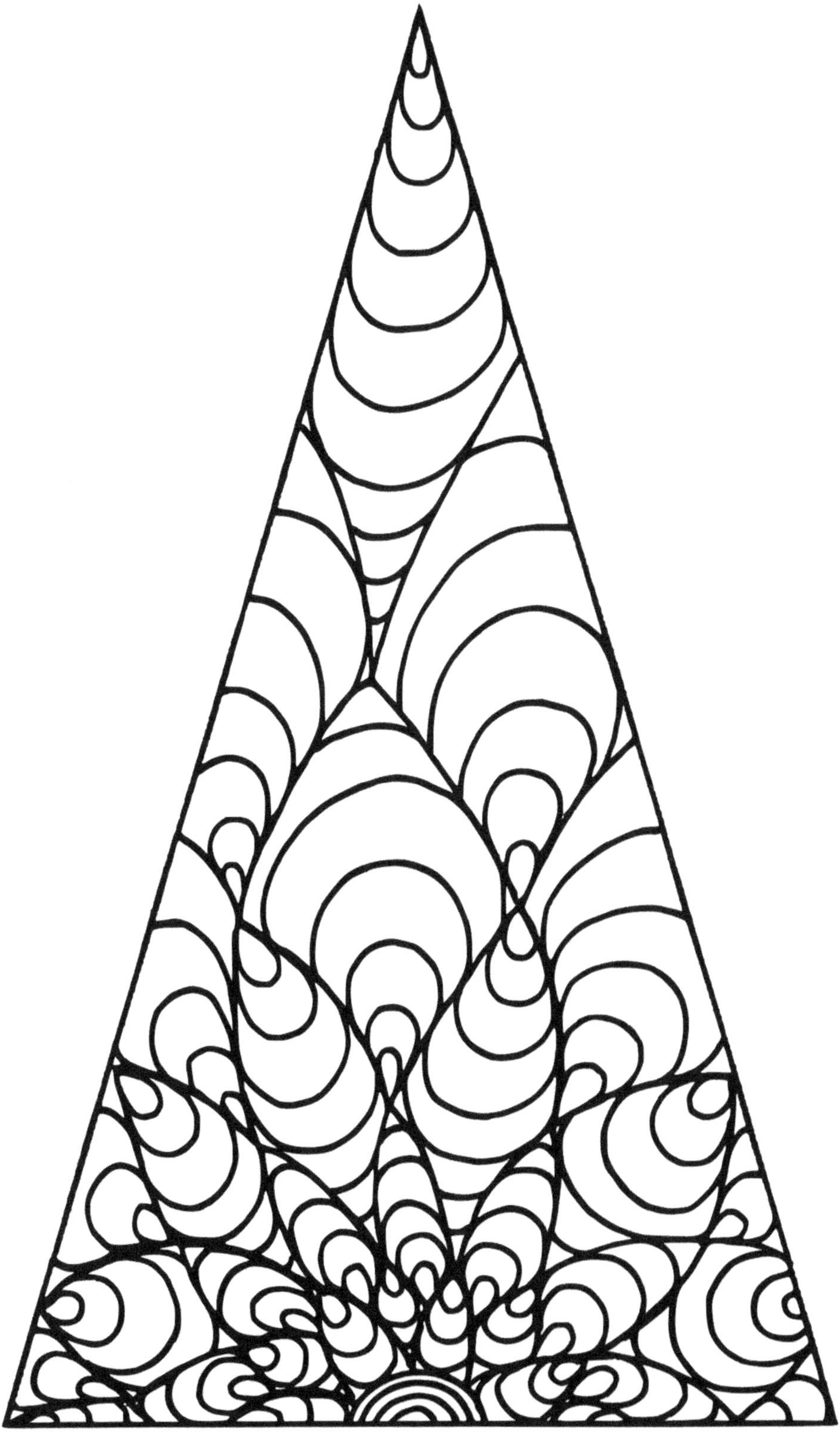

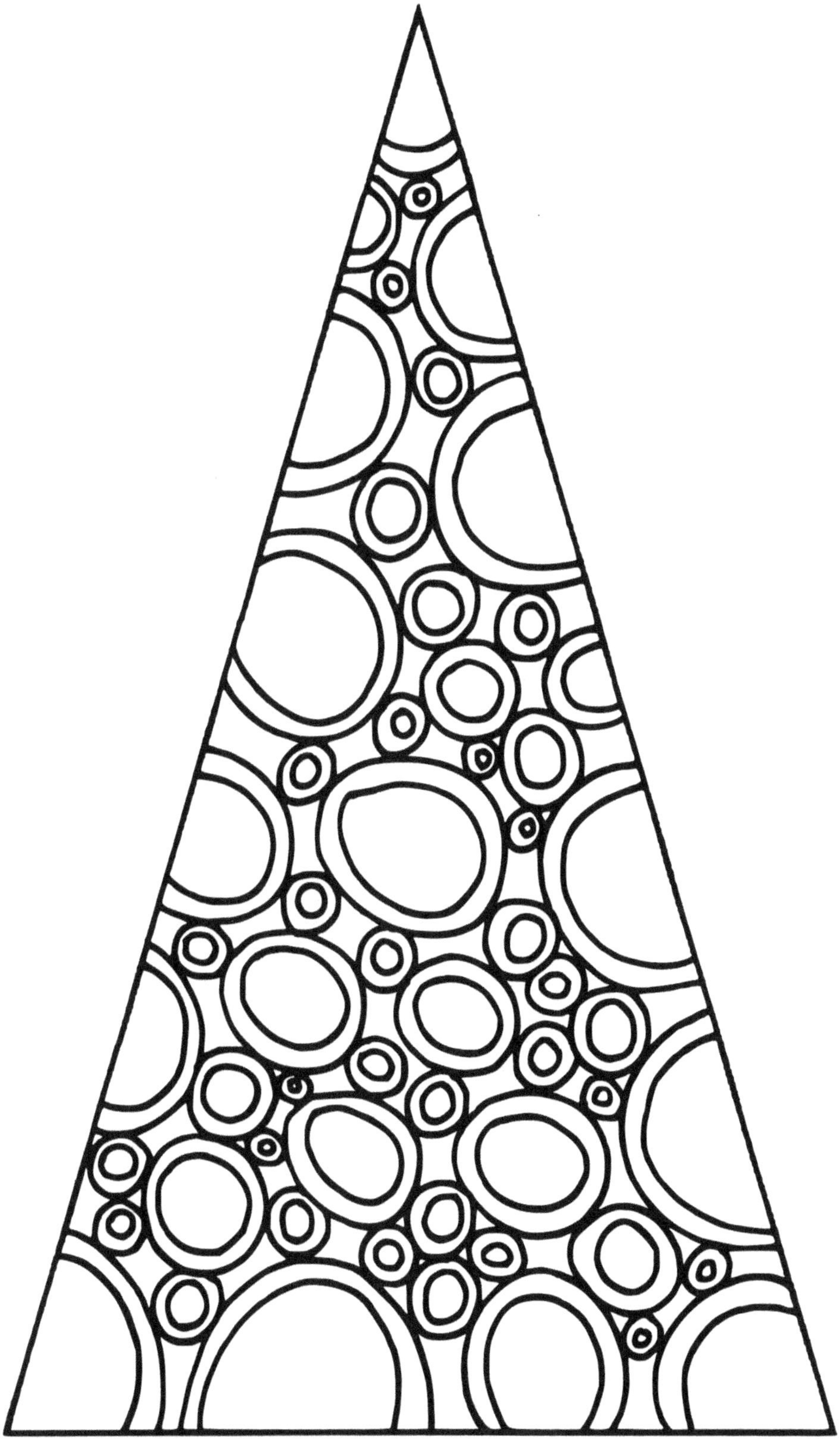

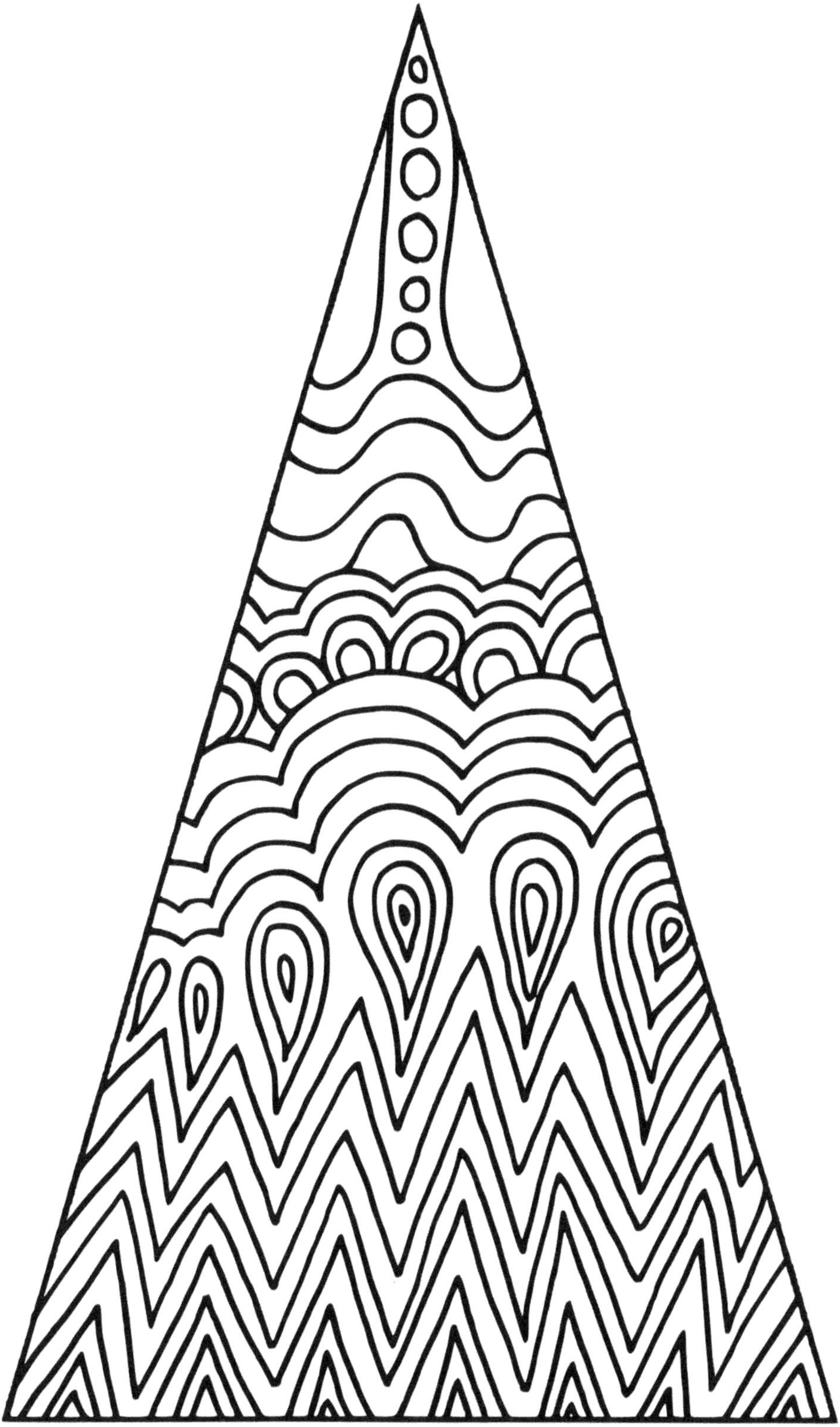

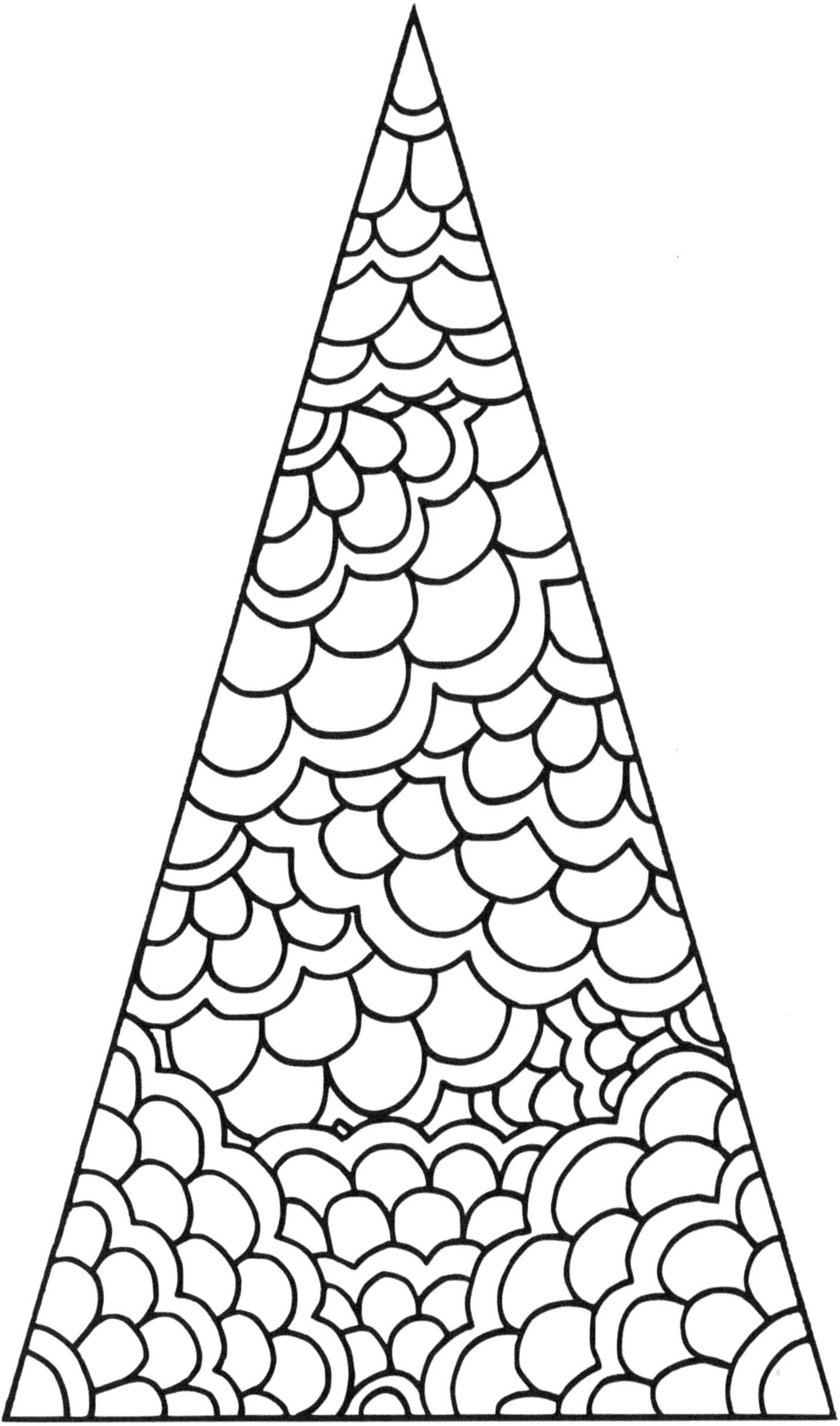

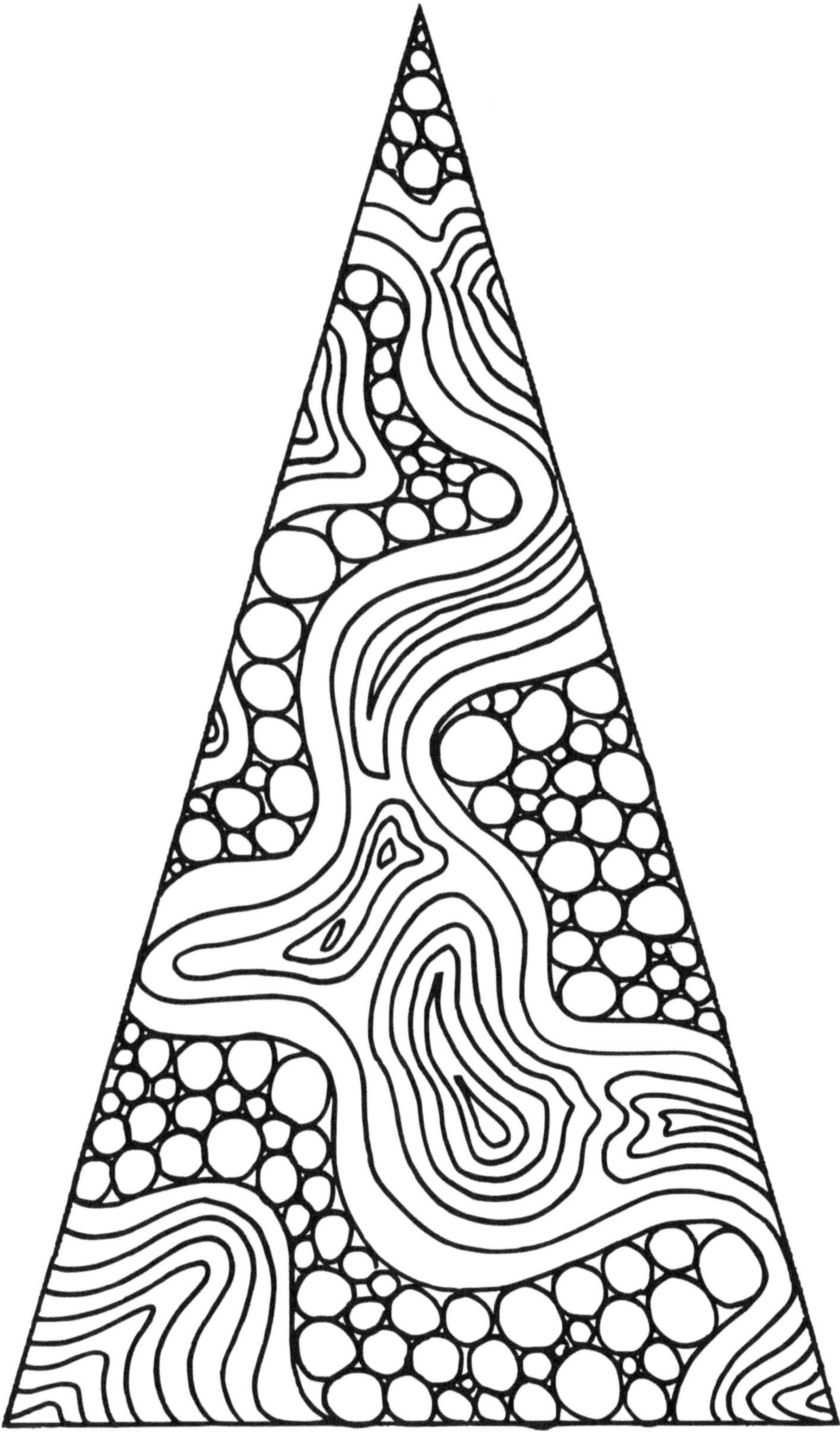

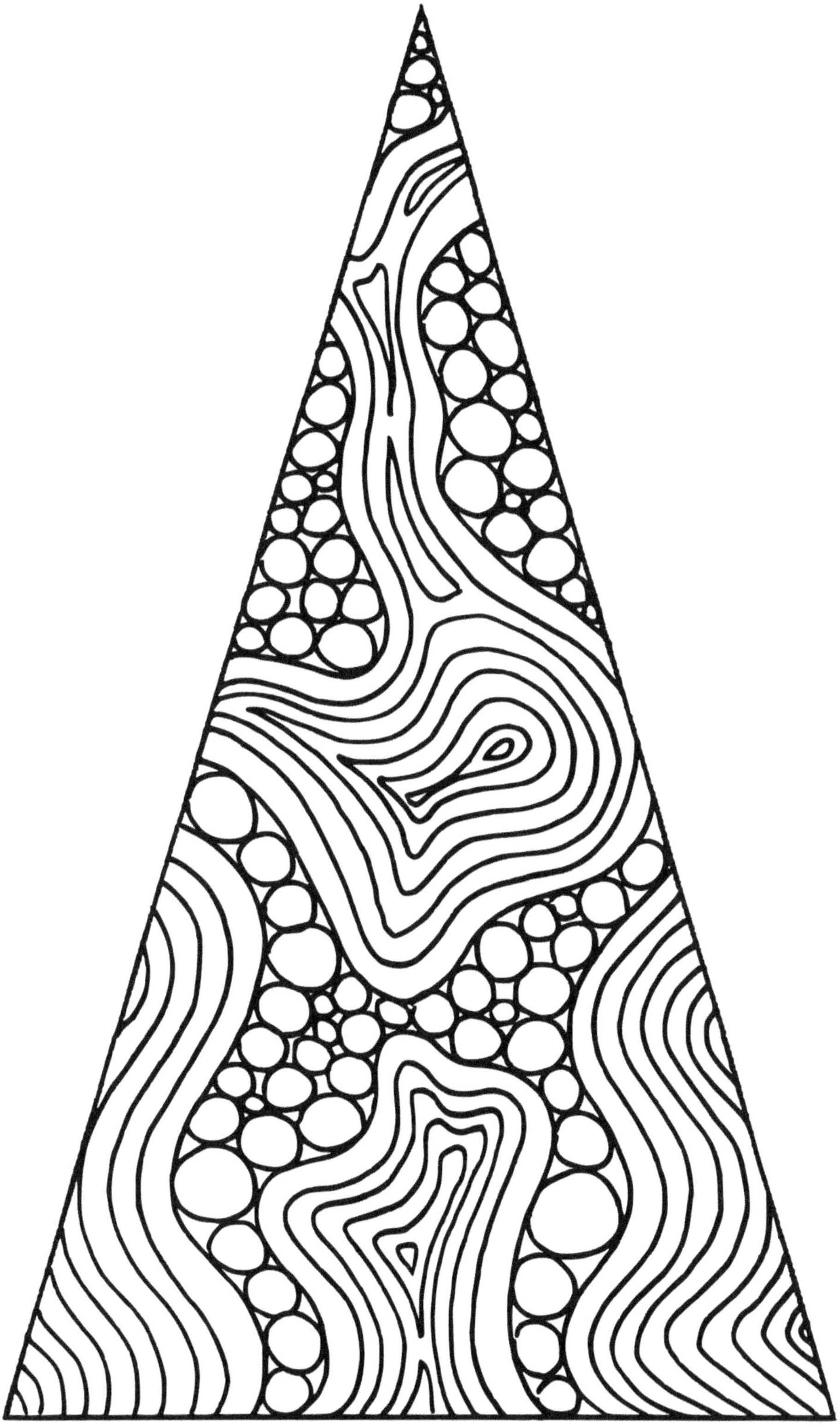

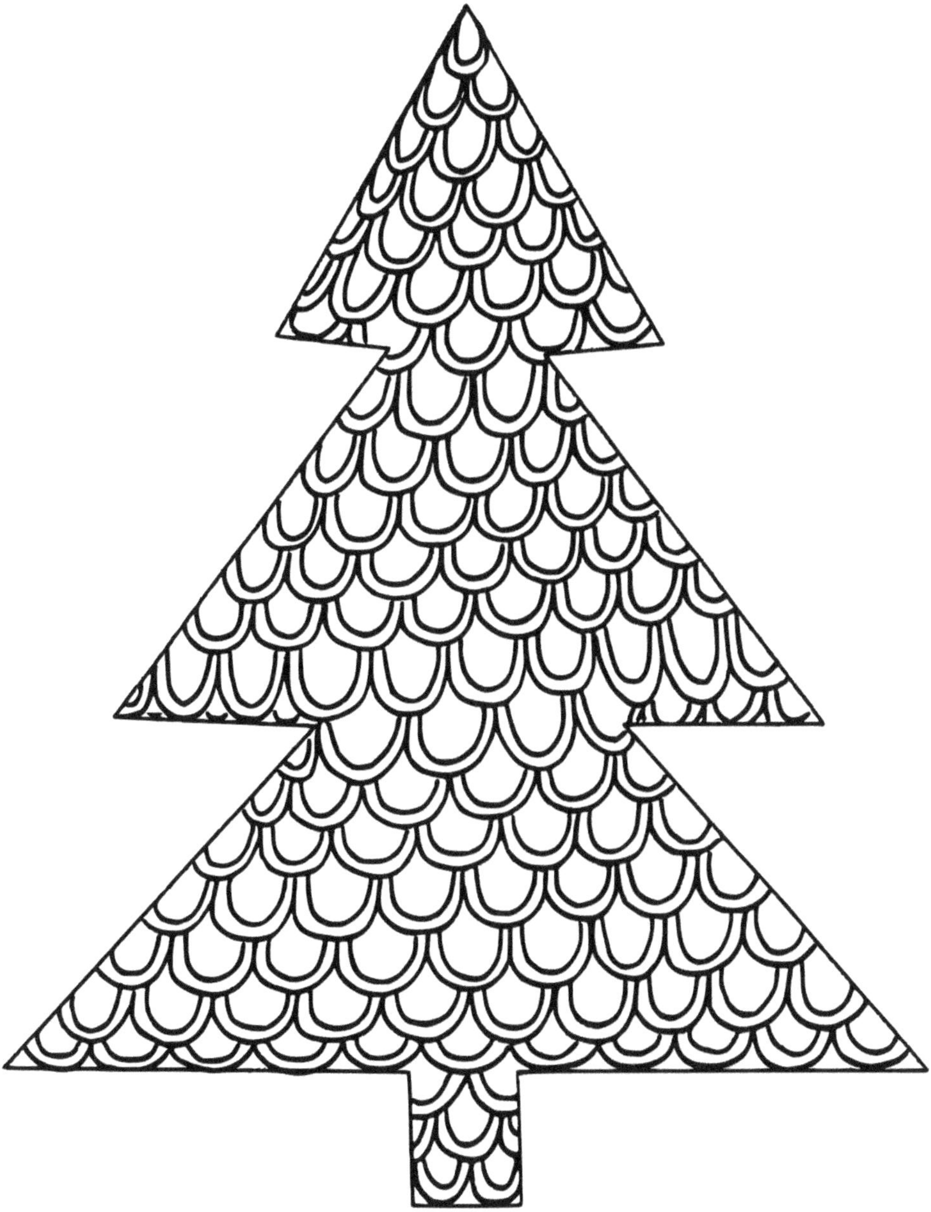

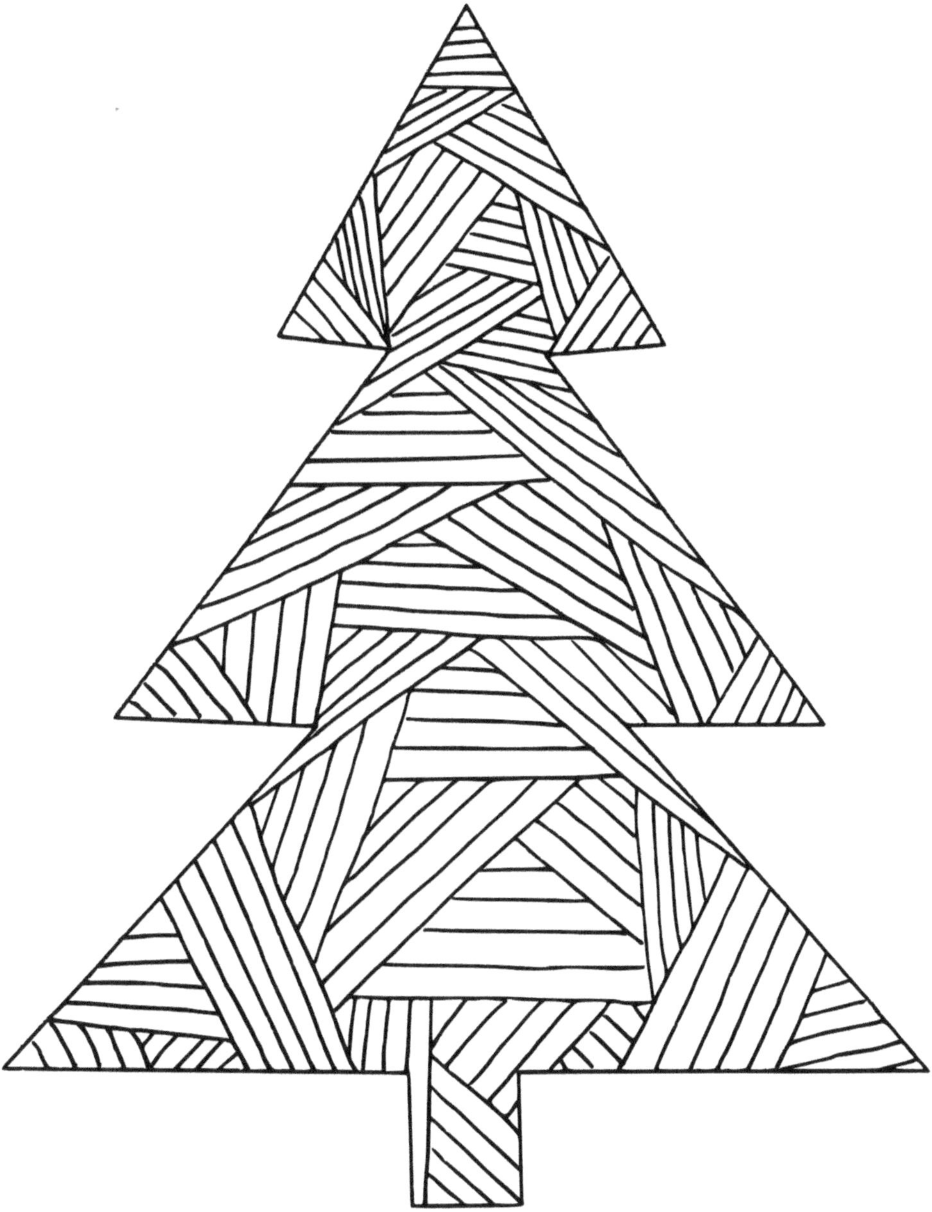

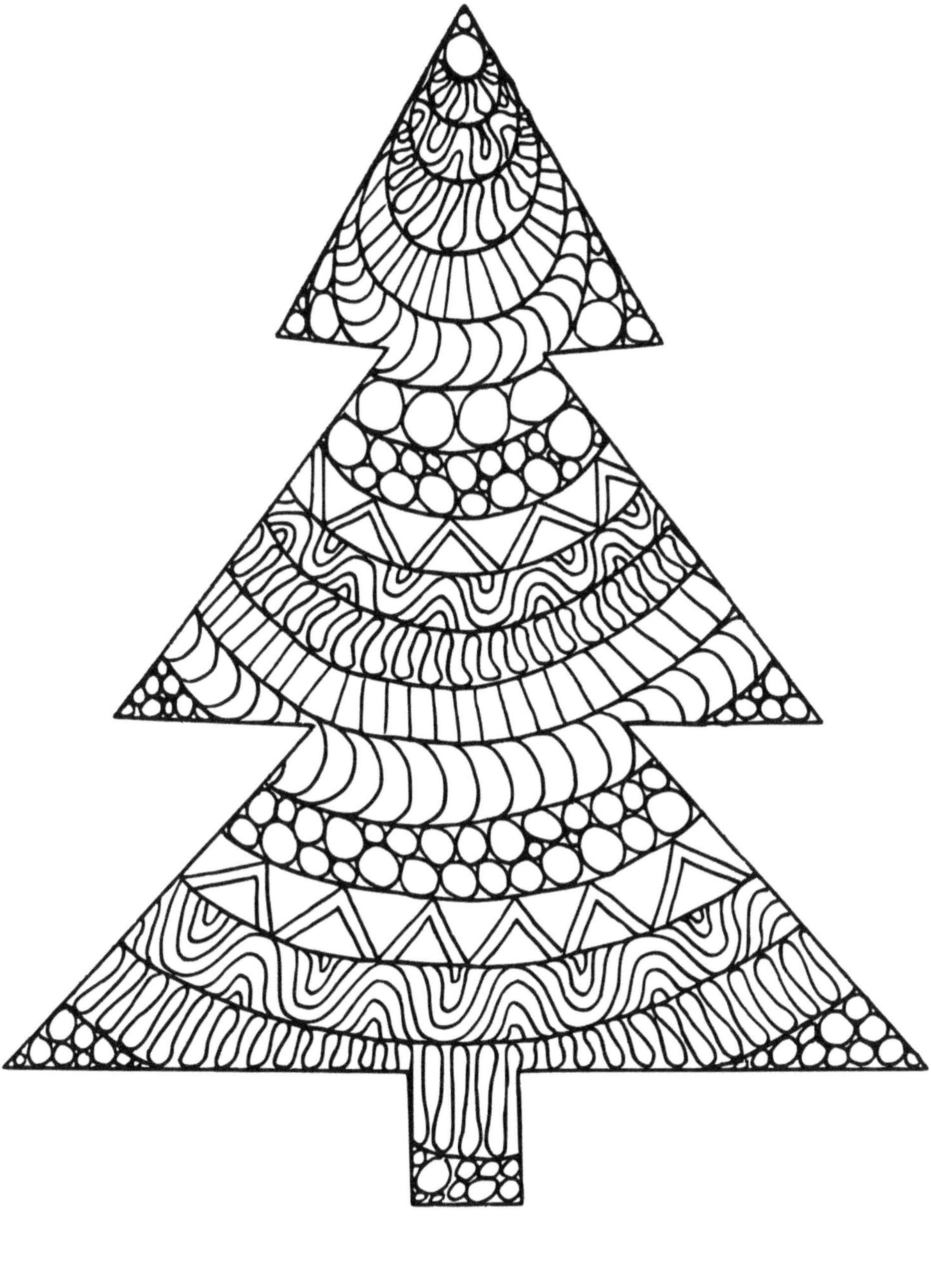

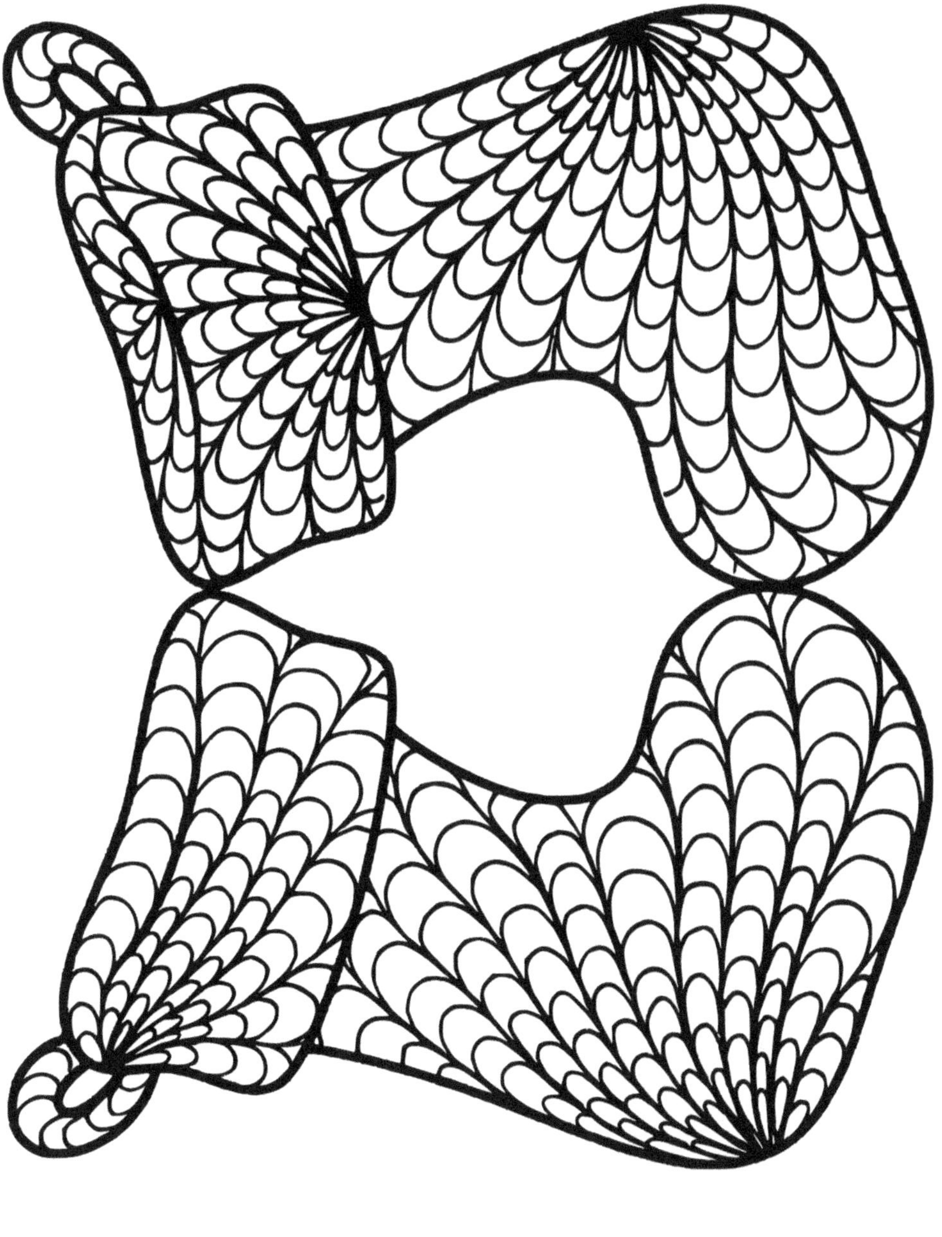

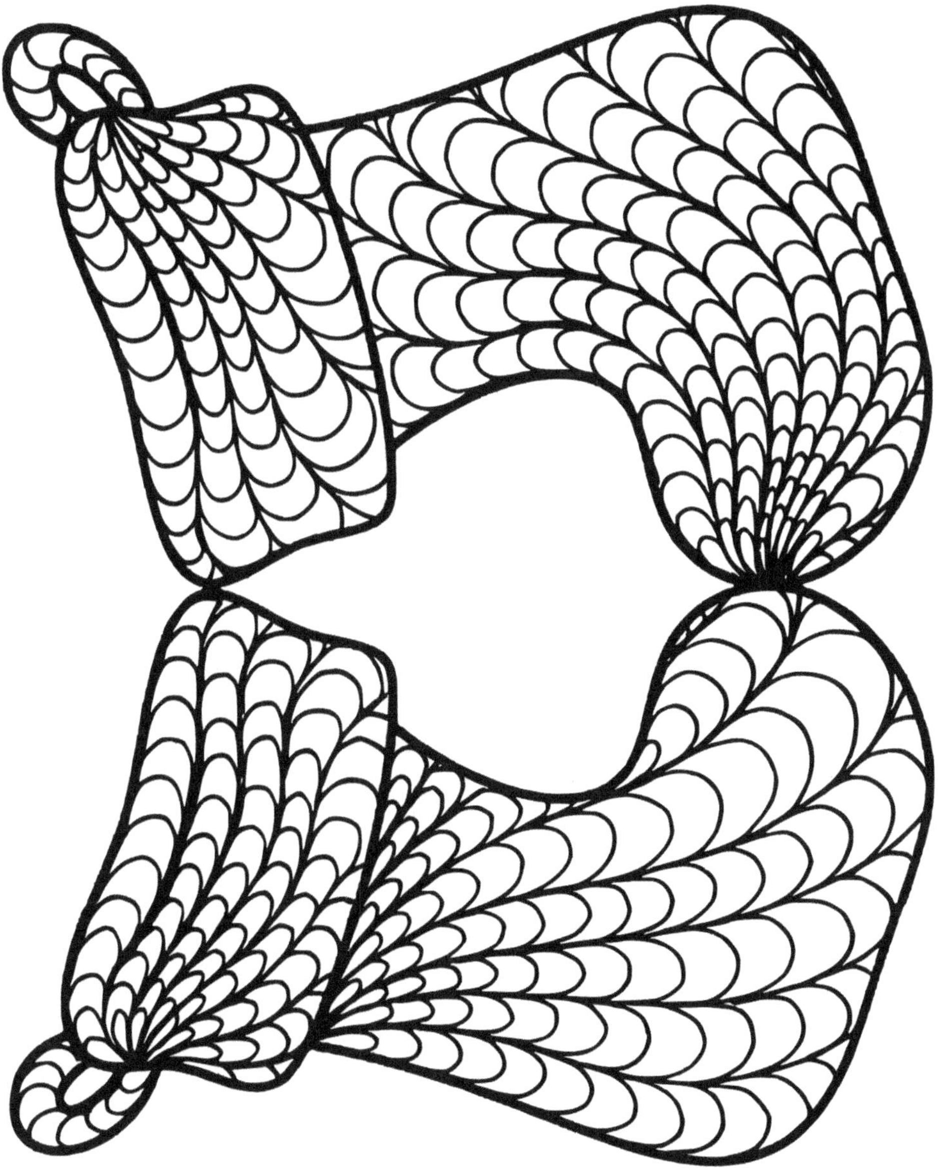

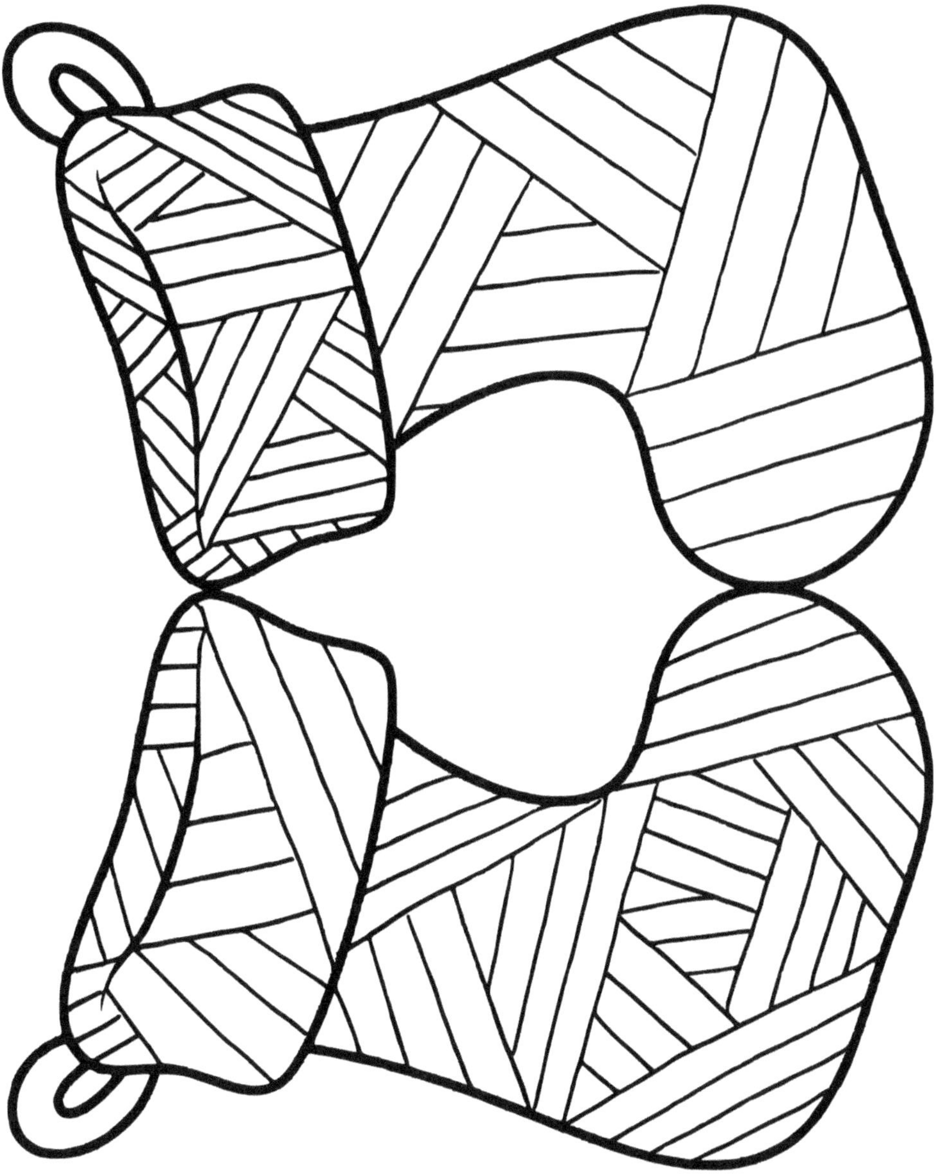

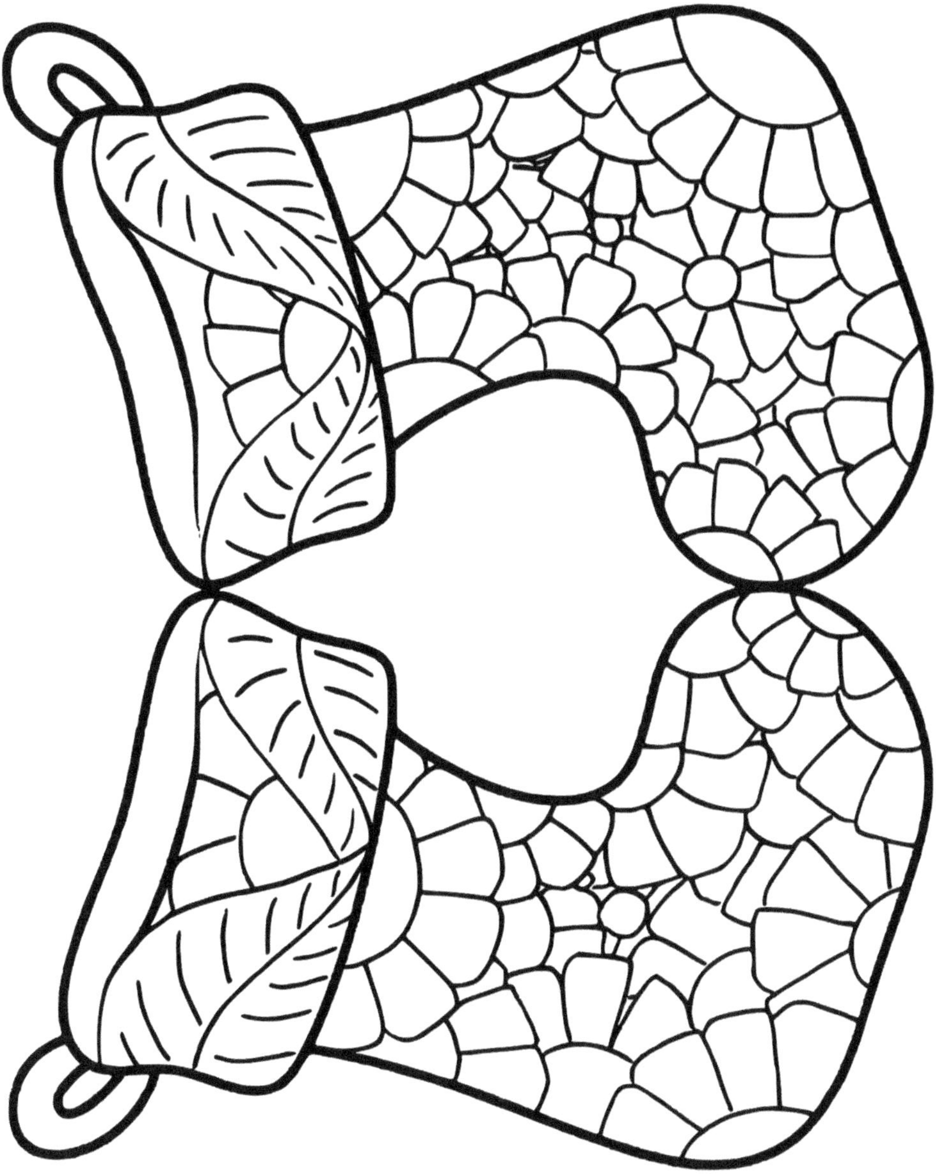

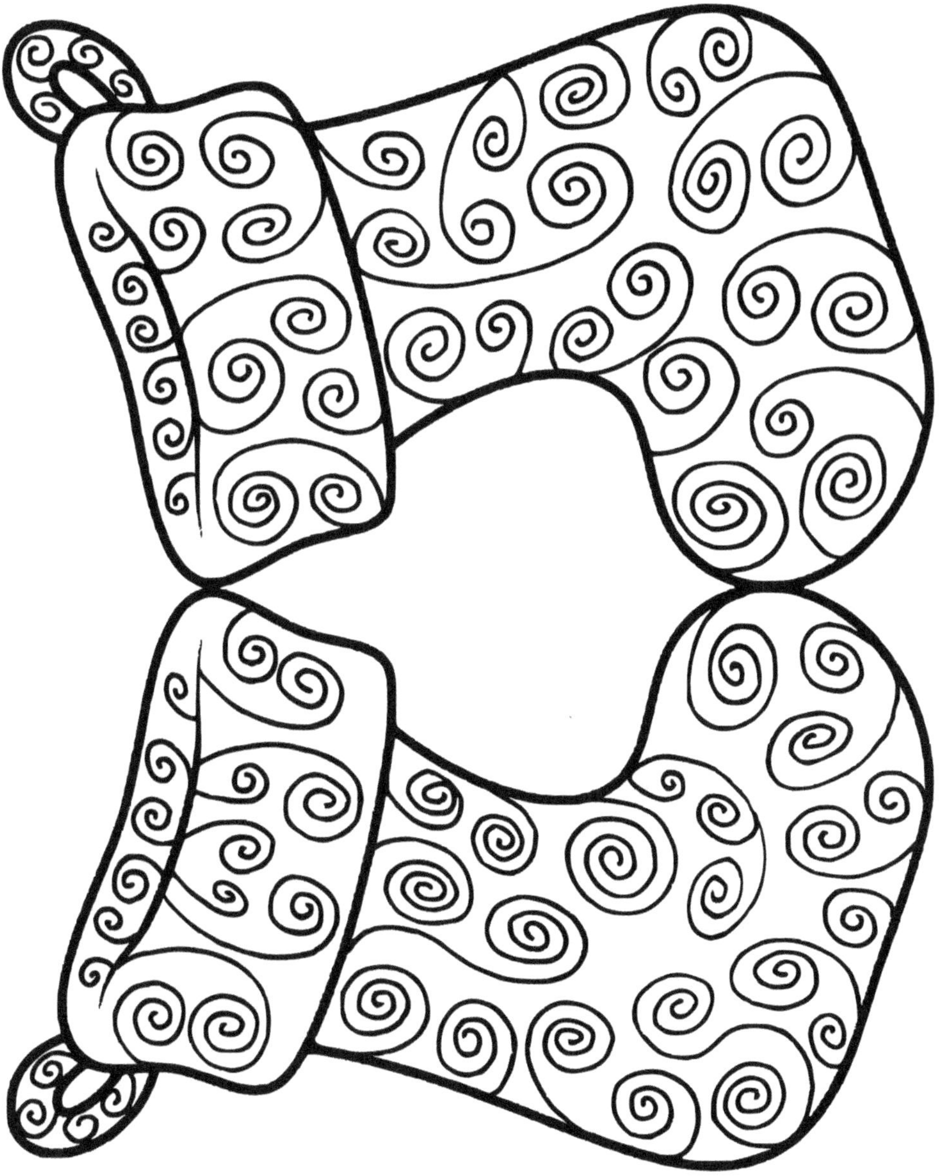

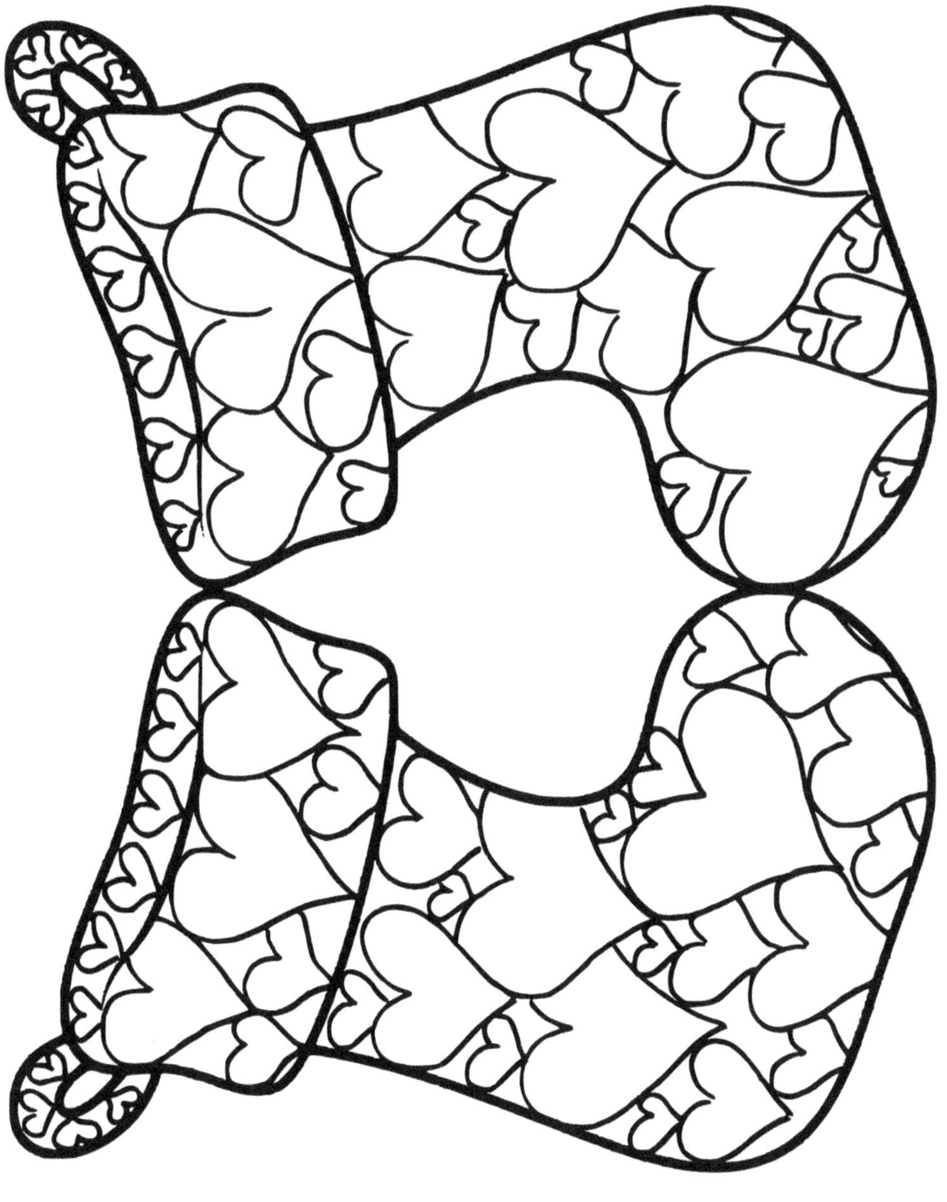

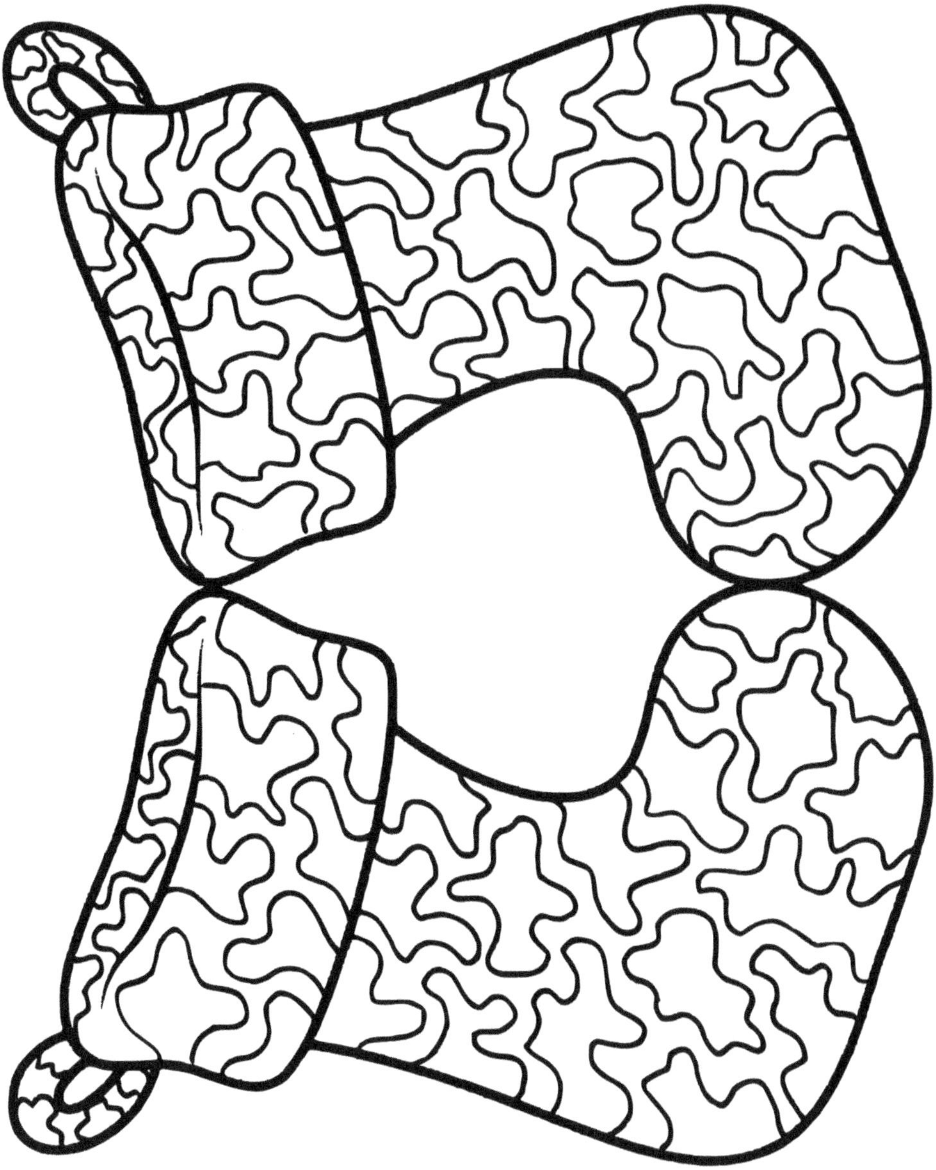

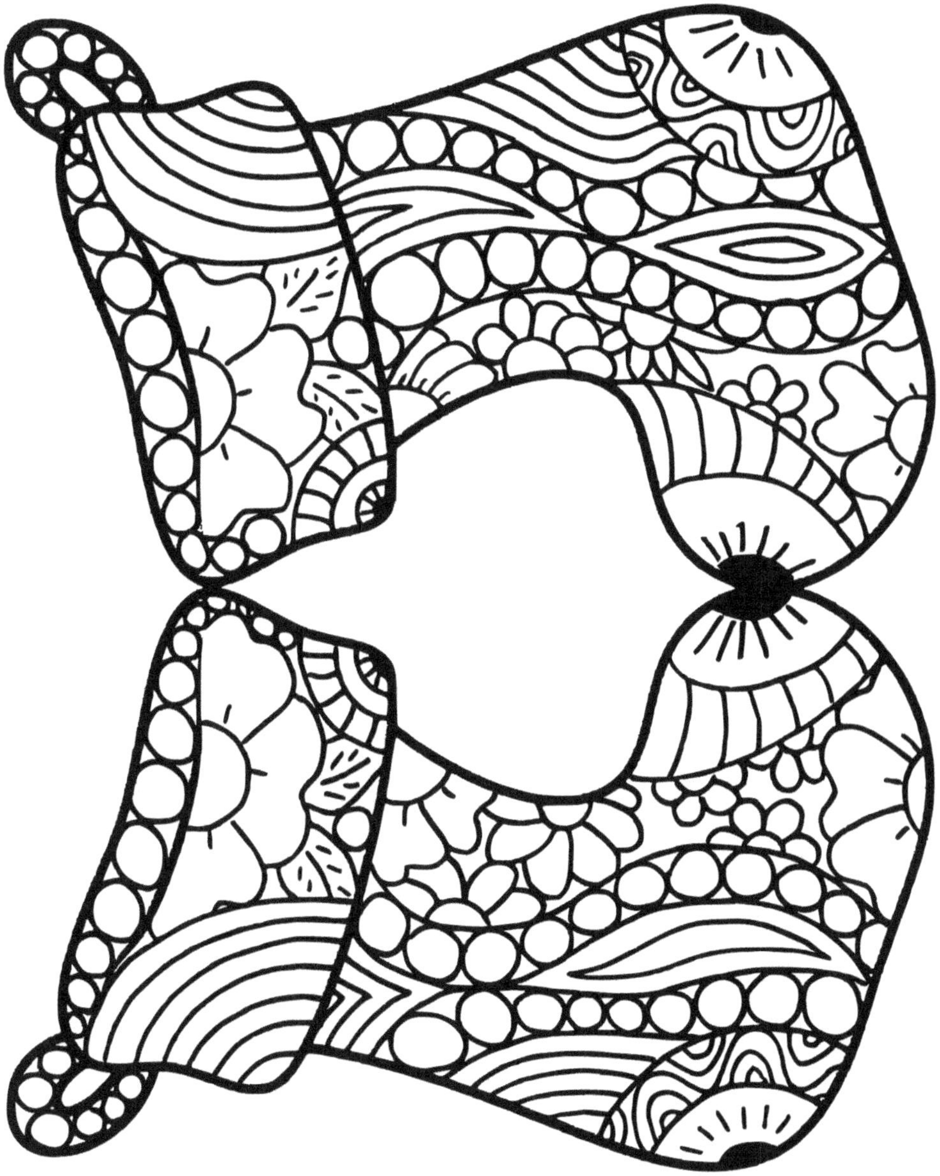

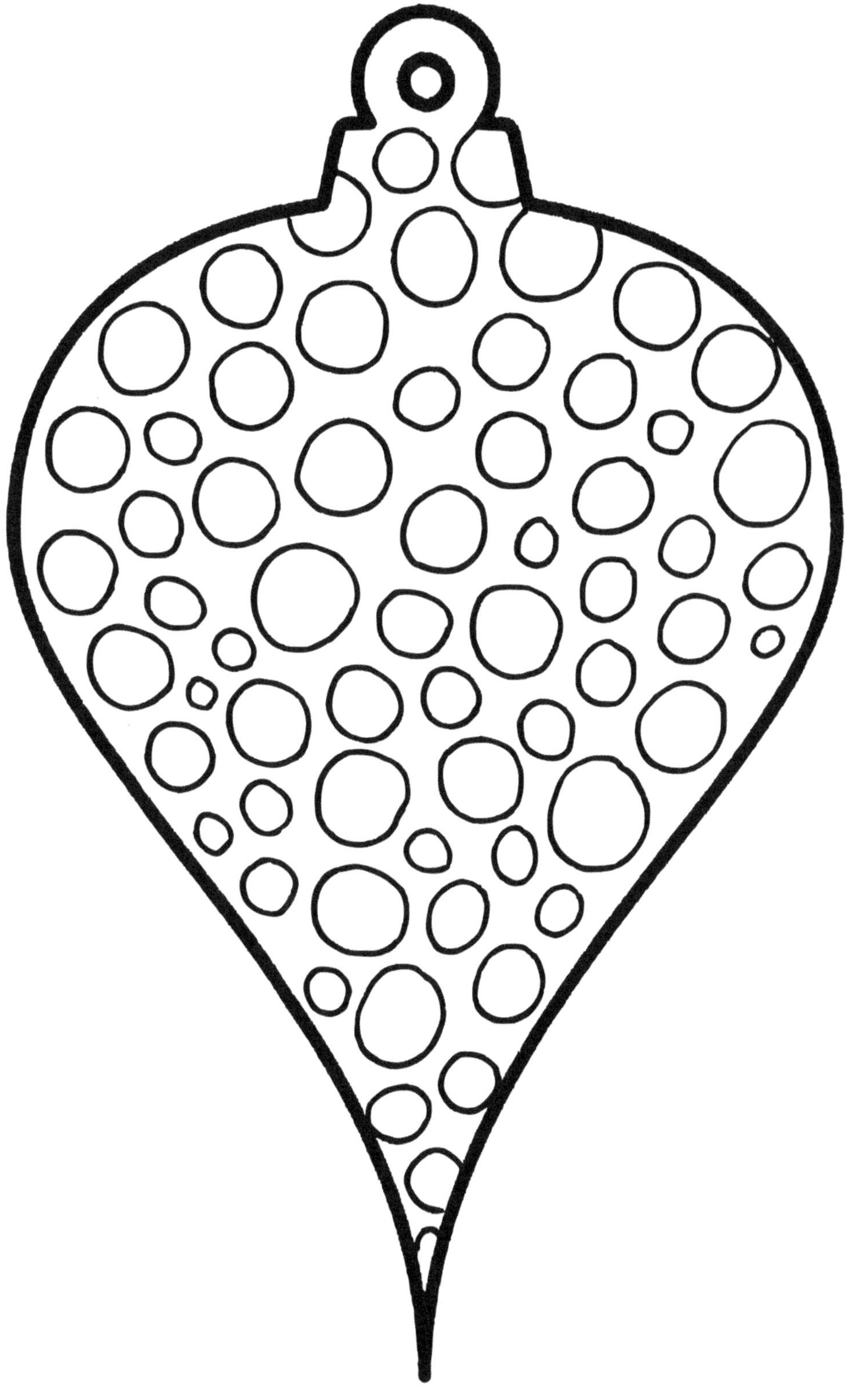

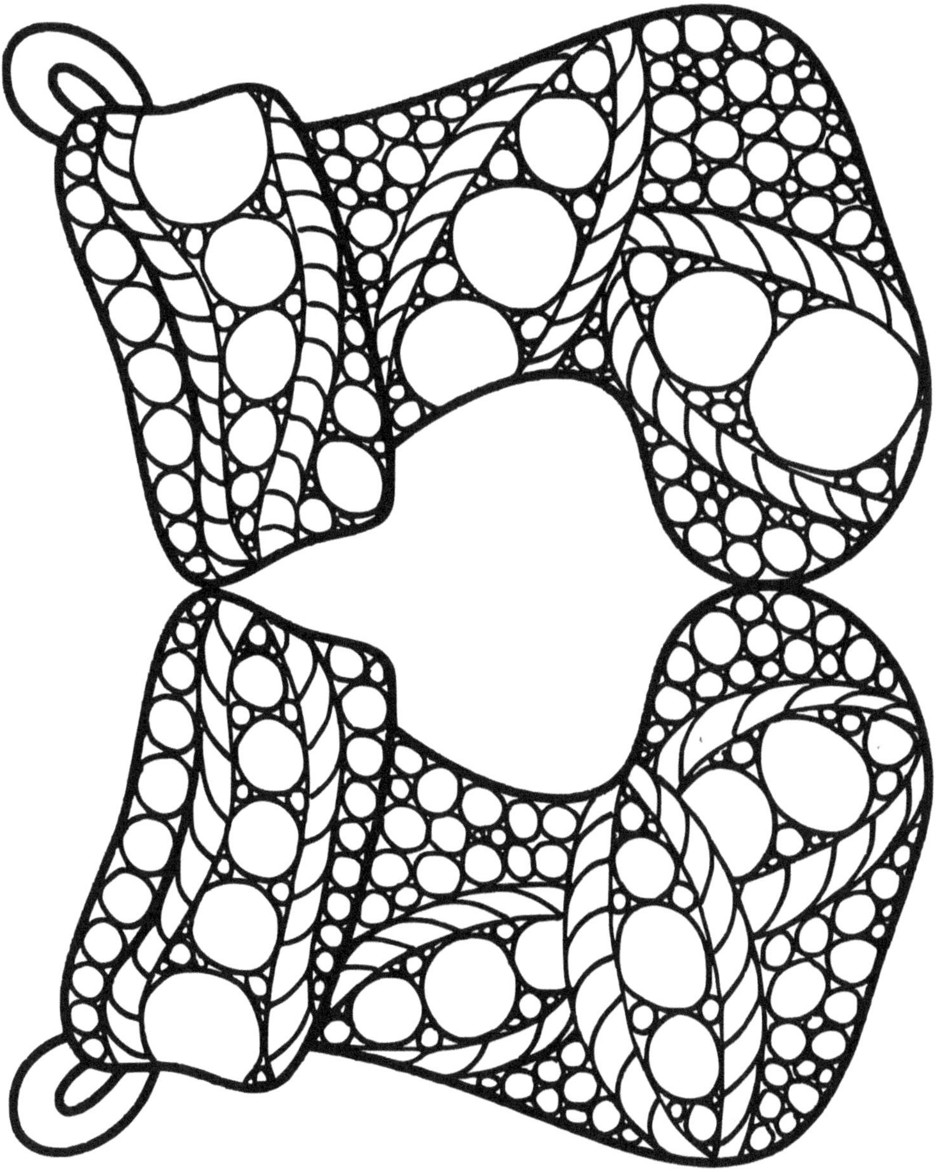

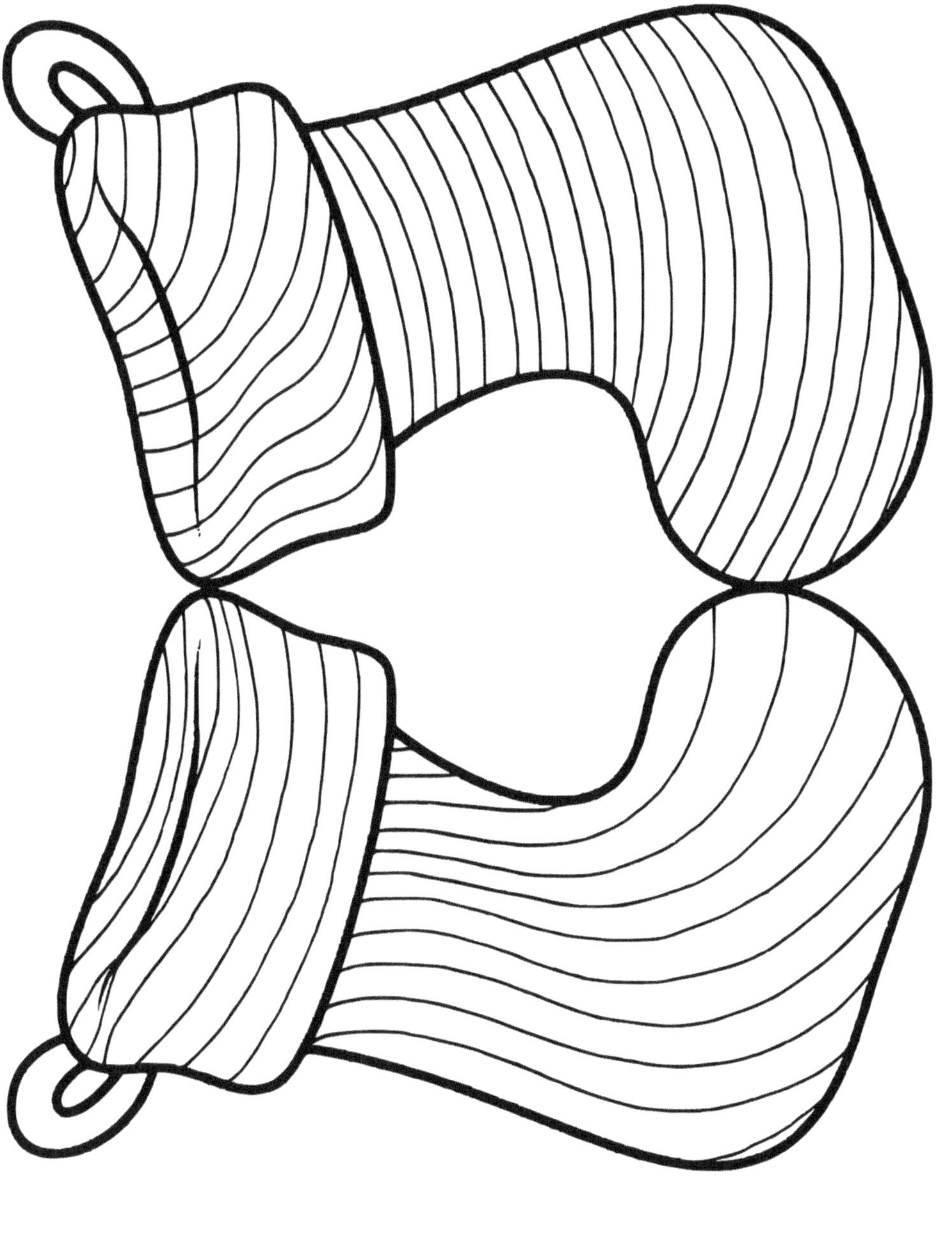

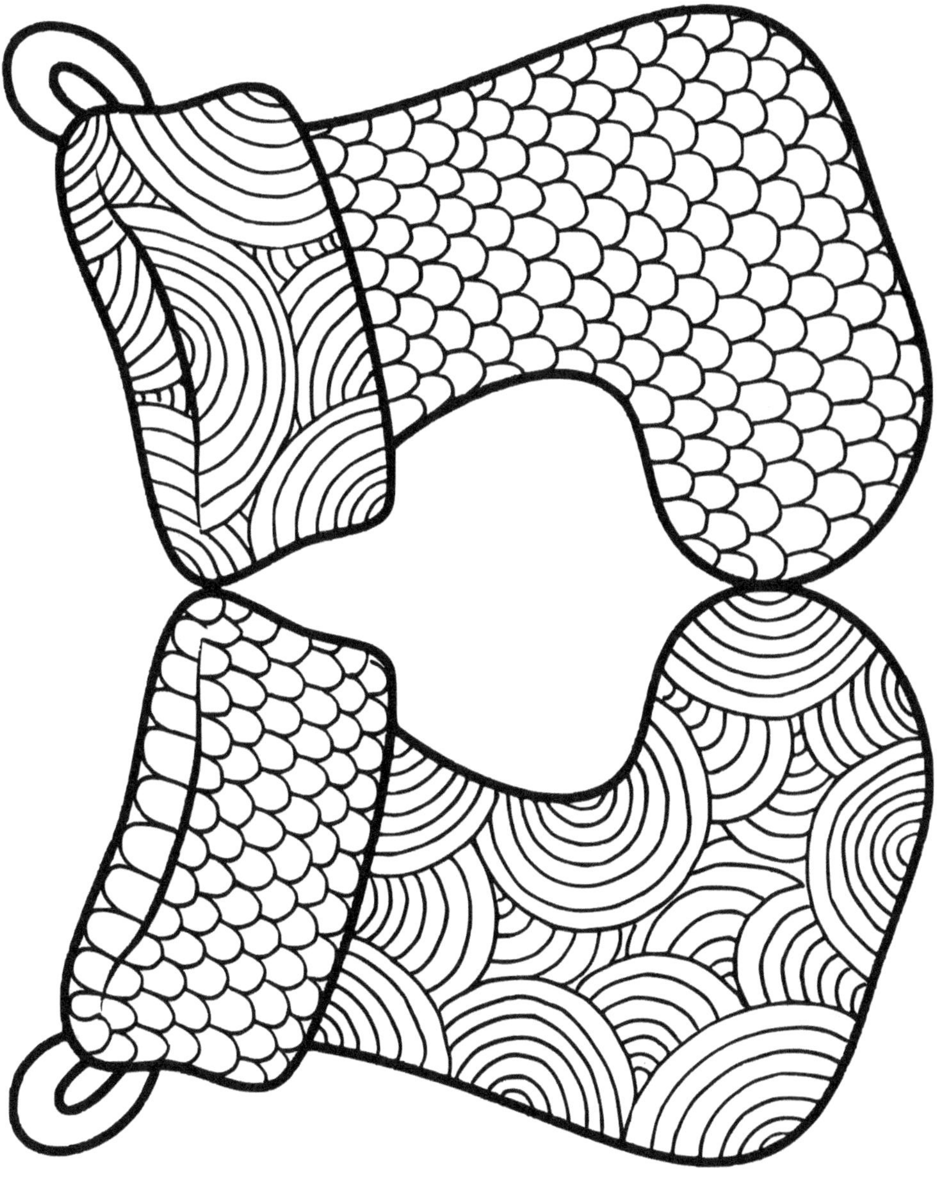

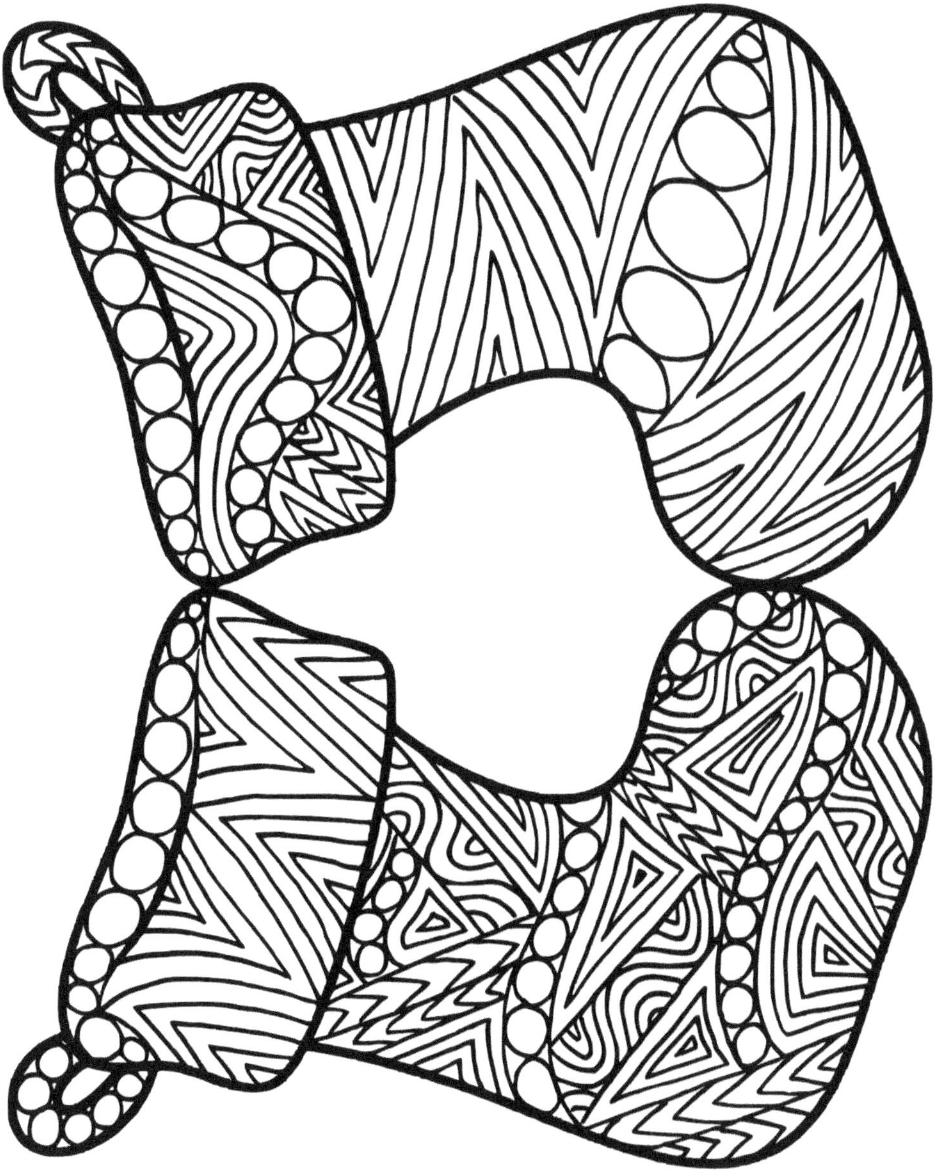

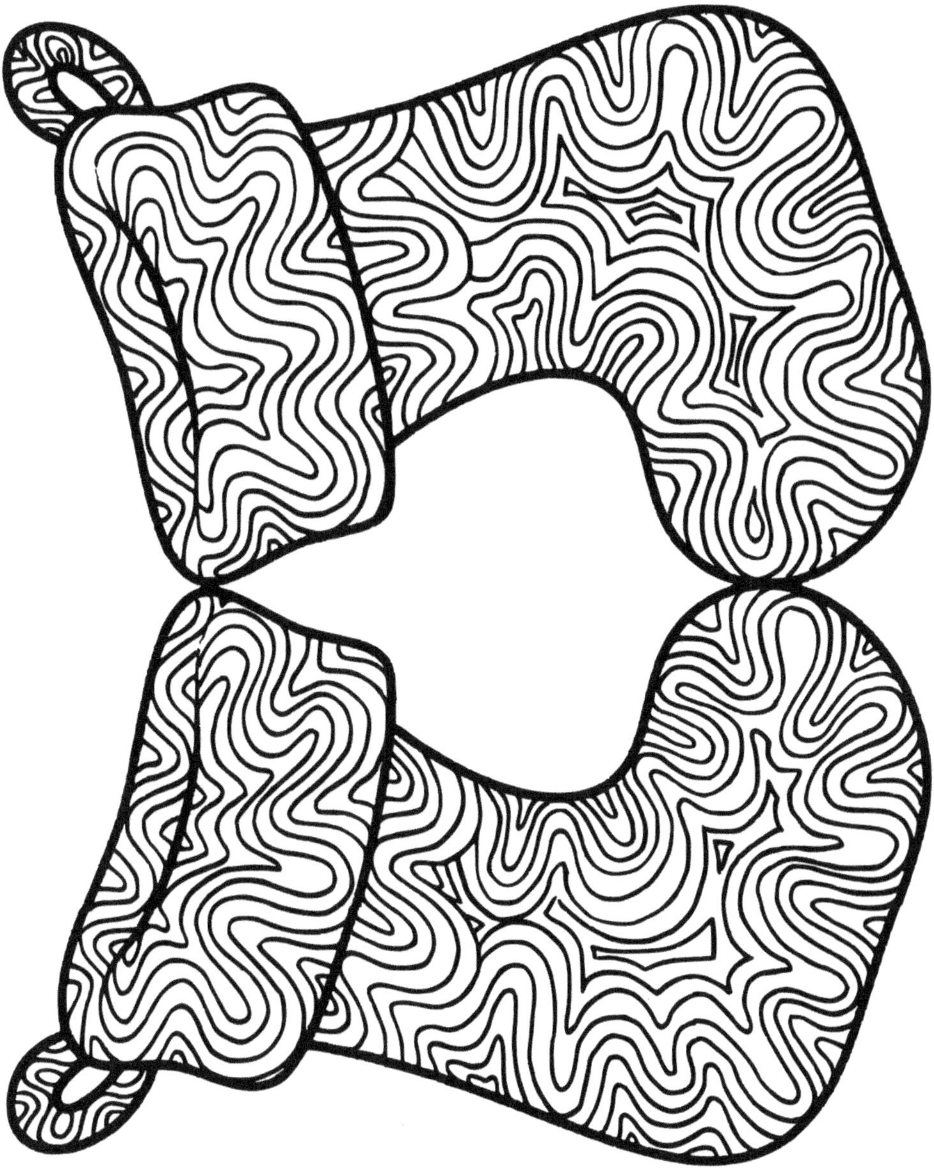

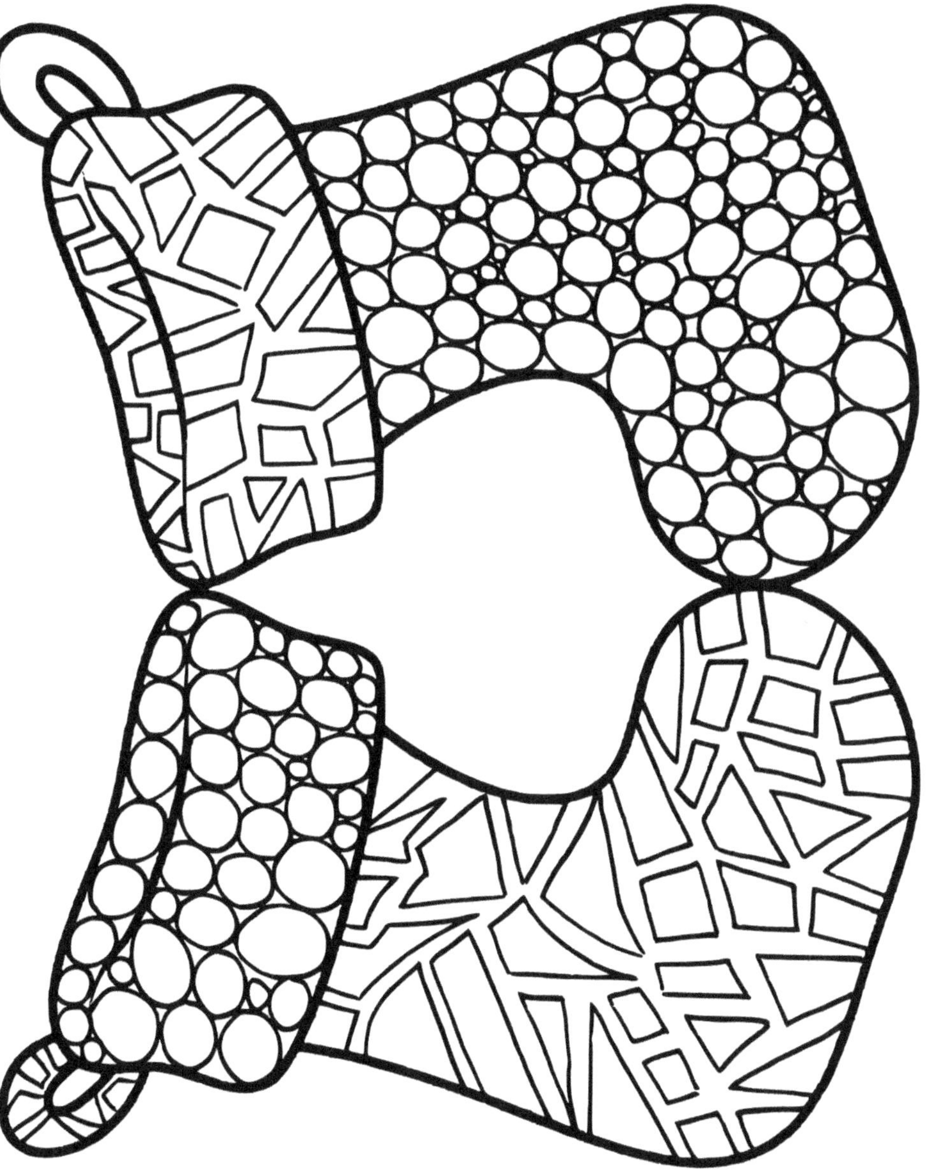

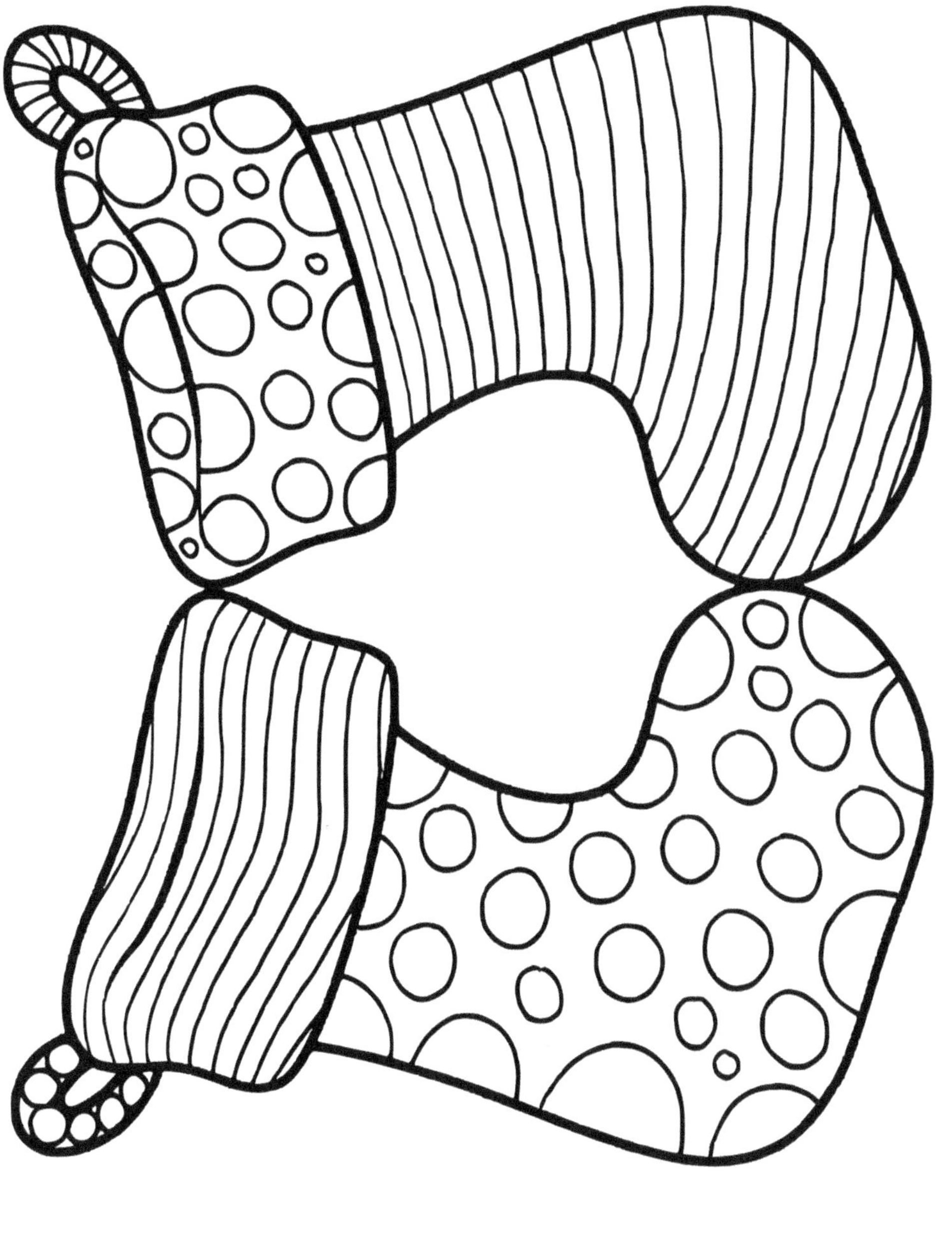

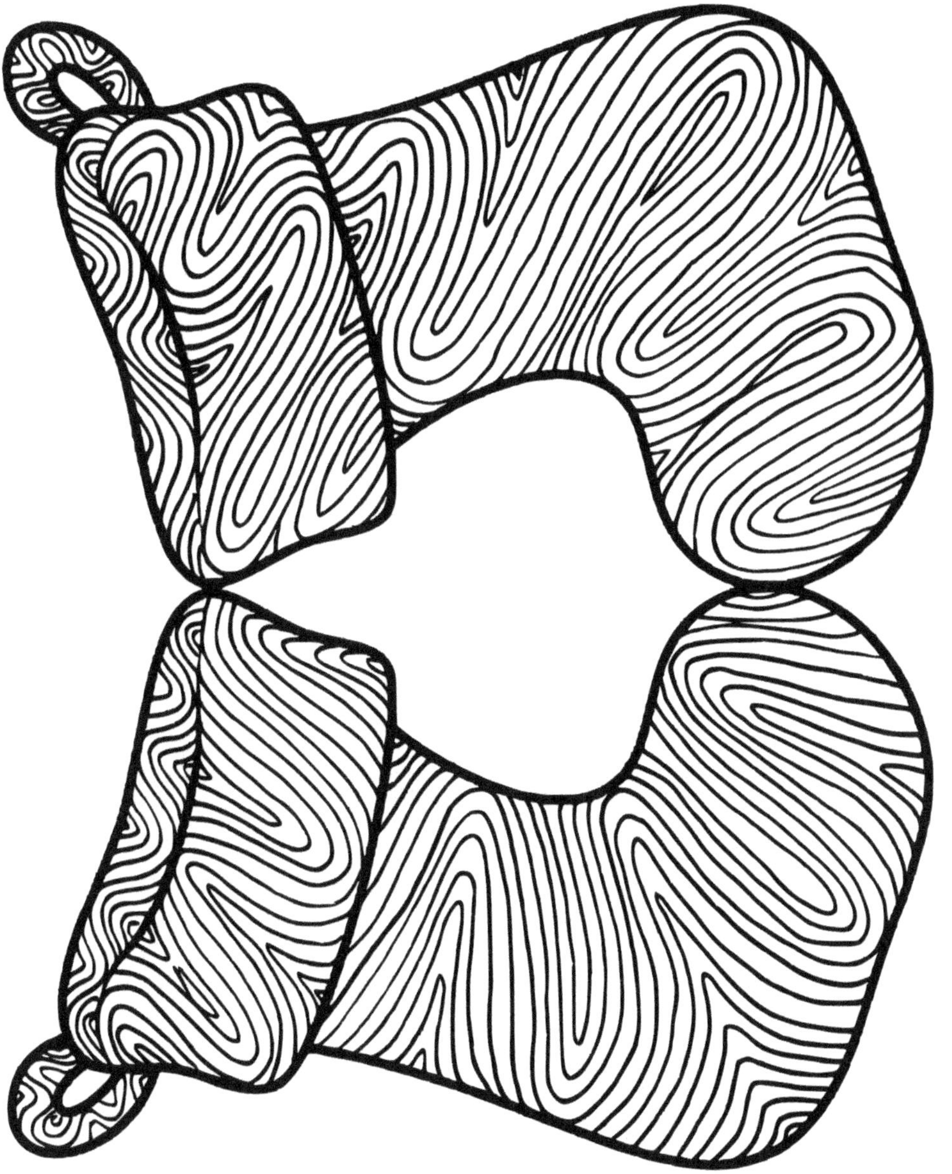

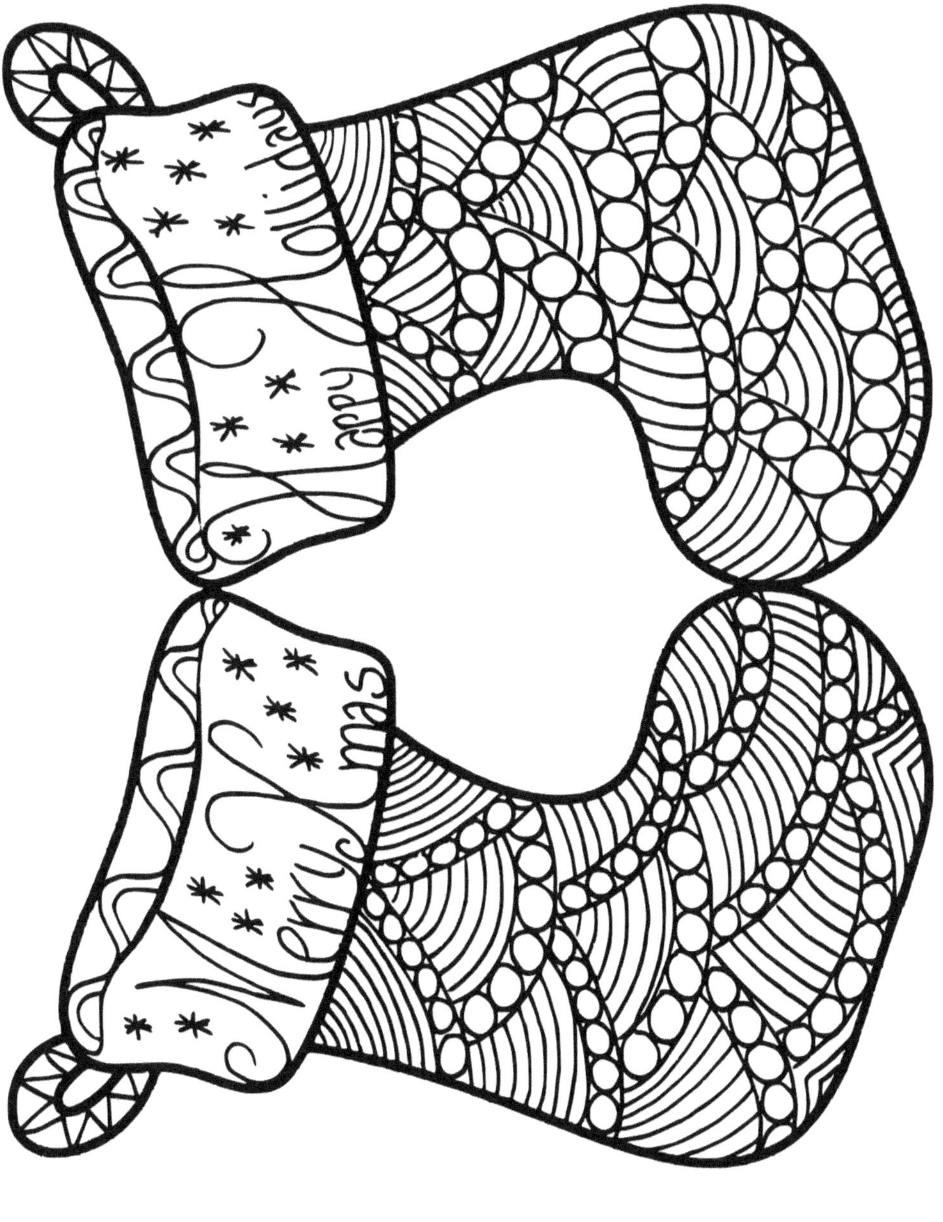
happy holidays
Merry Xmas

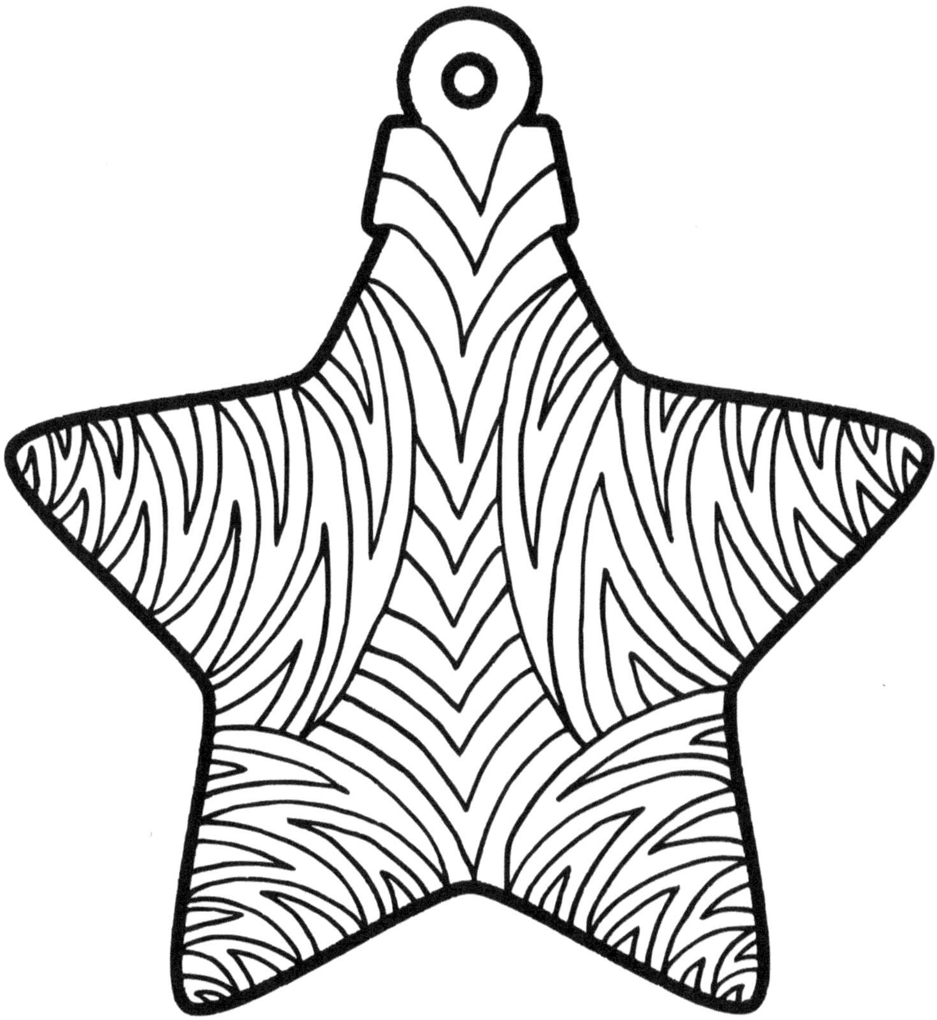

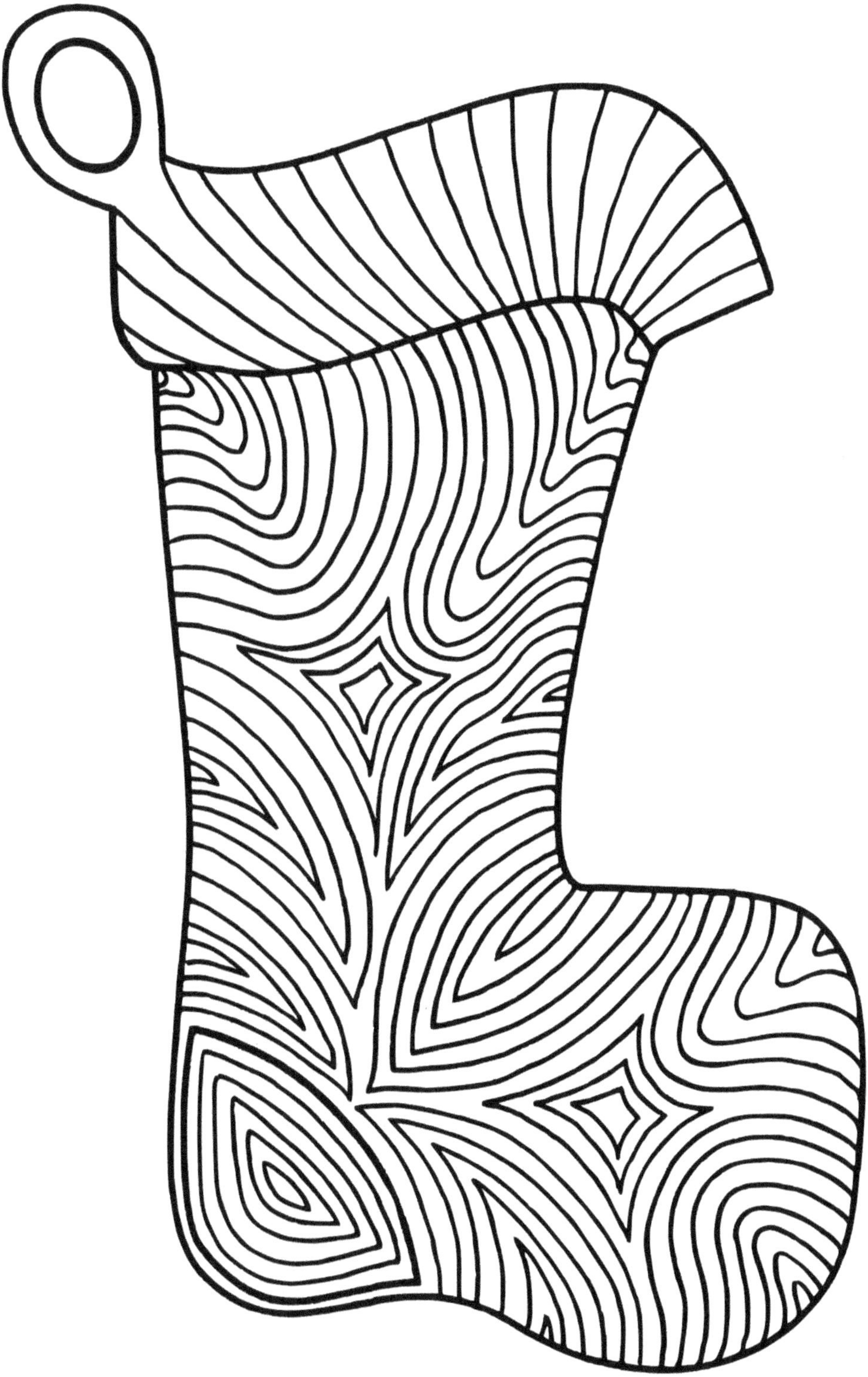

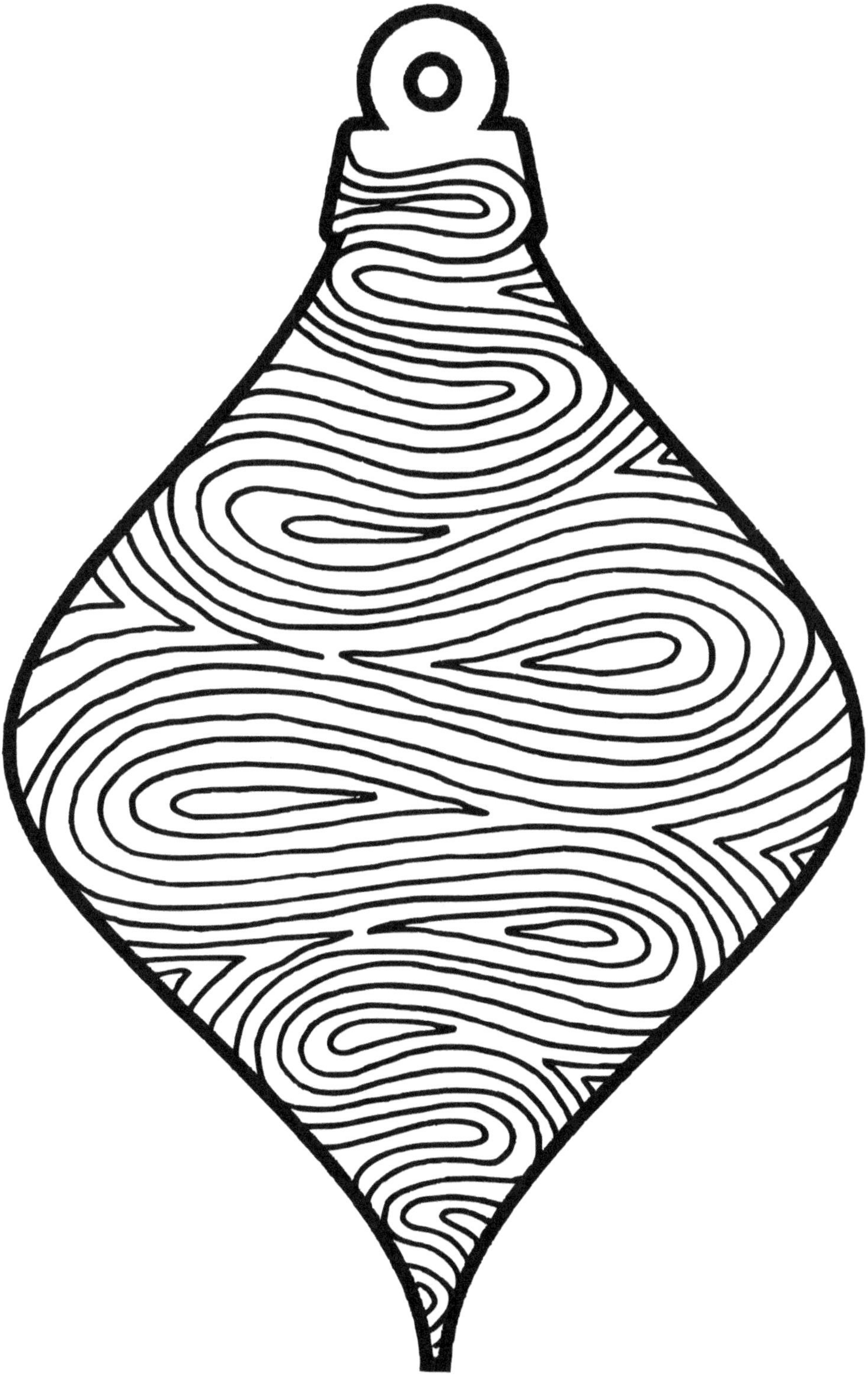

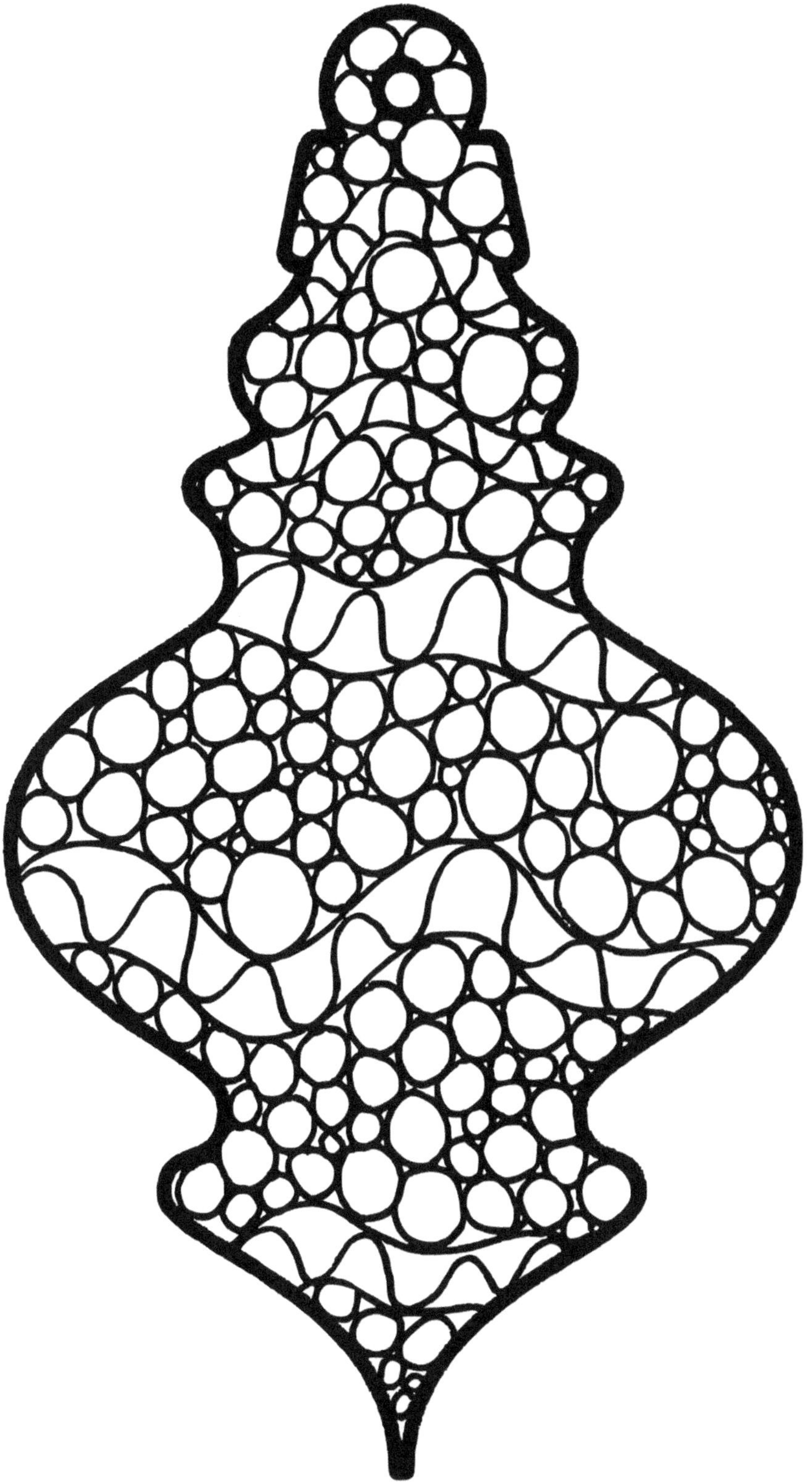

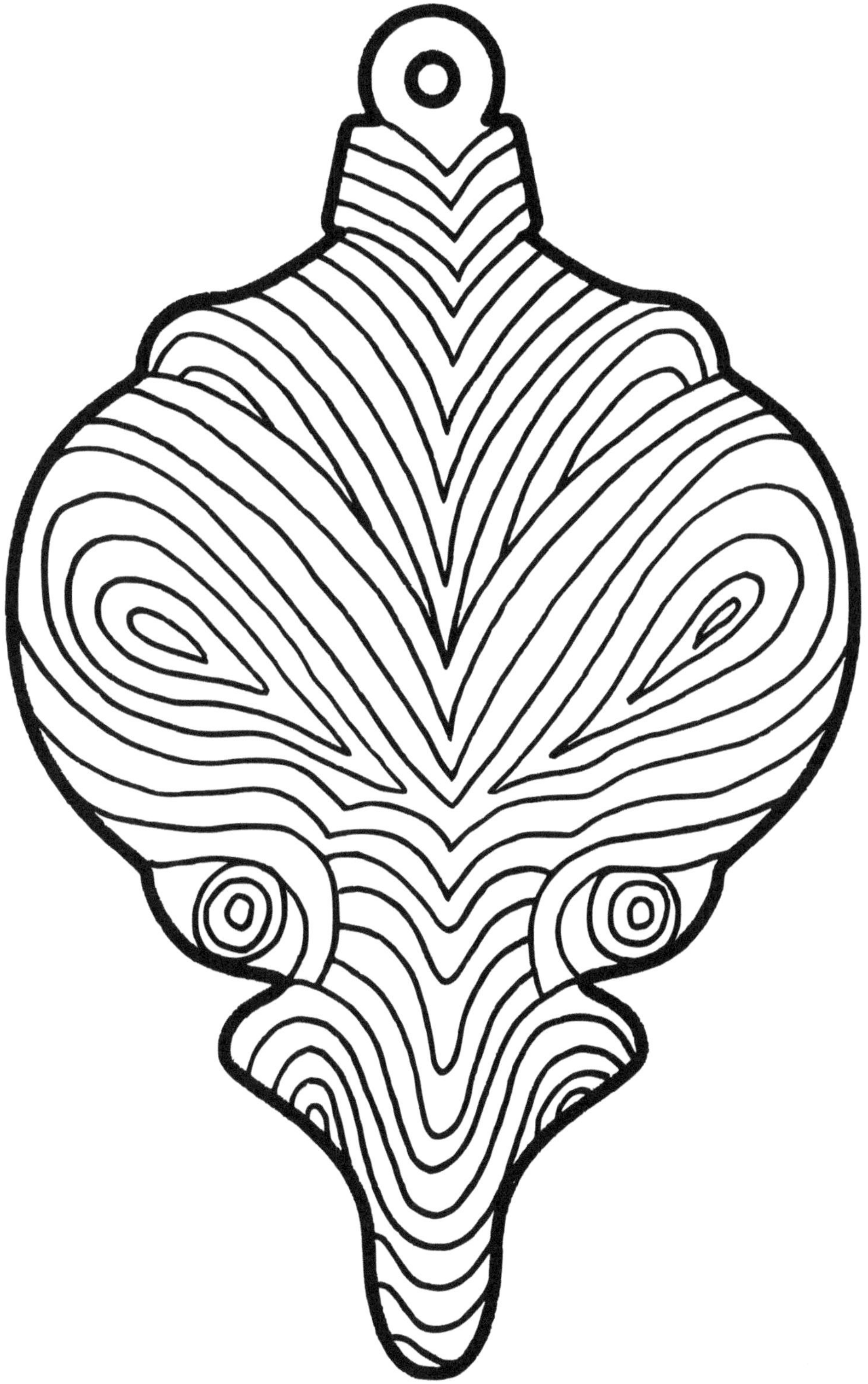

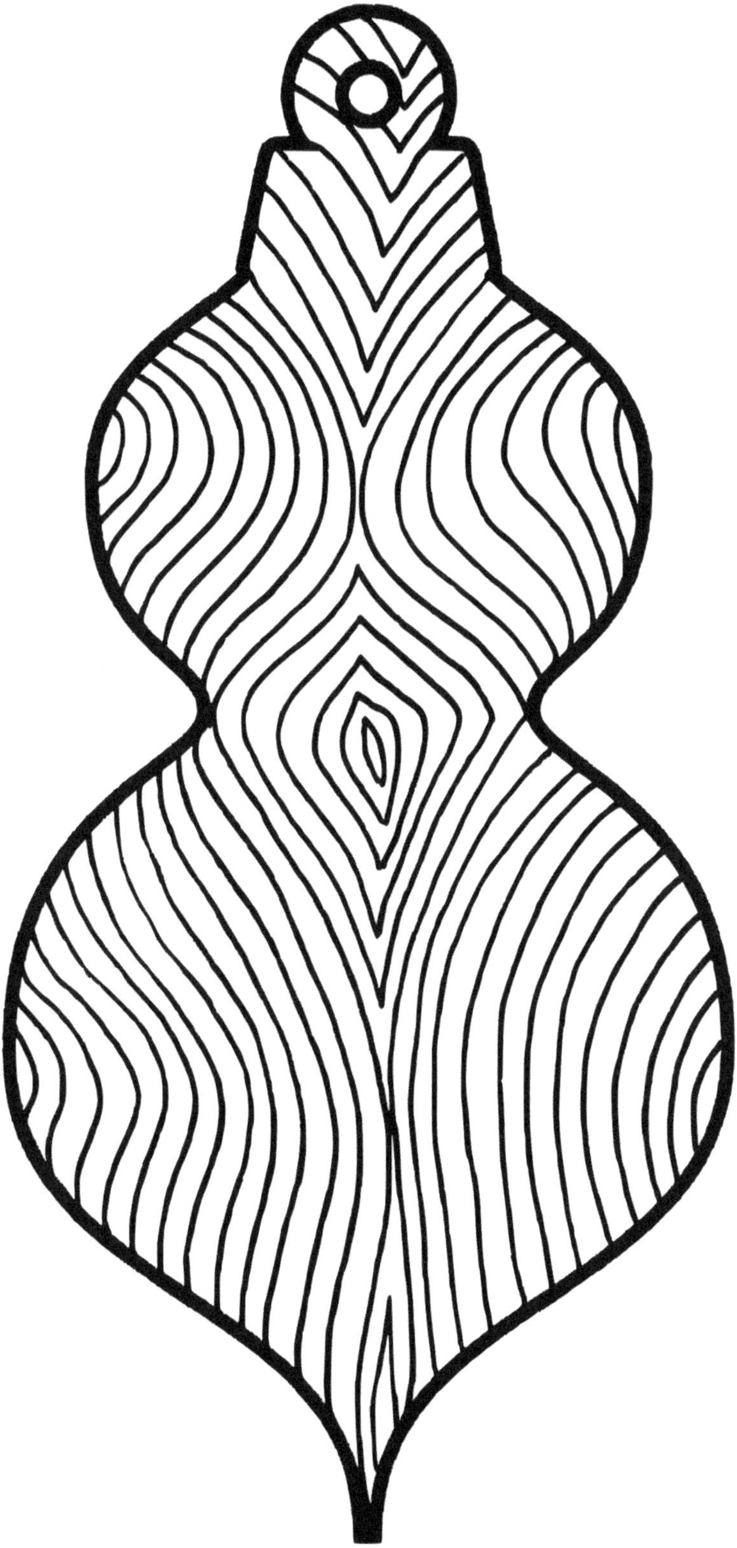

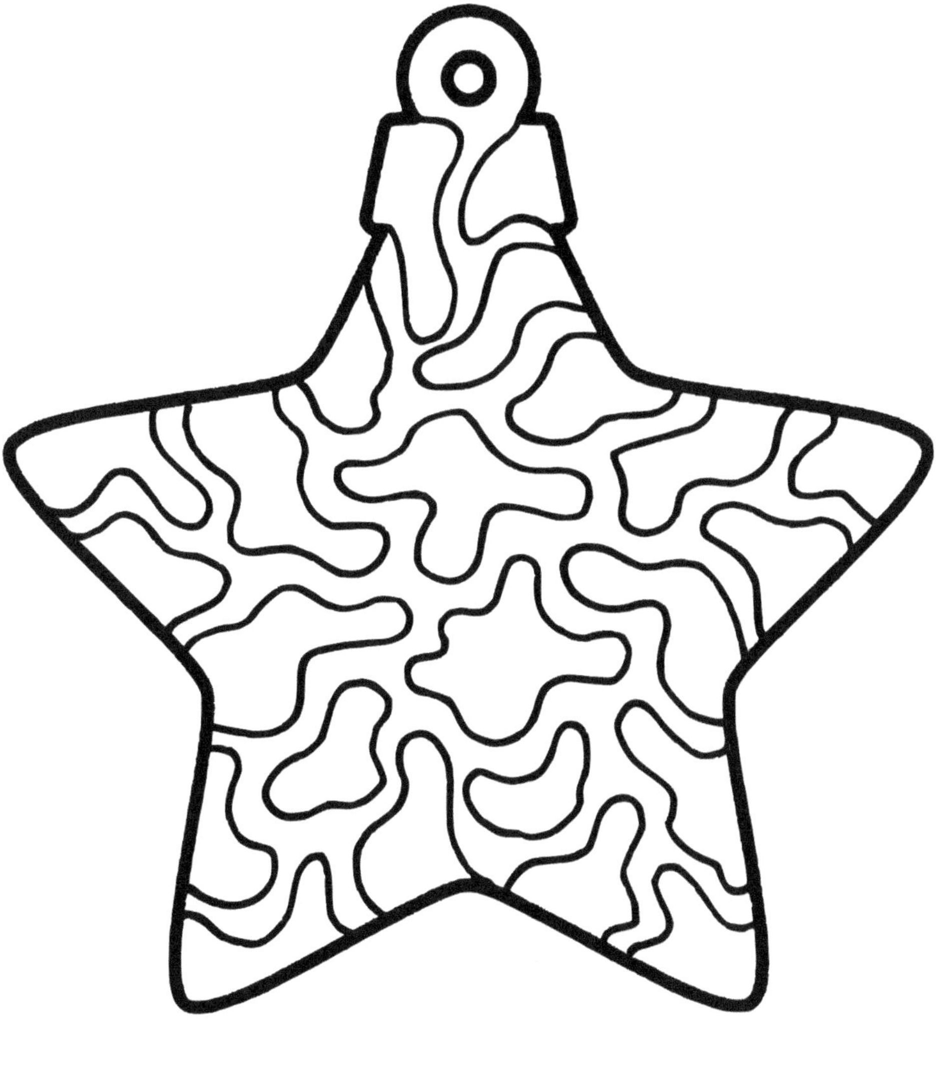

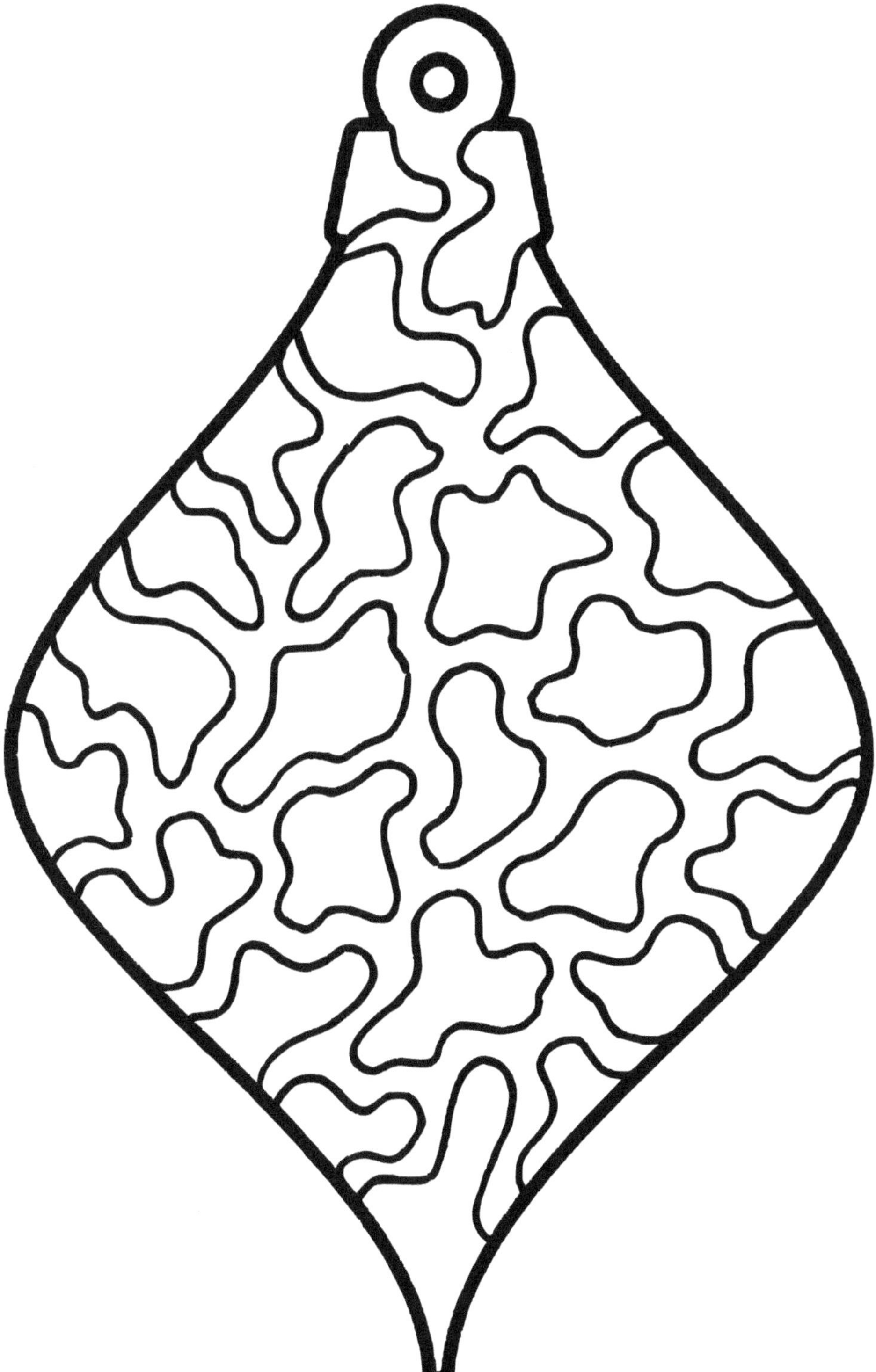

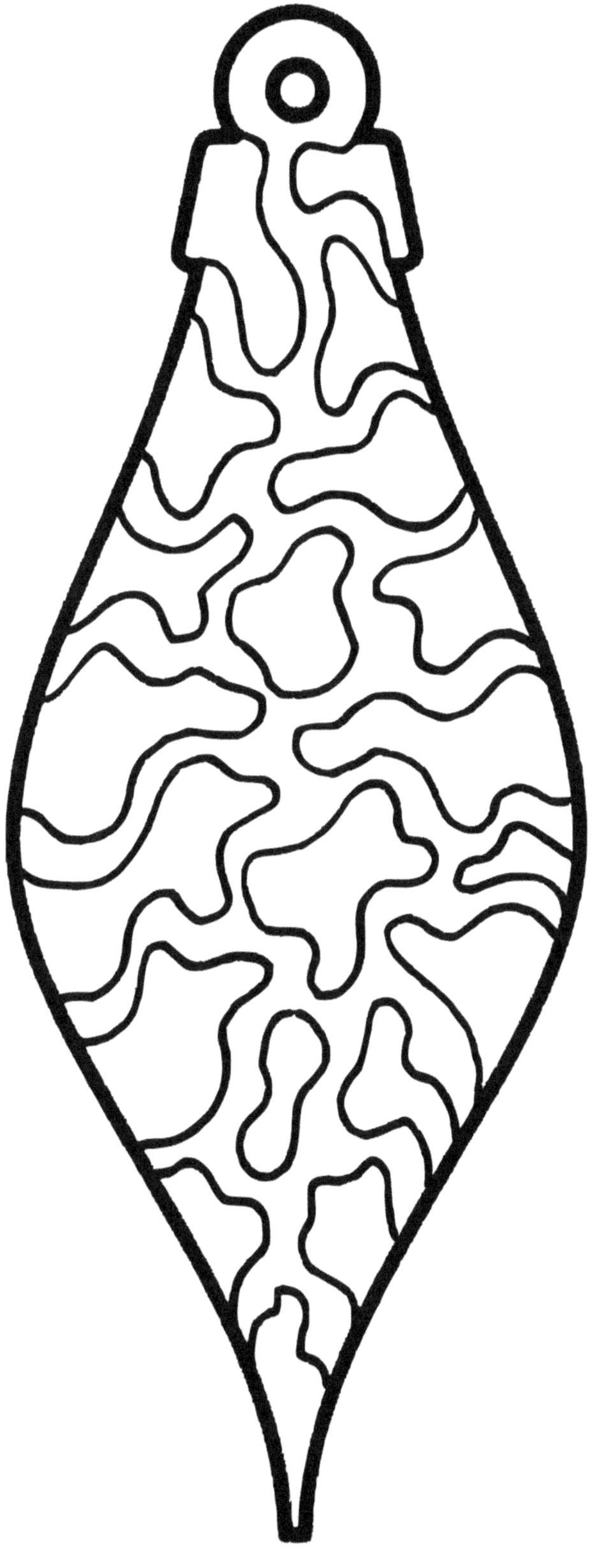

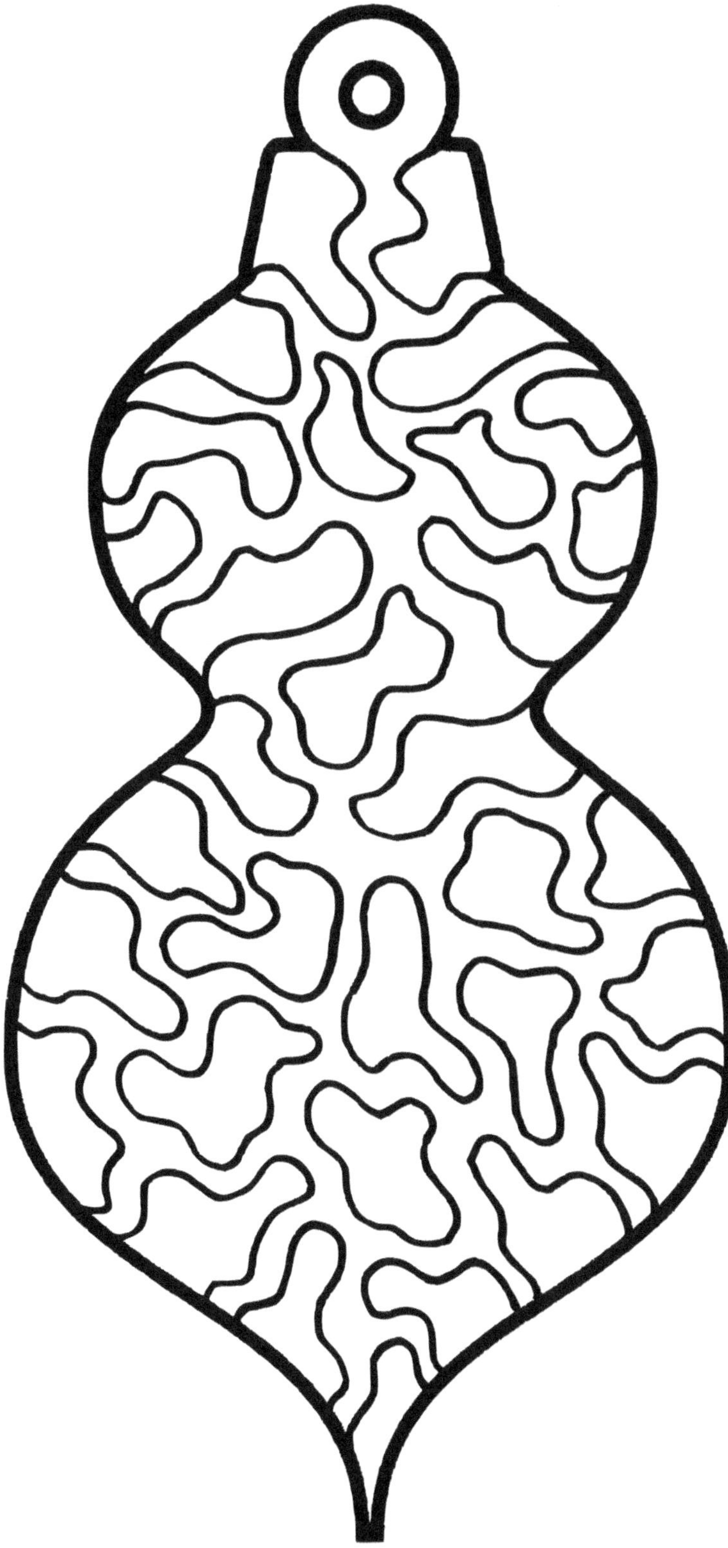

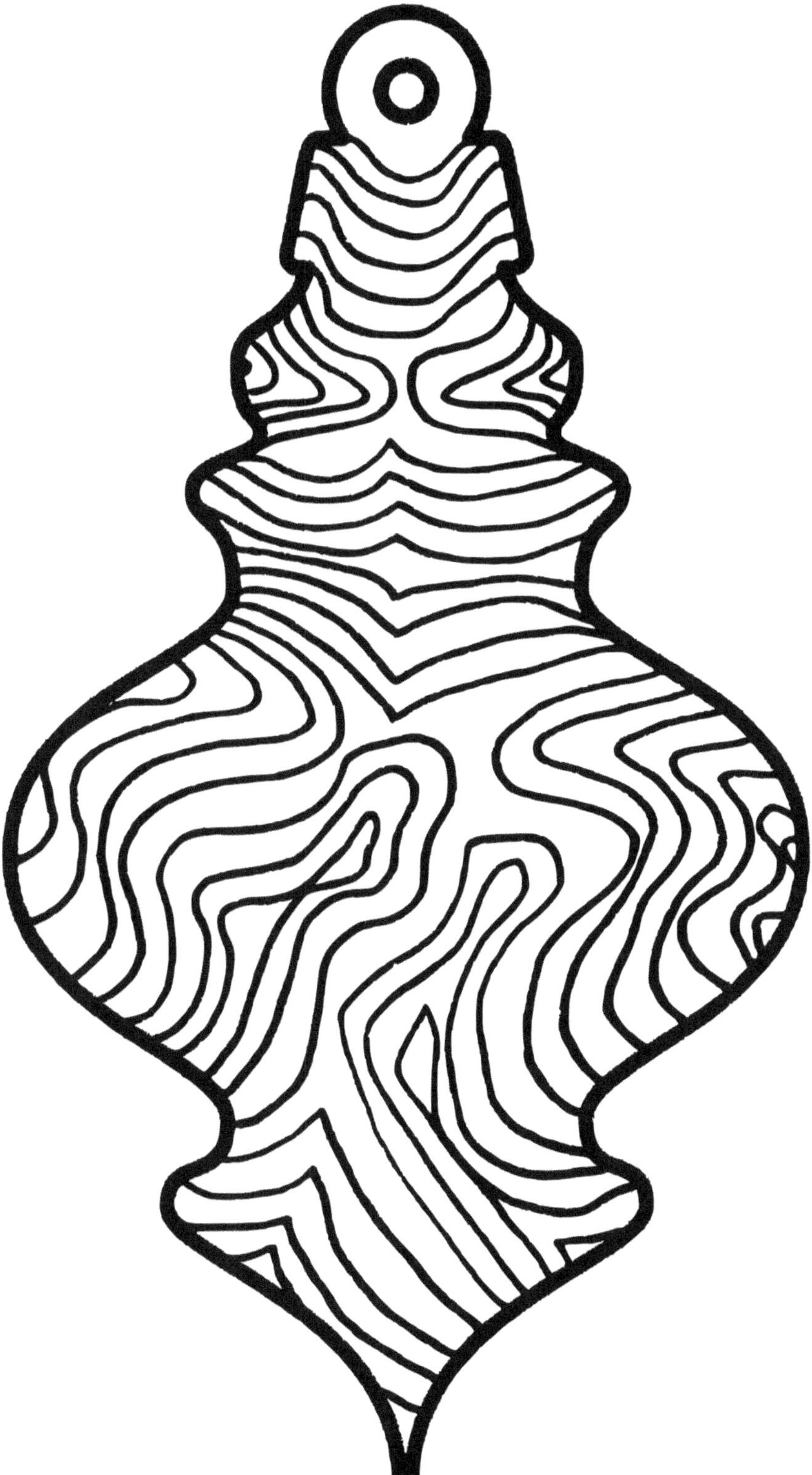

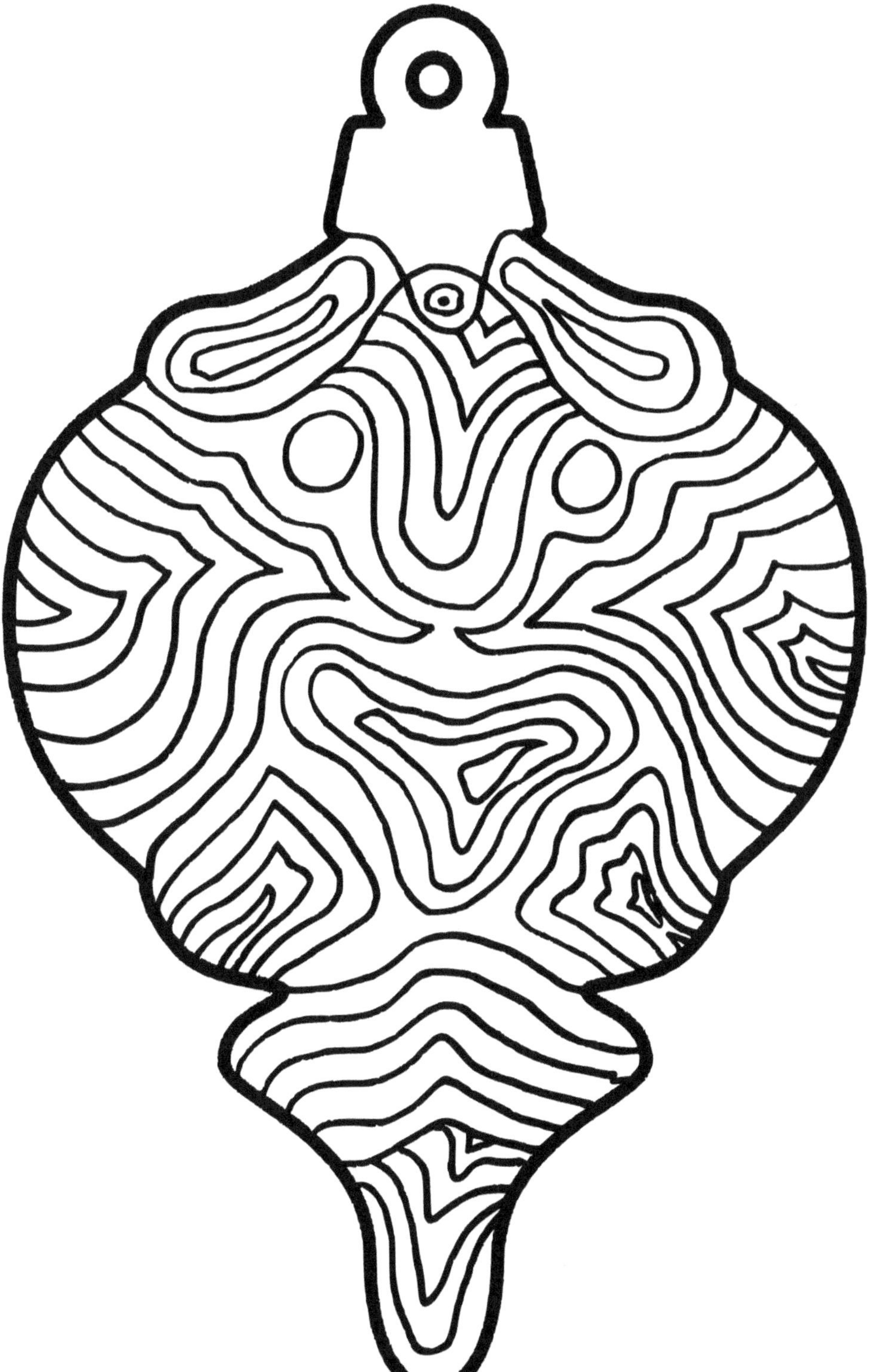

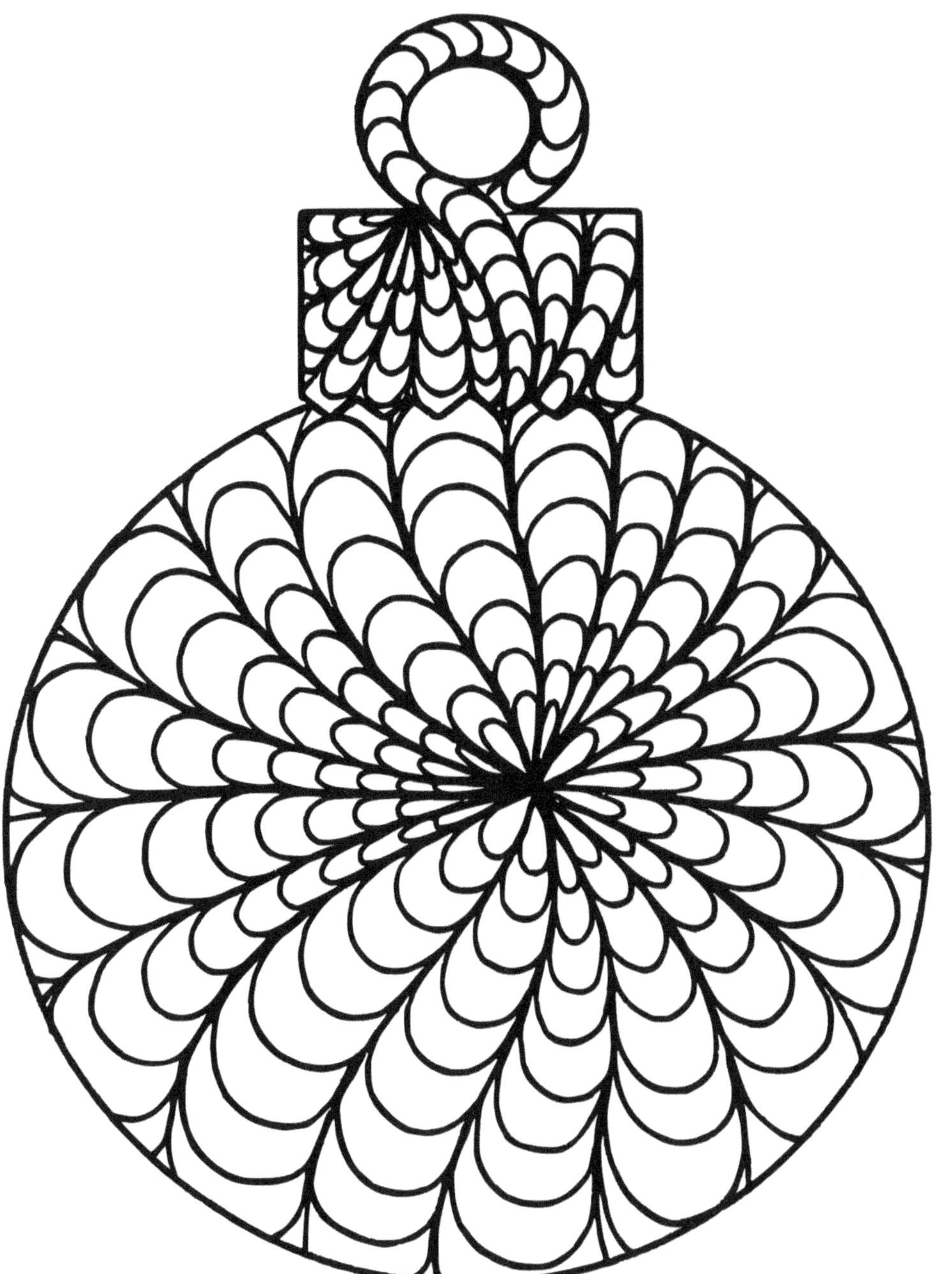

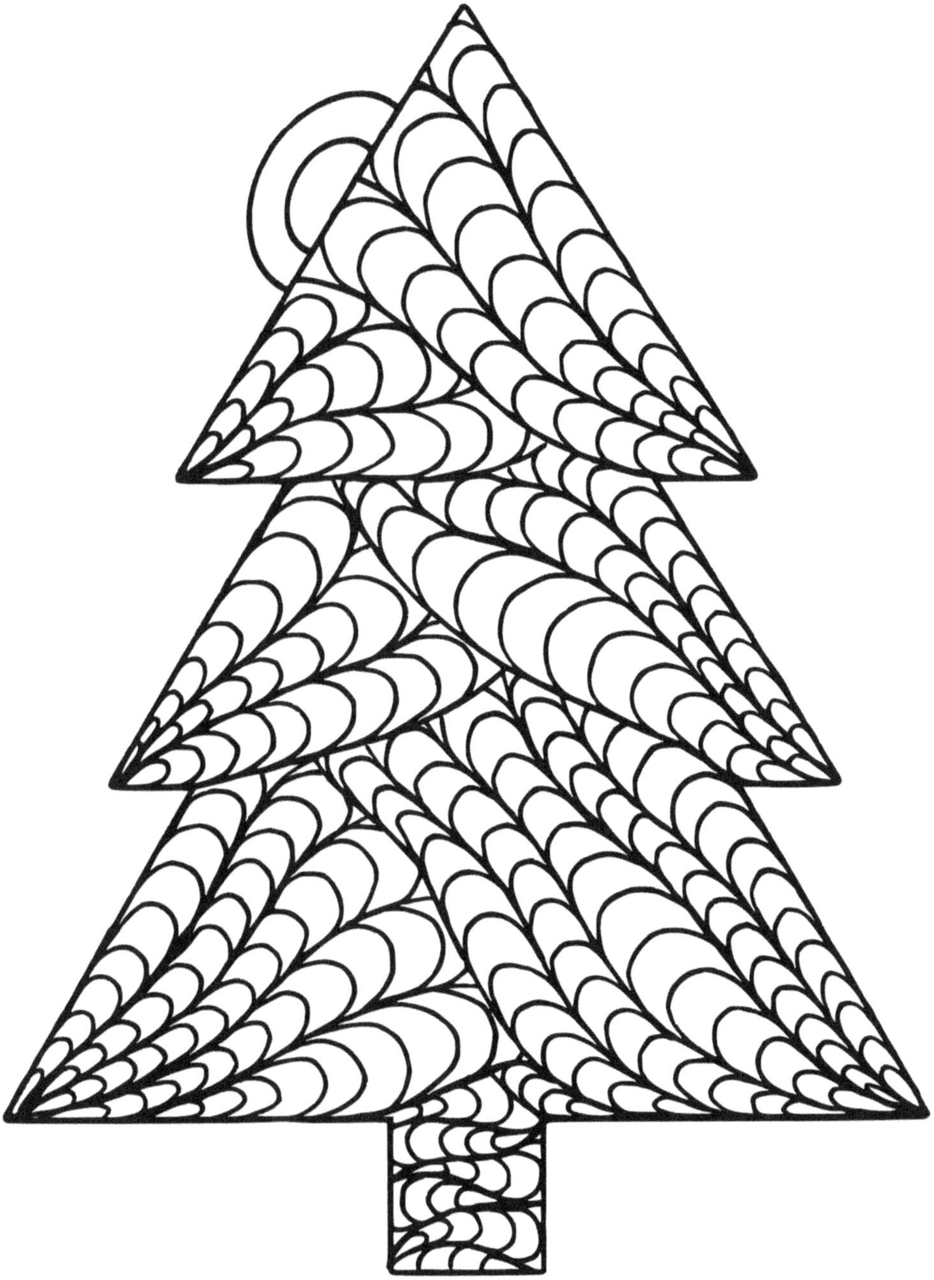

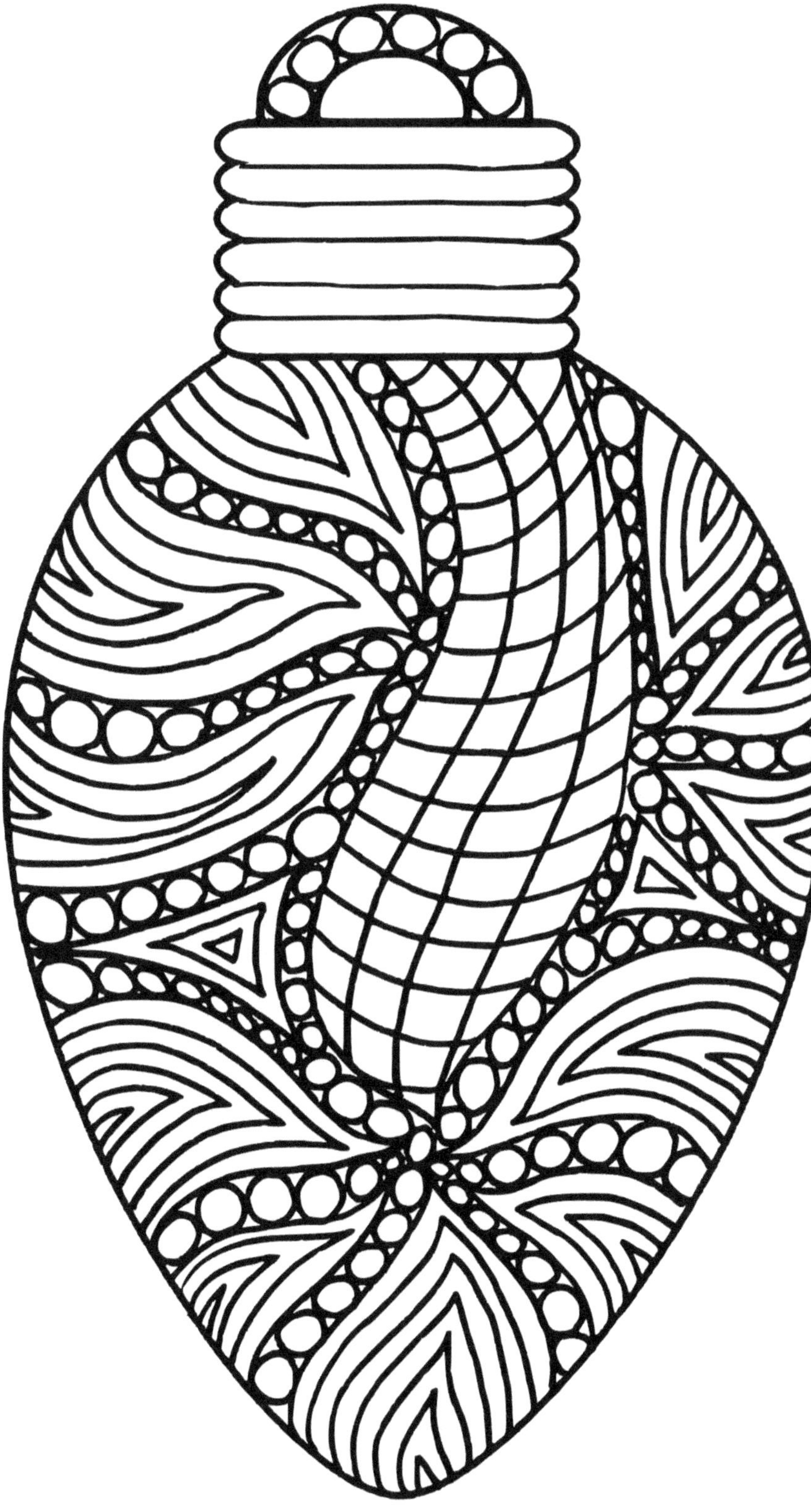

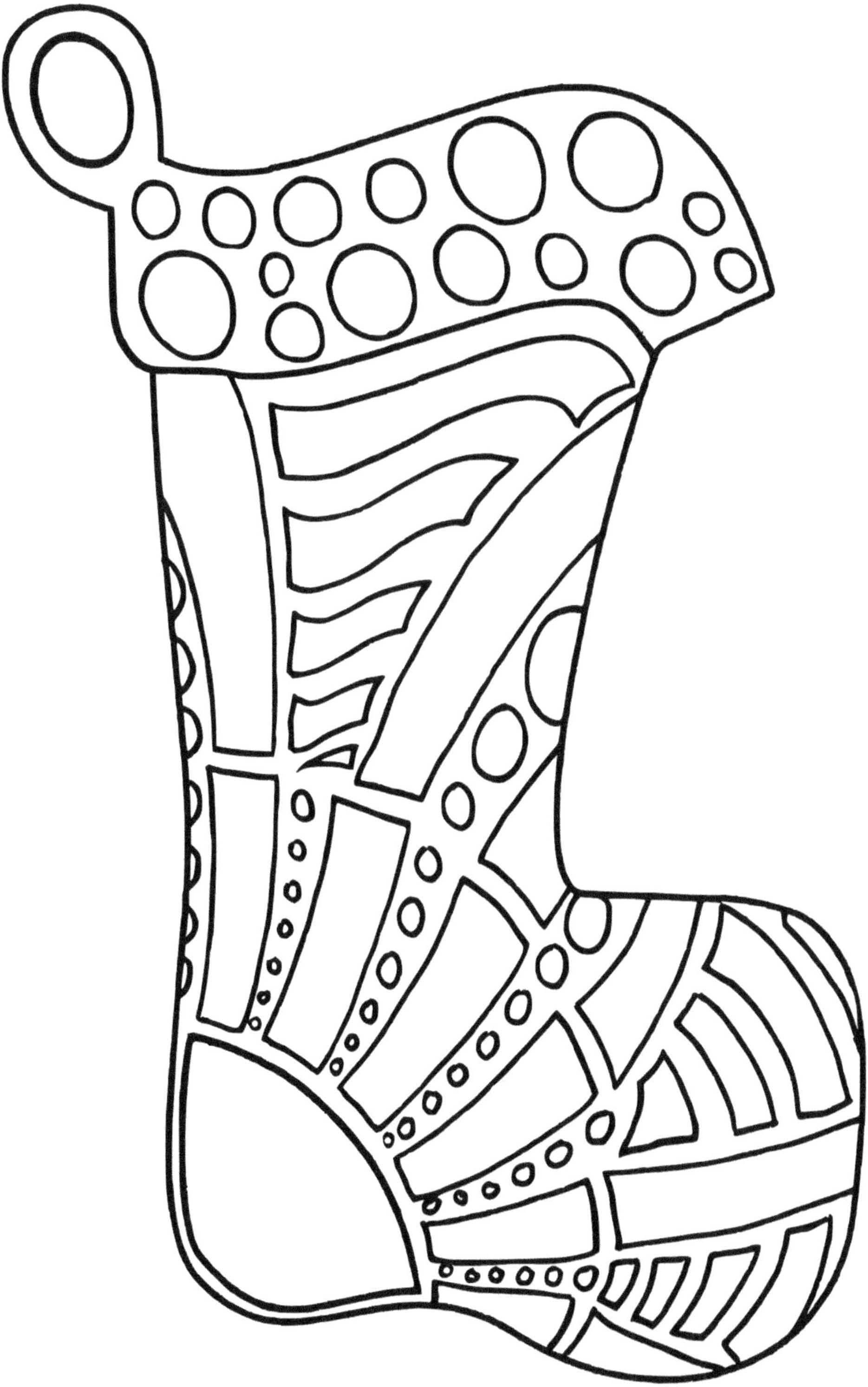

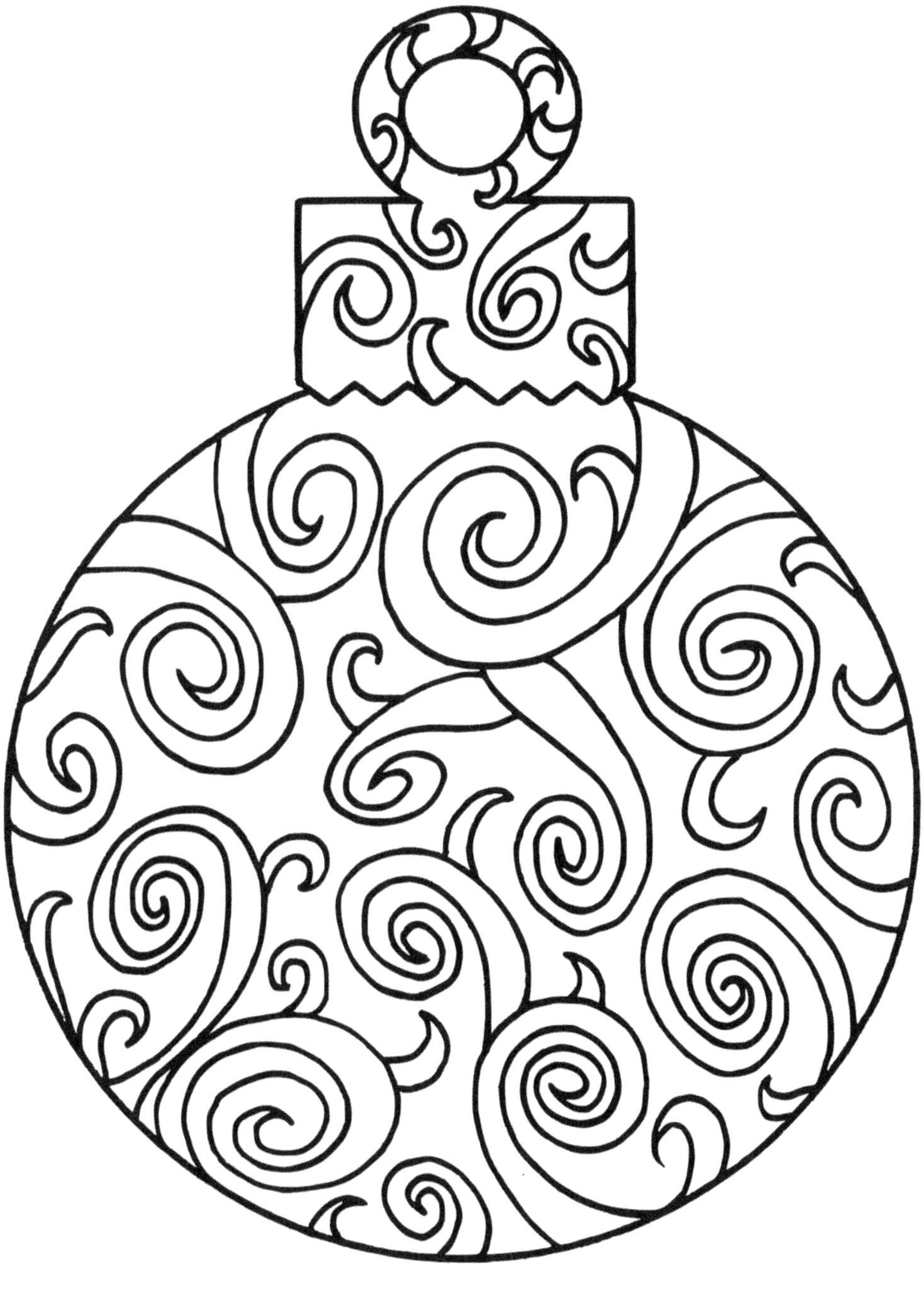

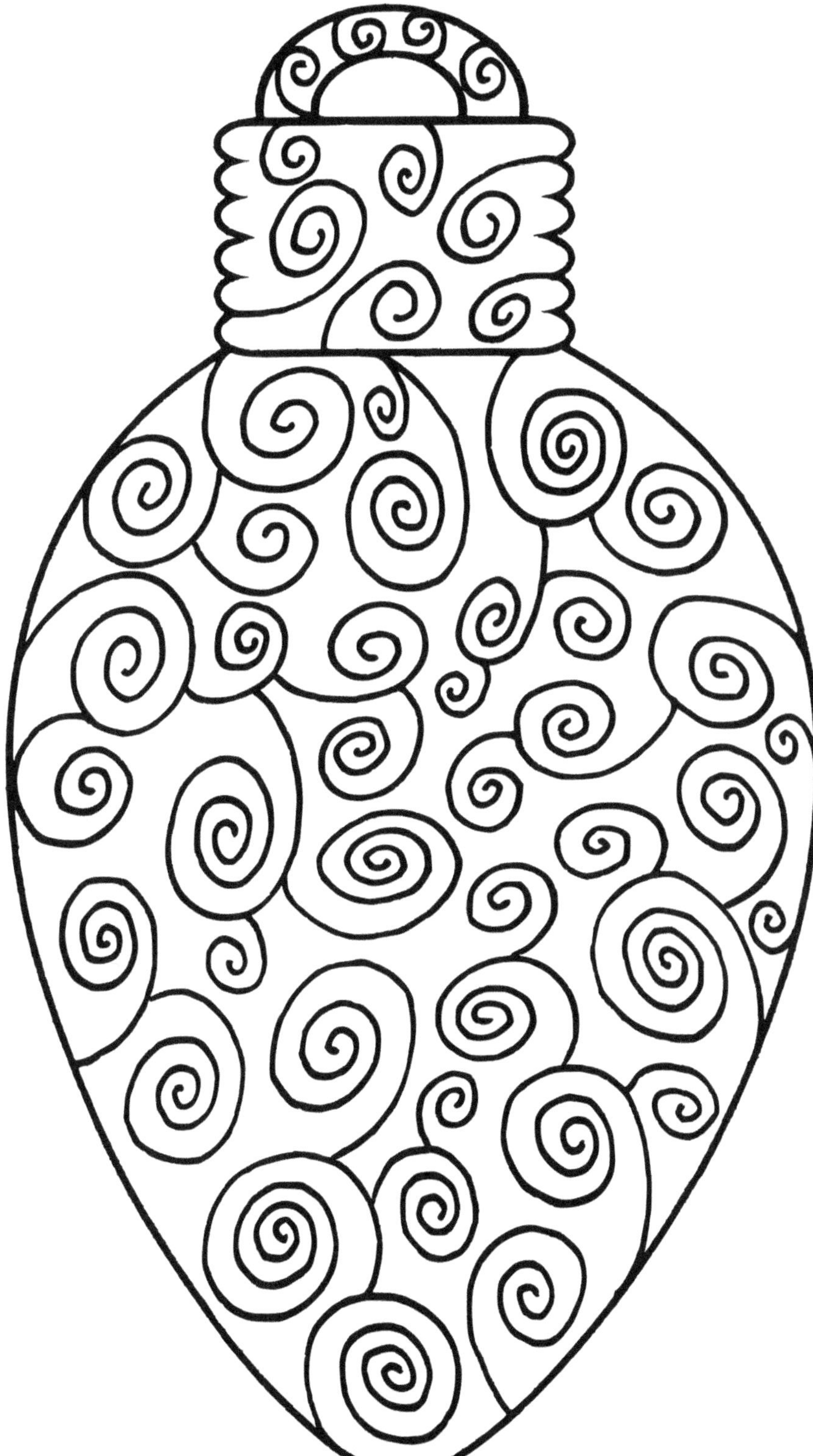

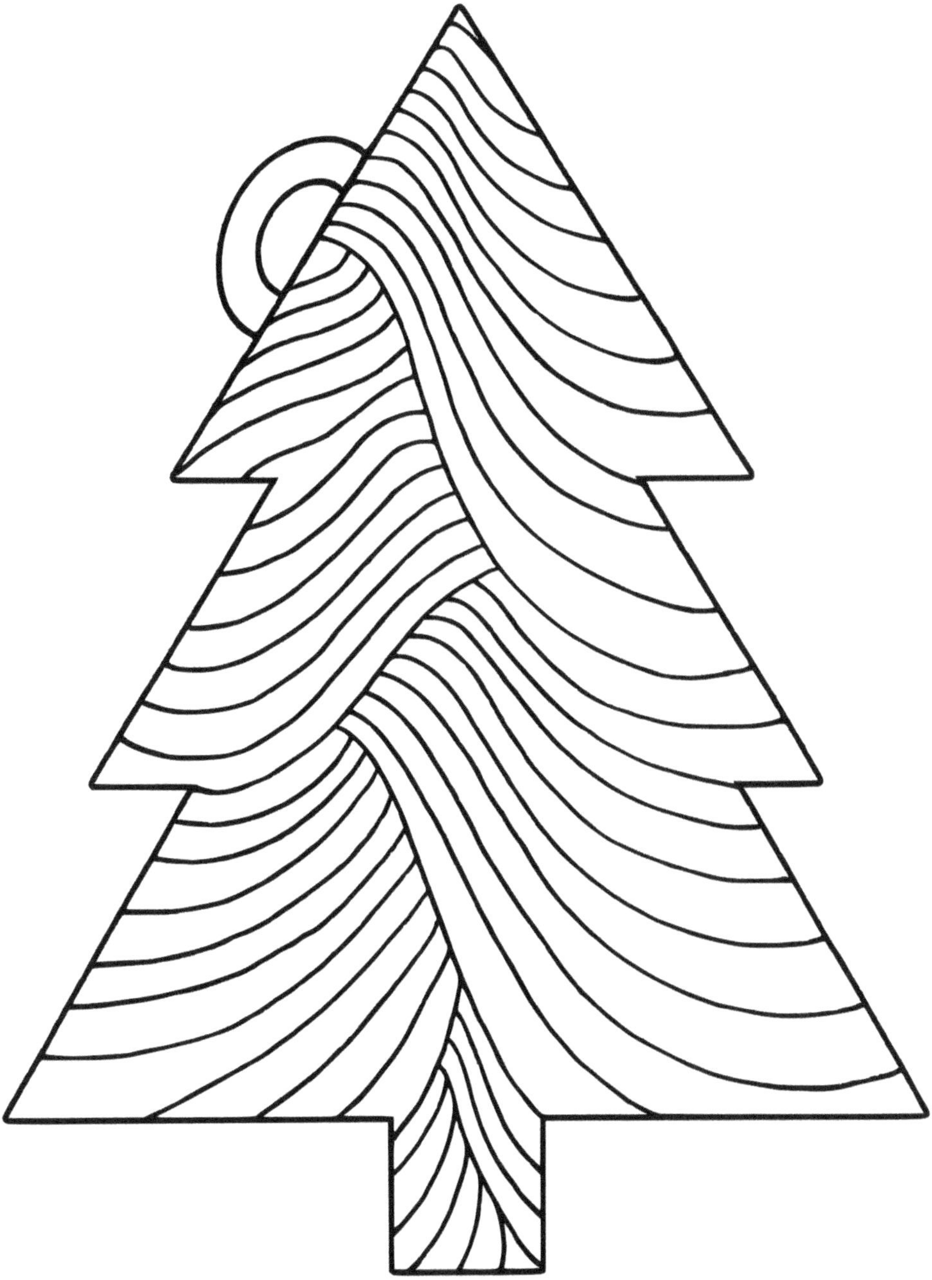

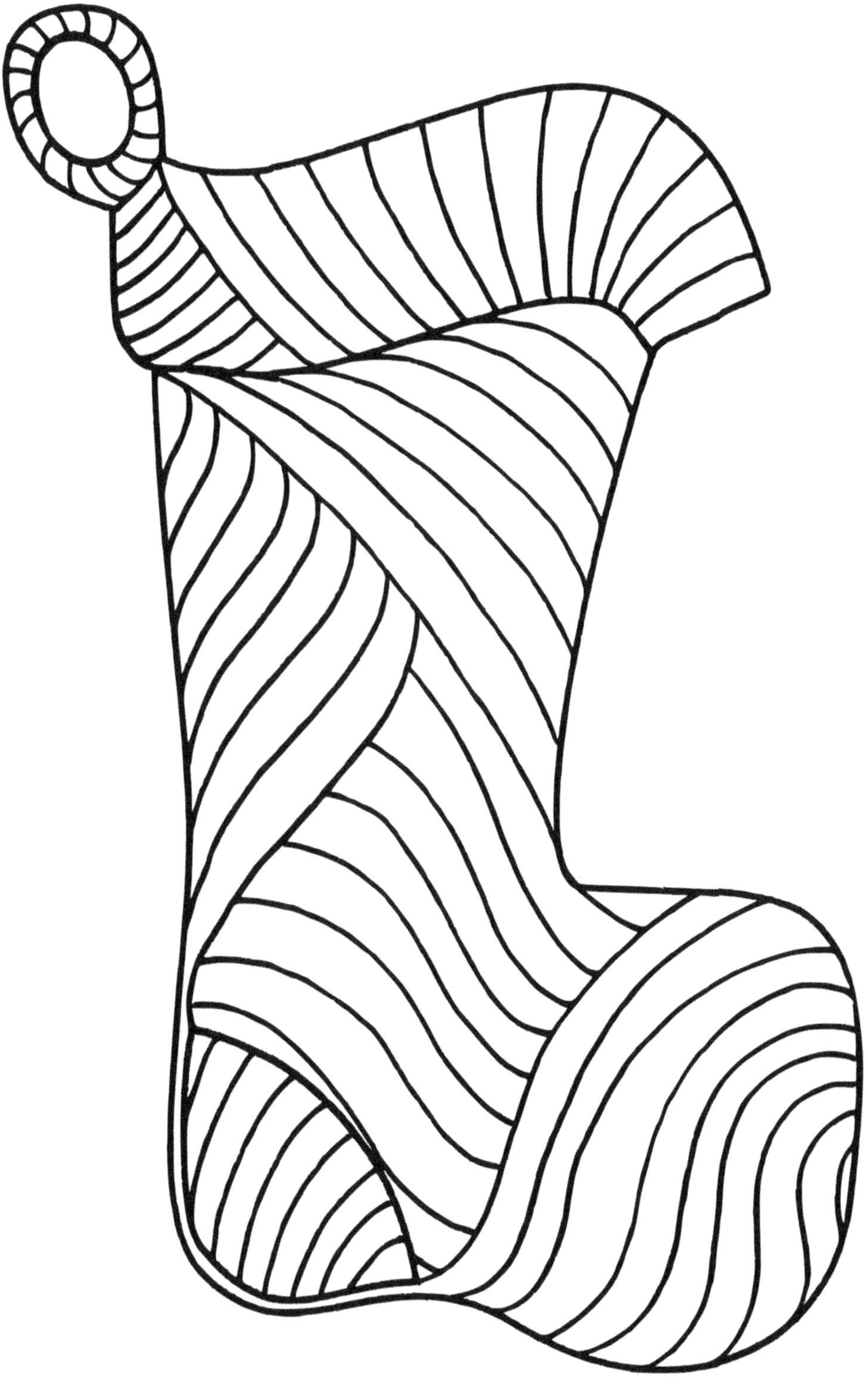

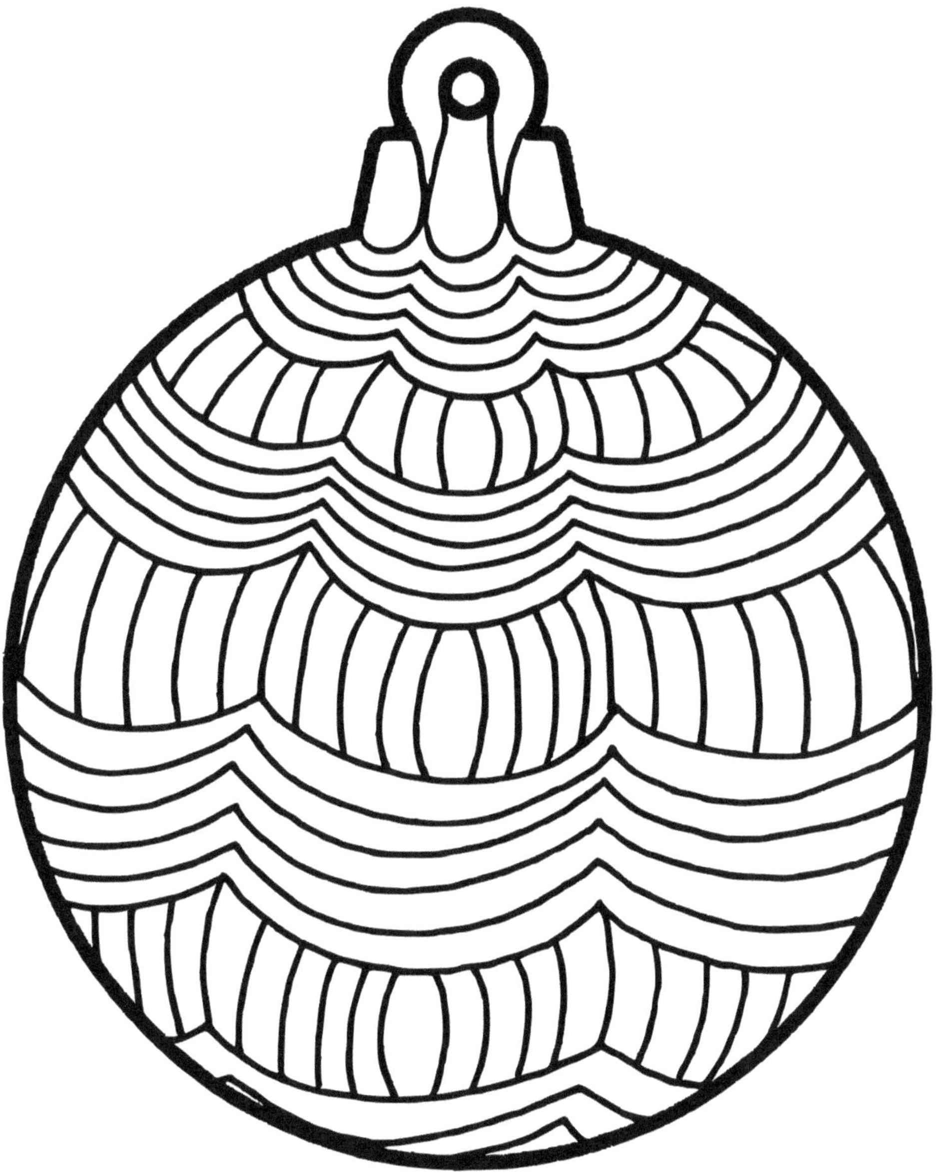

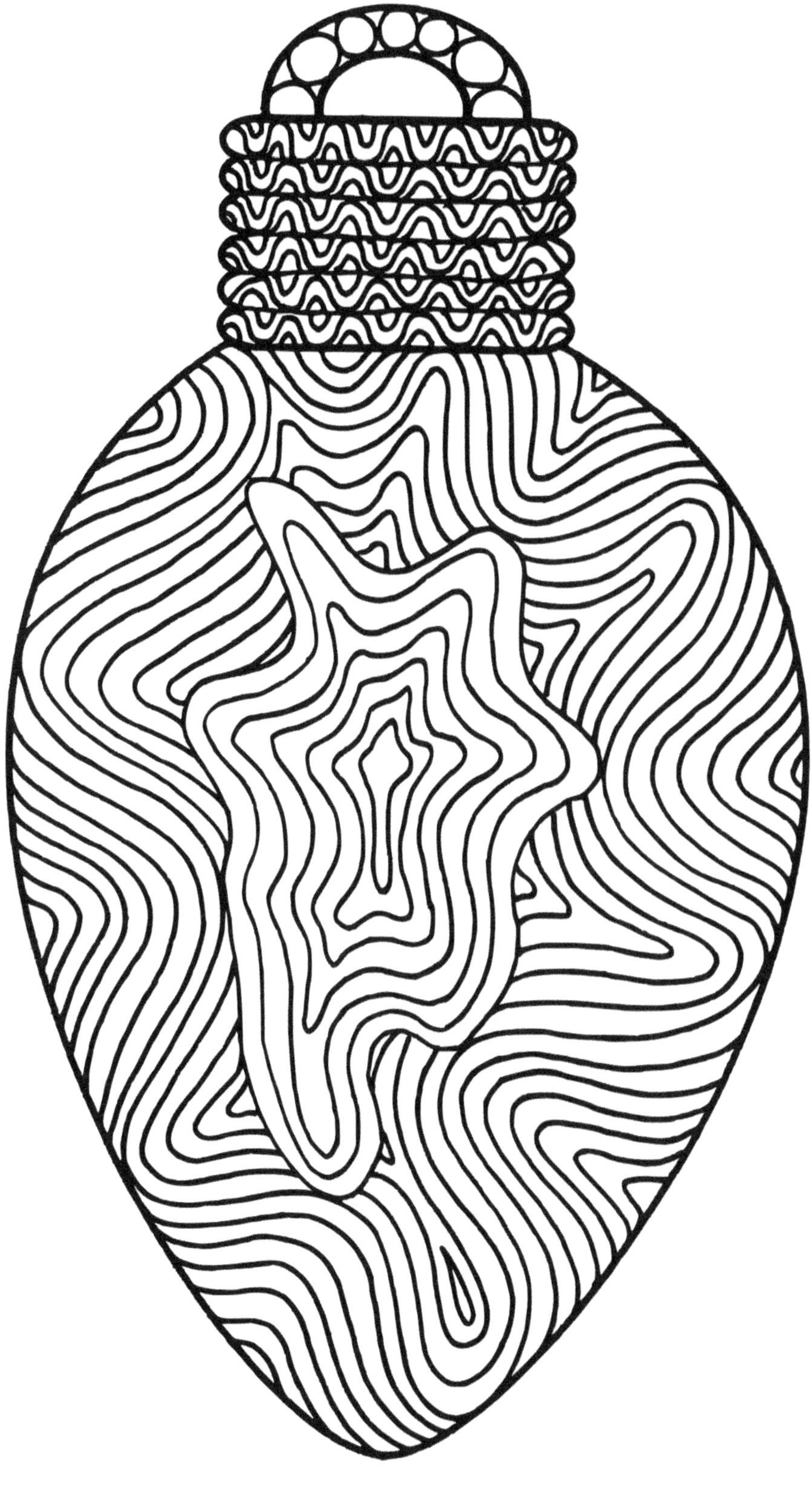

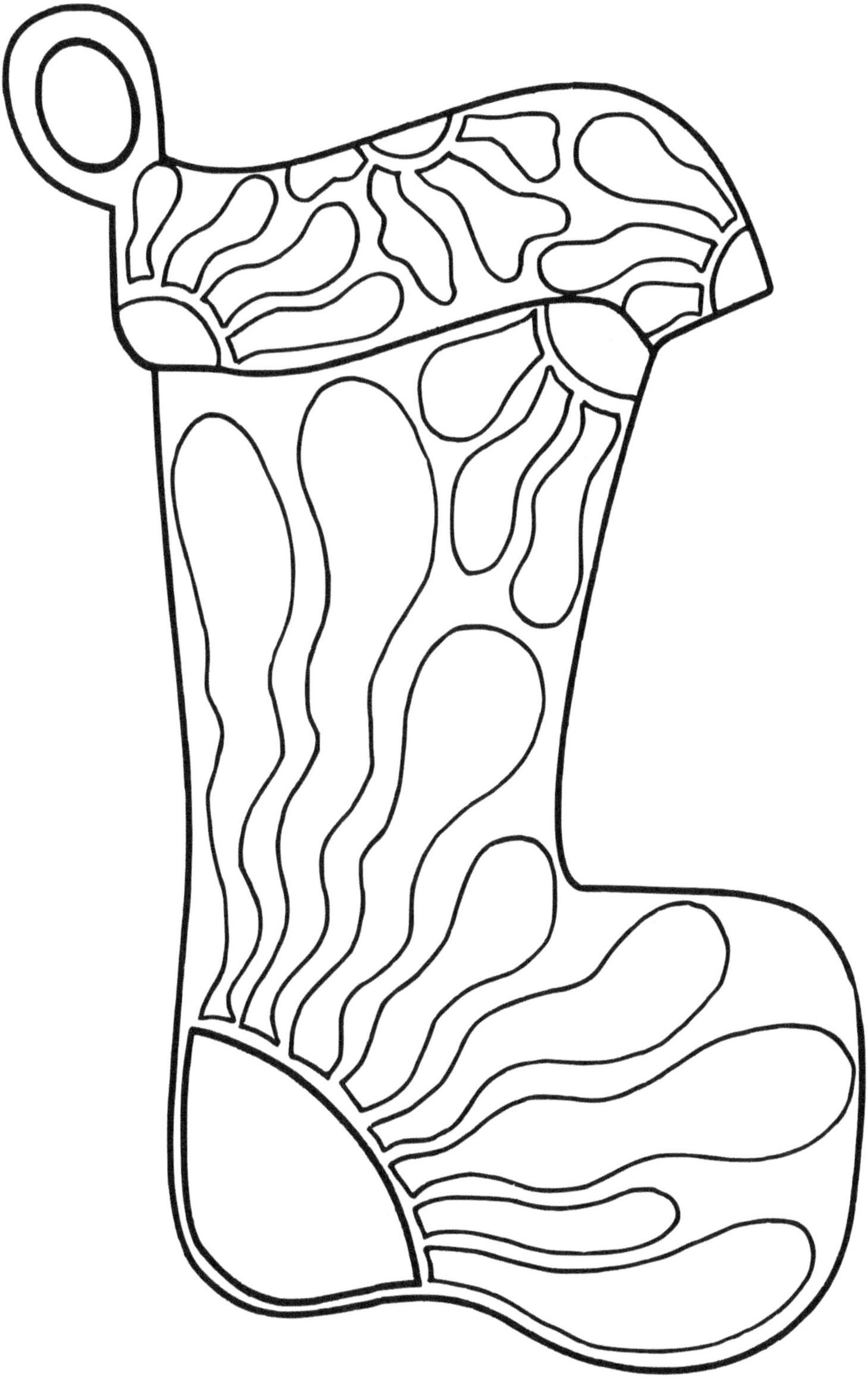

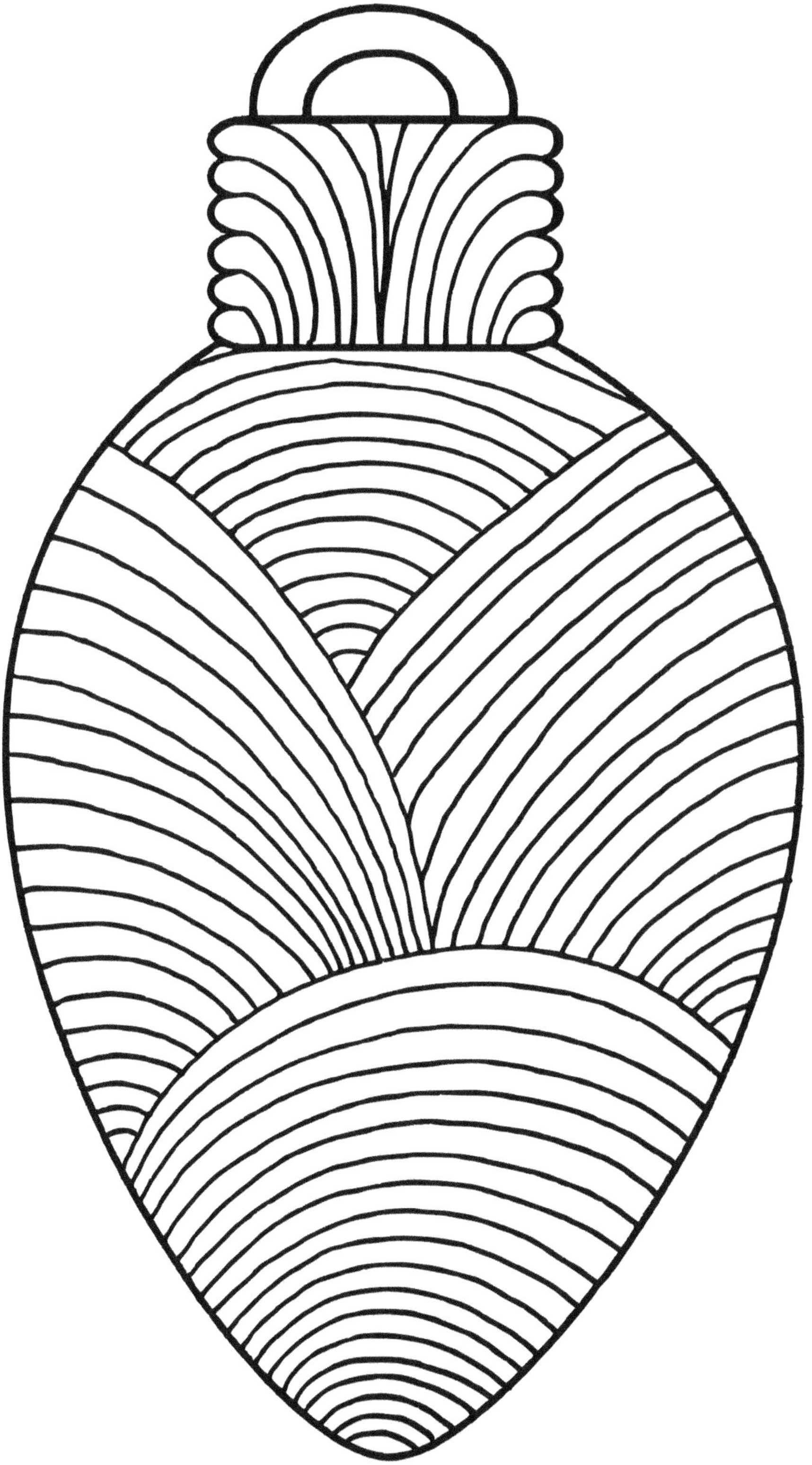

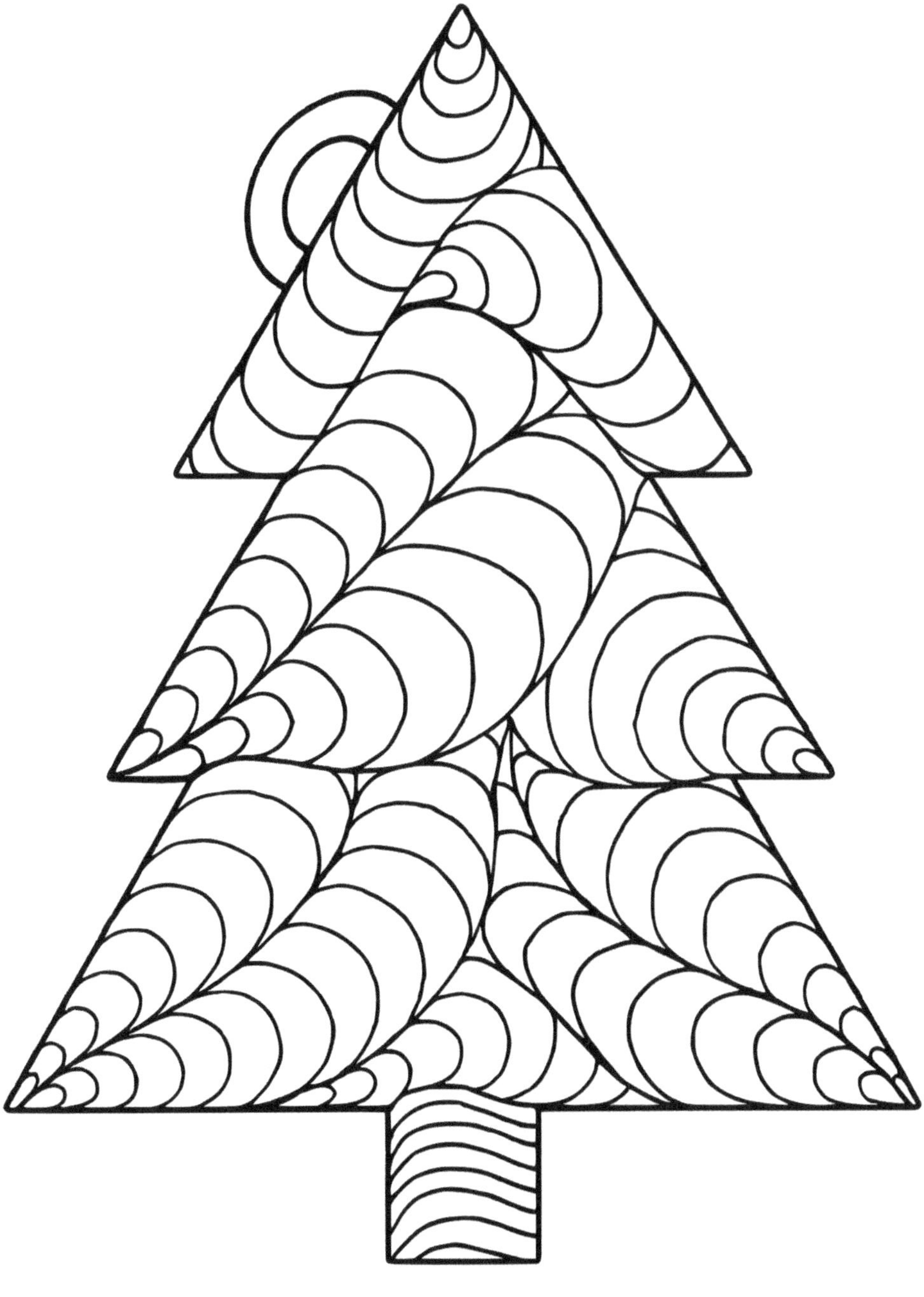

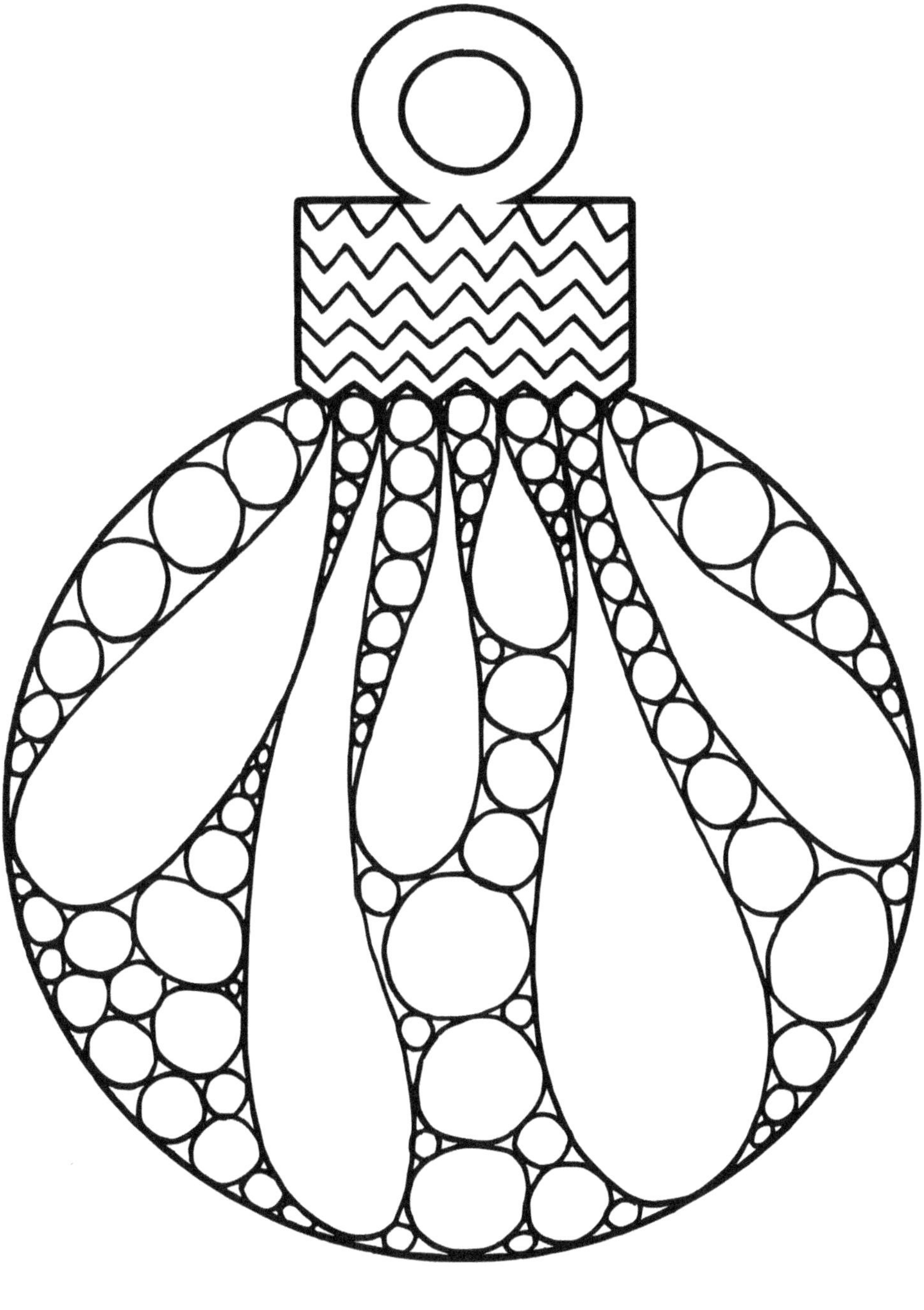

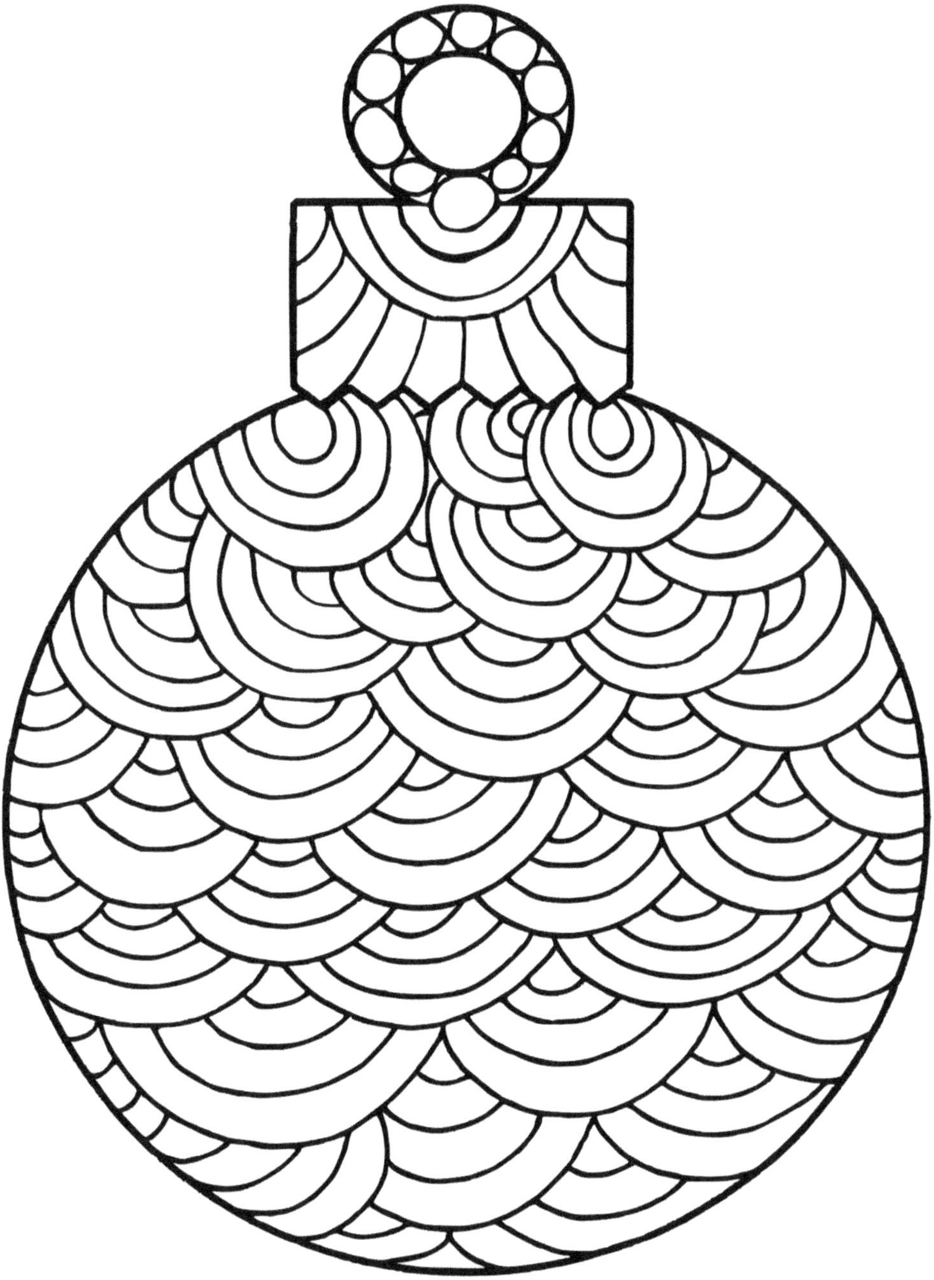

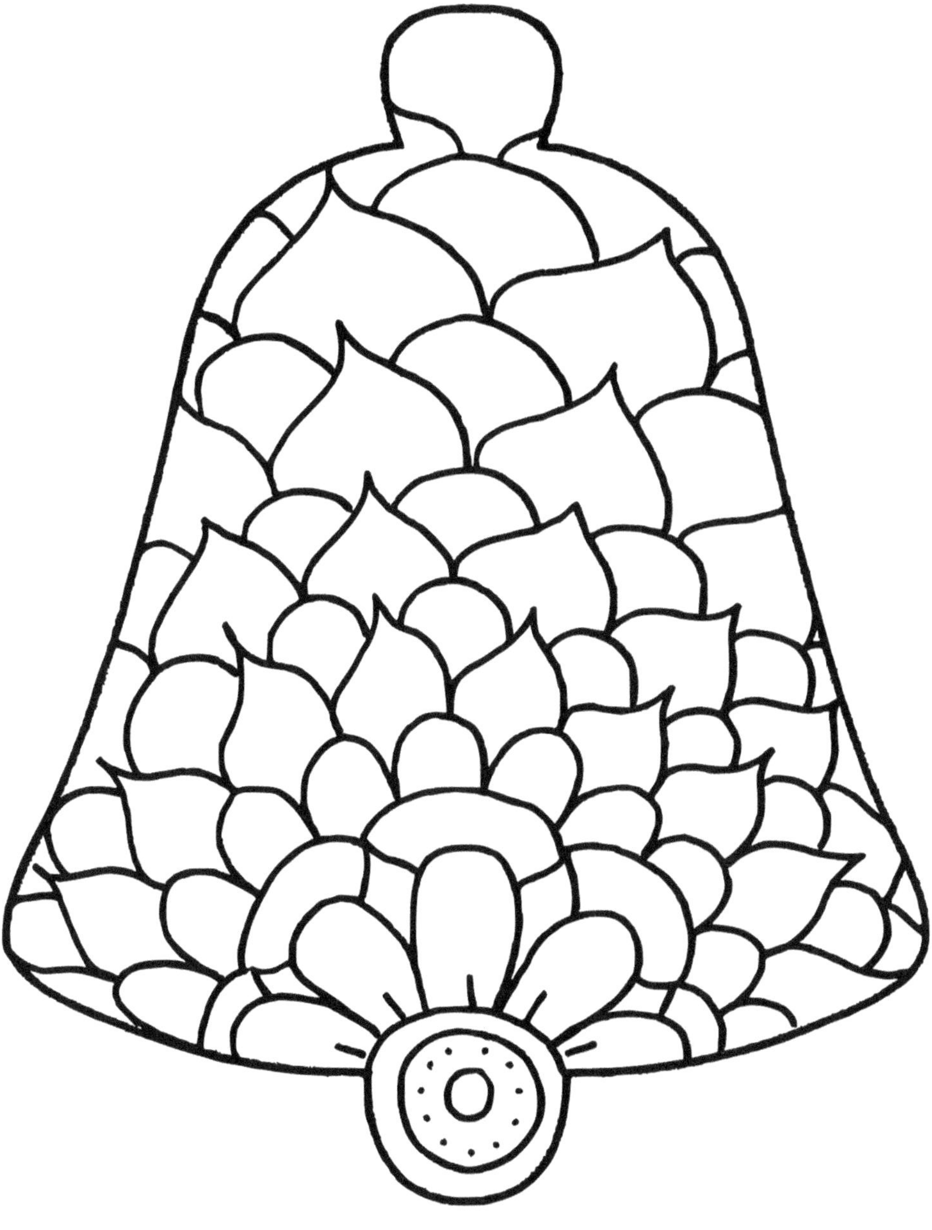

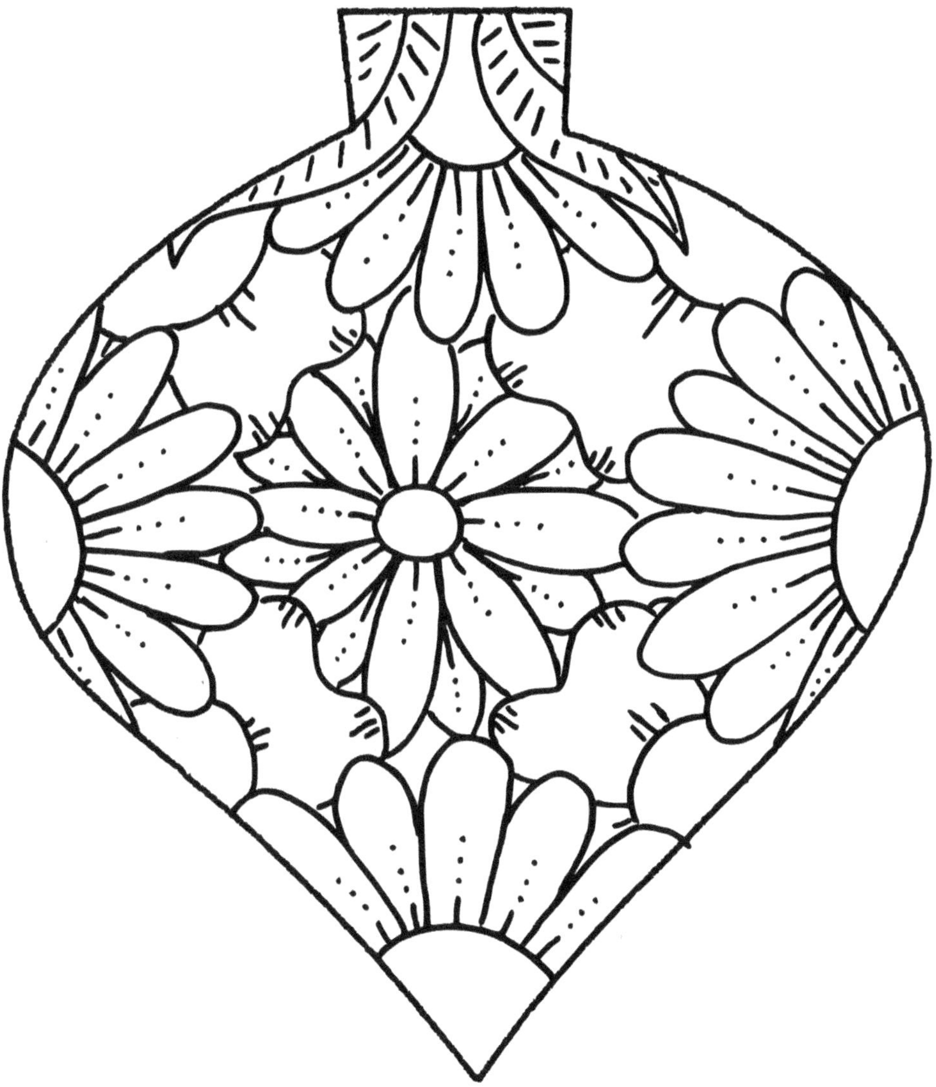

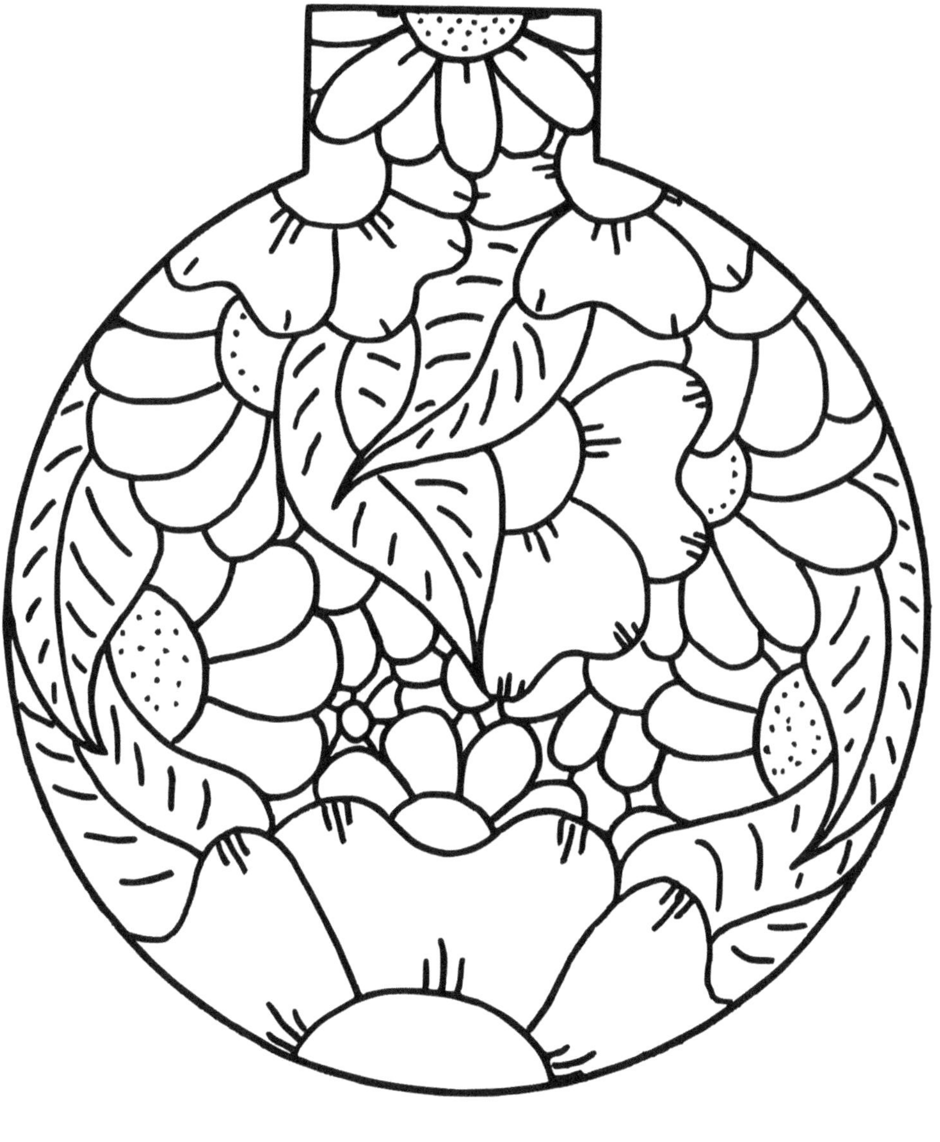

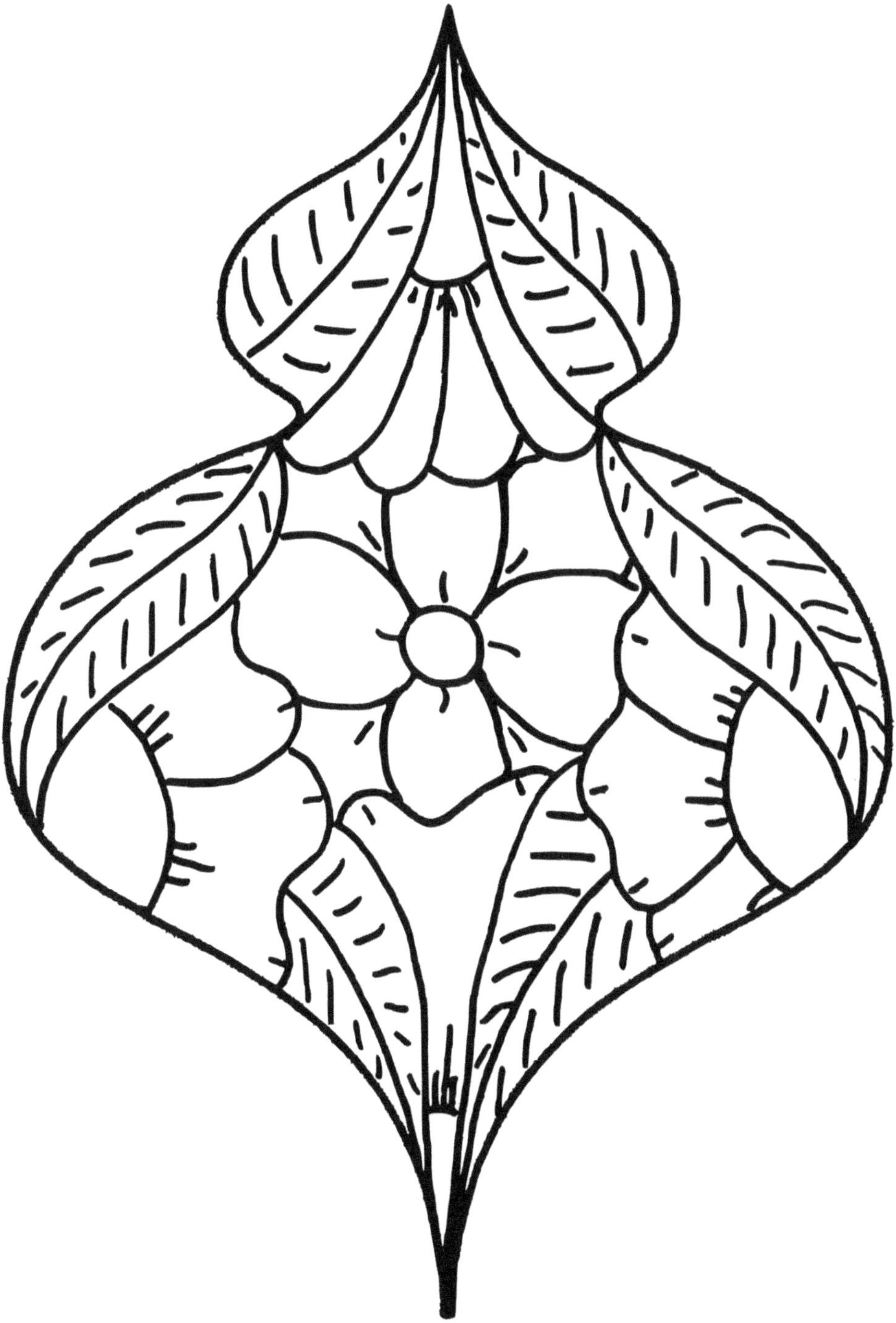

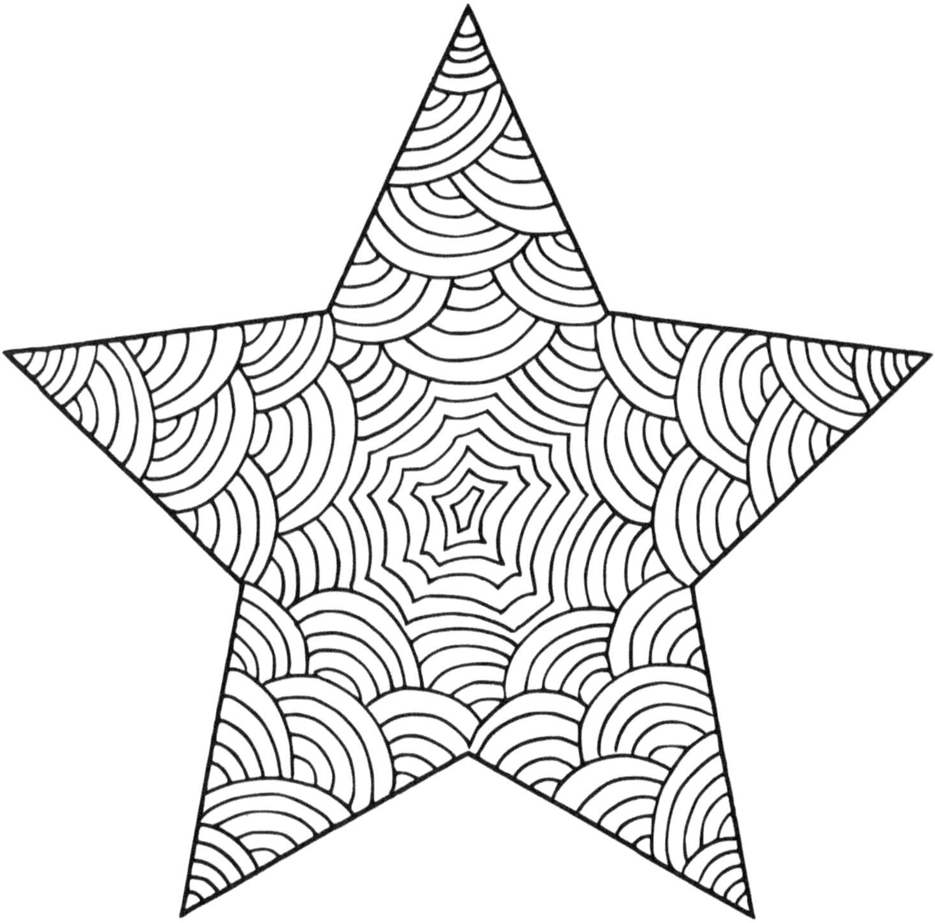

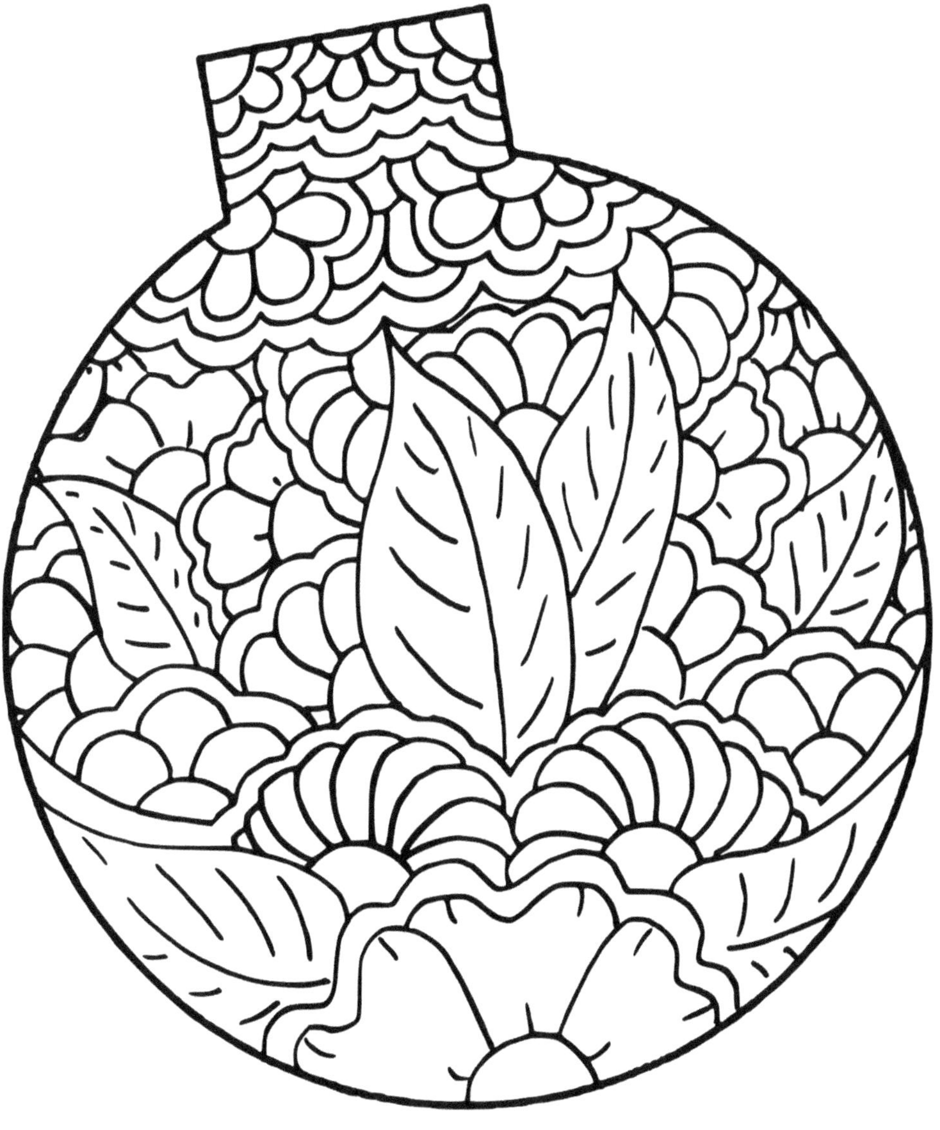

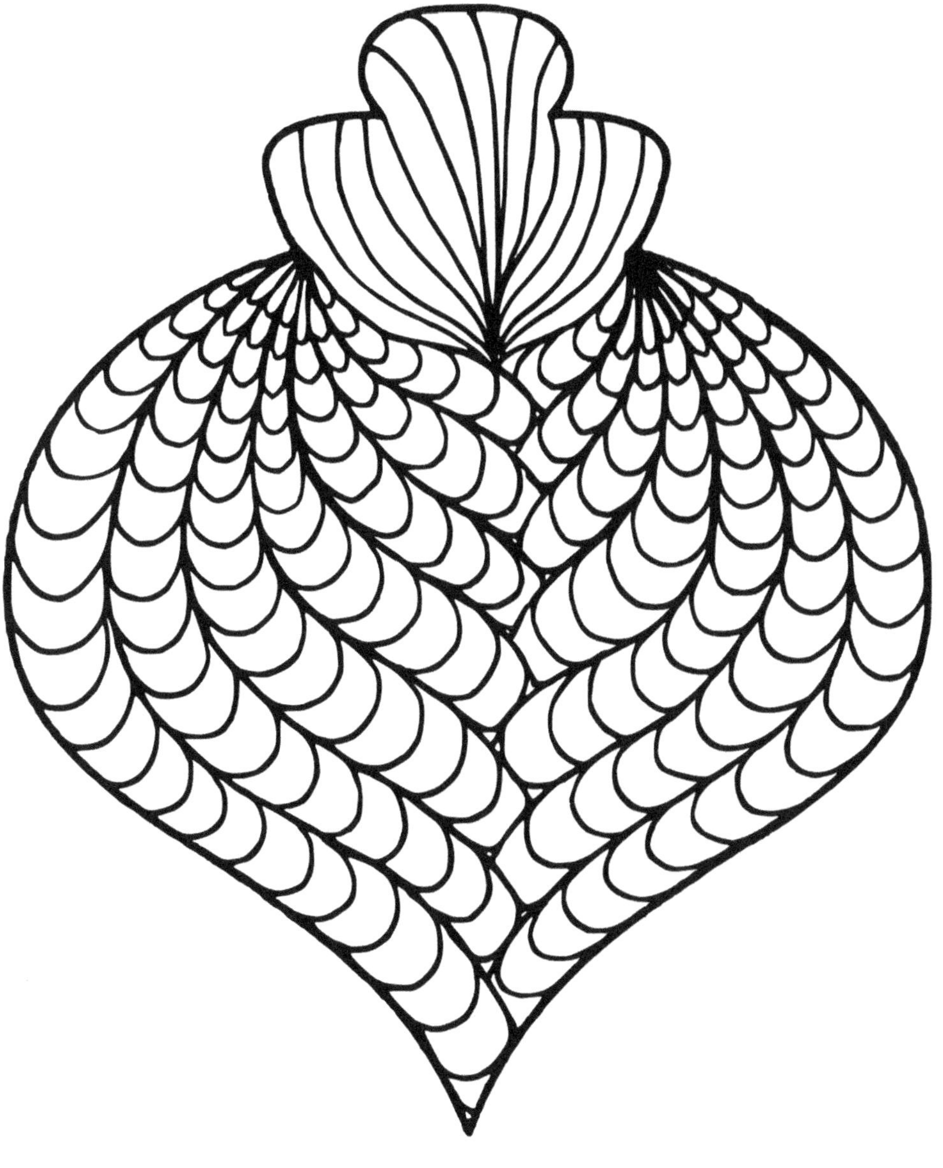

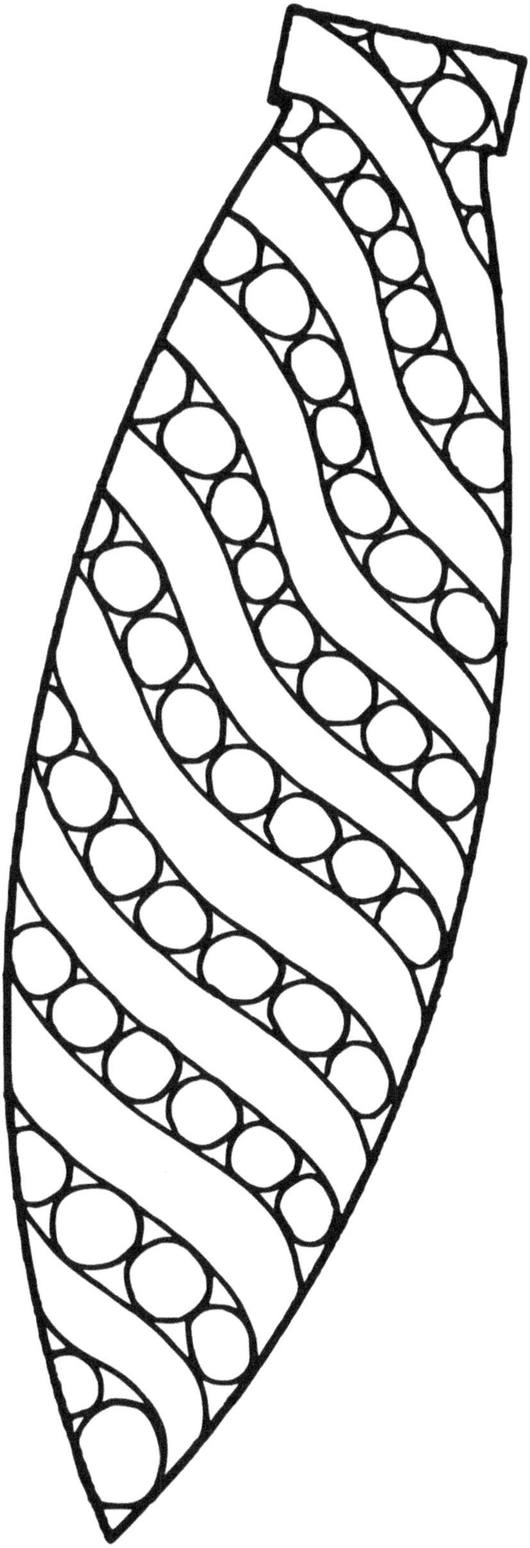

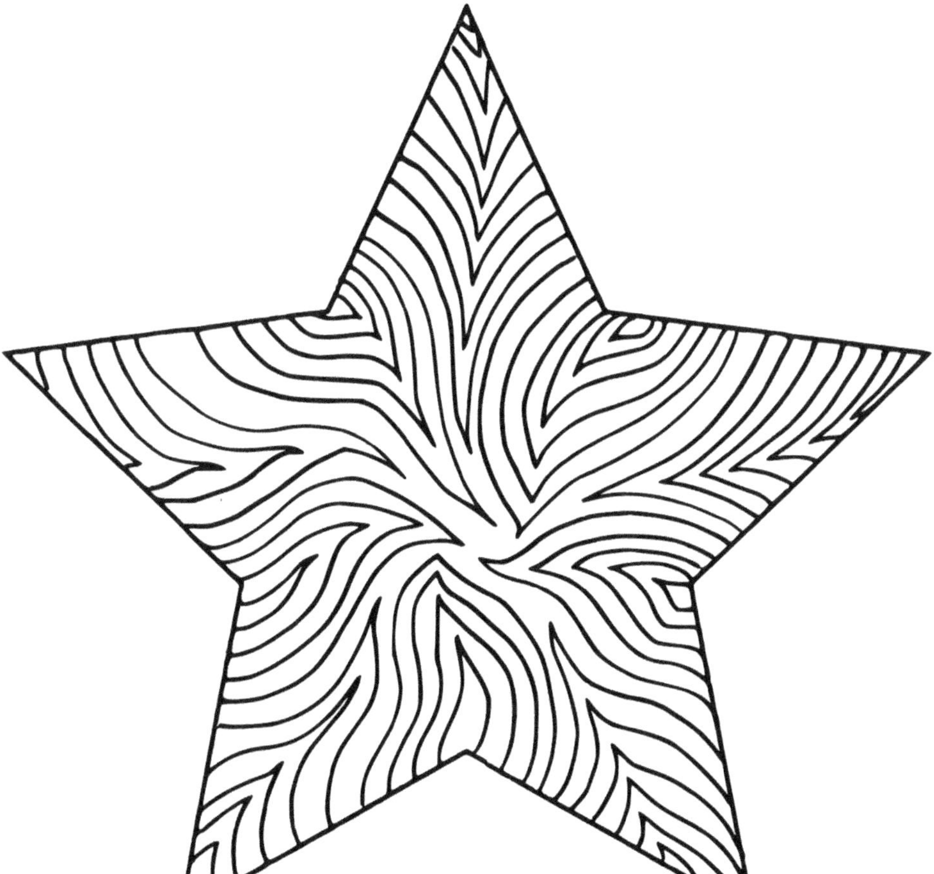

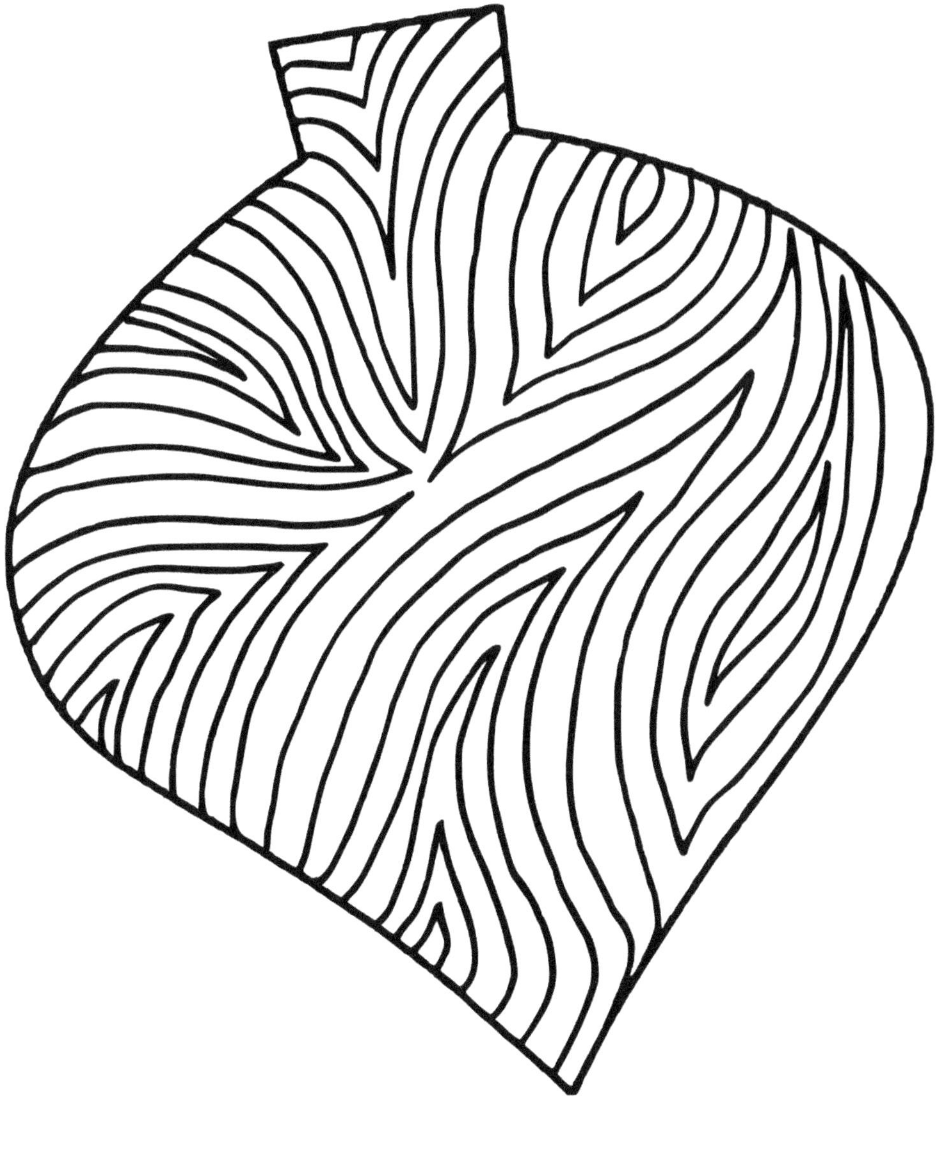

Test your colors here on the templates from

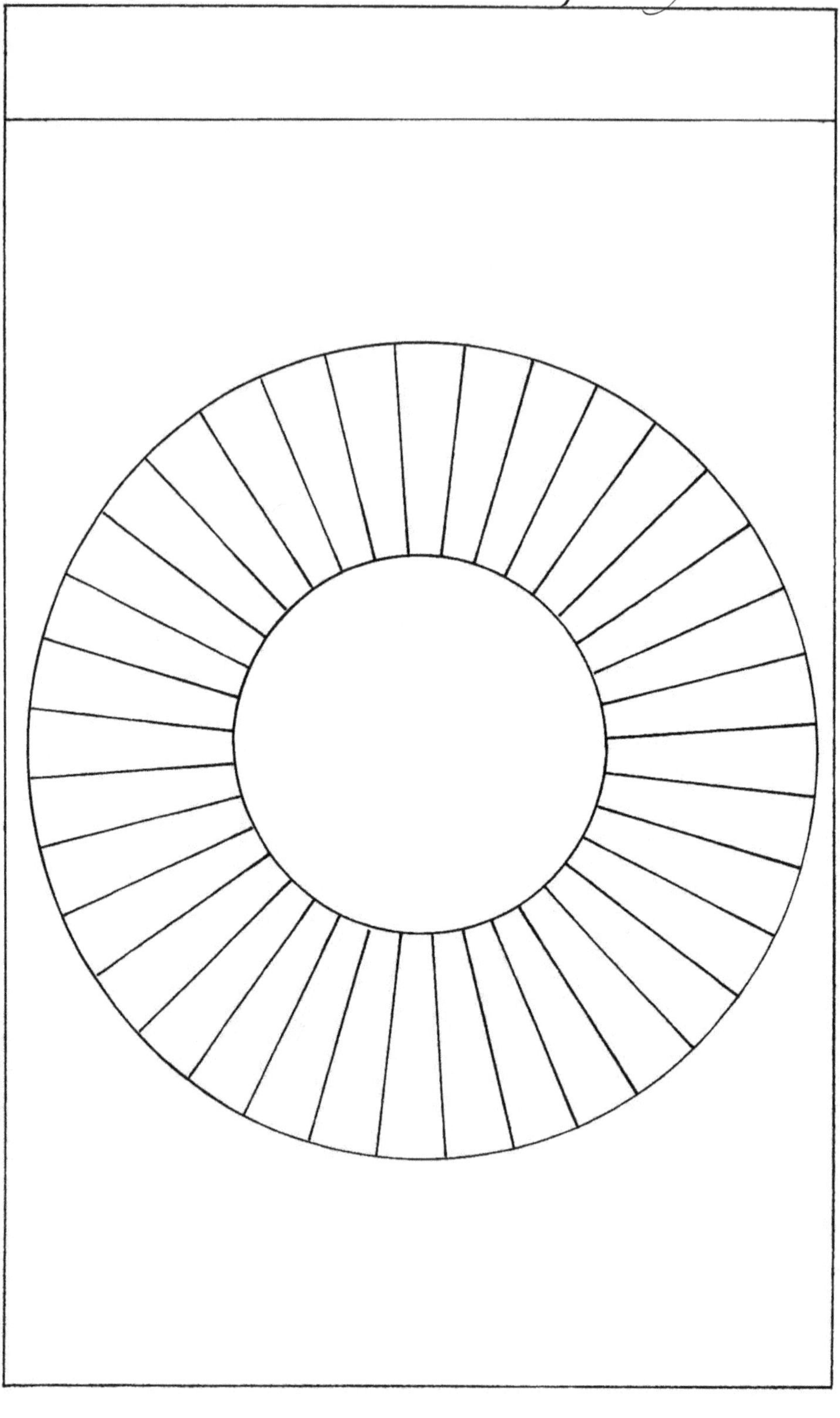

"My Pocket Coloring Companion"

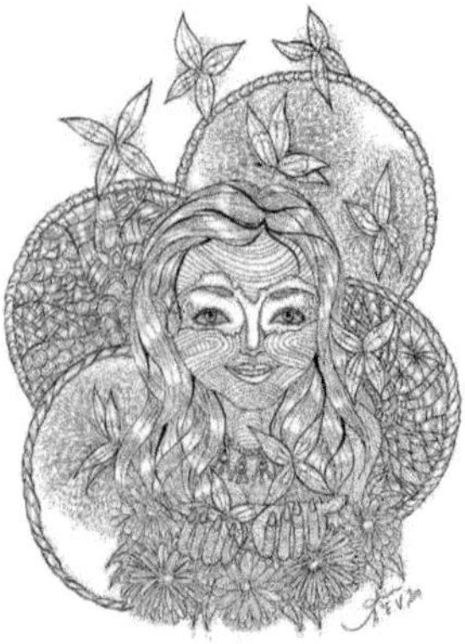

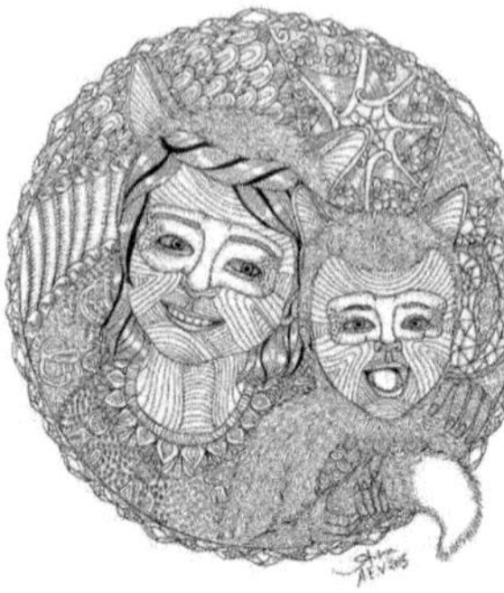

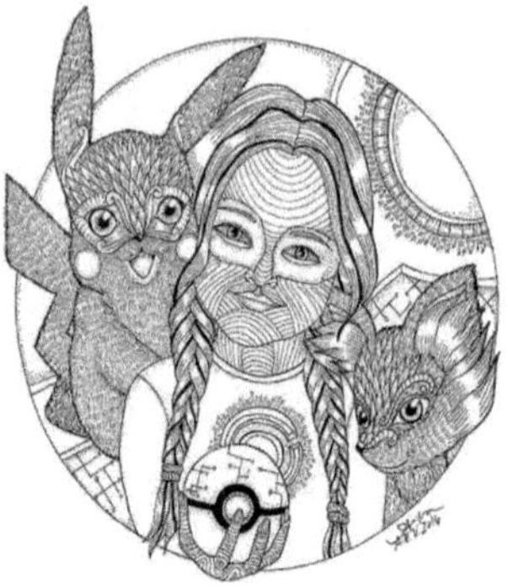

Interested in getting your own personal Coloring page ?

Digital Portrait commission by alfred
Size: 12”x18” in size
Format: high quality printable PDF files
Final pieces will be:
1 Black and white
1 colored piece in PDF formats
Both signed by the artist
Price: 40 dollars
Maximum 3 subjects on one commision piece
Inquiries just message on his Facebook page

Alfred E. Villanueva
Philippines
Facebook : viworksart2015

www.ingramcontent.com/pod-product-compliance
Lightning Source LLC
Chambersburg PA
CBHW050209230526
45470CB00001B/309
* 9 7 8 8 7 9 3 3 8 5 7 7 1 *